CREEPING FLESH

THE HORROR FANTASY FILM BOOK VOL 1

EDITED BY DAVID KEREKES

Critical Vision
An imprint of Headpress

www.headpress.com

A Critical Vision Book
Published in 2003
by Headpress

Headpress/Critical Vision
PO Box 26
Manchester
M26 1PQ
Great Britain

[tel]   +44 (0)161 796 1935
[fax]   +44 (0)161 796 9703
[email] info.headpress@zen.co.uk
[web]   www.headpress.com

British Library Cataloguing in Publication Data
A catalogue record for this book is available from the British Library

ISBN 1-900486-36-9

CREEPING FLESH
The Horror Fantasy Film Book Vol 1
Text copyright © Respective contributors
This volume copyright © 2003 Headpress
Layout/Design/Proofing/Etc: David Kerekes
World Rights Reserved

Front cover photo: *Tower of Evil* (1972)
Title page: *Whistle and I'll Come To You* (1968)

Images are reproduced in this book as historical illustrations to the text, and grateful acknowledgement is made to the respective filmmakers, studios and distributors.

Acknowledgements

This book would be somewhat less satisfying (and thinner) if not for the dedication of all those involved, some of whom came to it via the fine Mausoleum Club website [w] www.the-mausoleum-club.org.uk. Particular thanks go to Phil Tonge, whose unbridled enthusiasm and unsolicited hand-written deliberations on small screen fantasy, were inspiring. Thanks to Gary Ramsay who hit on the title, *Creeping Flesh*. (For a long time this book was *Three-Legged Dog*, a reference to Hannah, the pooch in *Killer's Moon* — the one concession to which now is the motif at the beginning of each chapter.) Andrew Screen [w] www.action-tv.org.uk came up with some much needed images without very much notice, as did Oliver Tomlinson, David Slater and Harvey Fenton. Harvey, it should also be noted, does a sterling job in bringing genuine curios — like *Sleepwalker* and *Killer's Moon* — back into the public eye, courtesy of his FAB film festivals. Likewise, Andy Murray, who organises the annual Darkness Over Britain Halloween weekends at the Cornerhouse cinema, Manchester. Many thanks to those people who gave up their time for interviews, those people who worked to make those interviews happen and those people who supplied materials for review (no less Jill Reading at the BFI).

CREEPING CONTENTS

INTRODUCTION

CREEPING FLESH has a history which stretches back a couple of decades, to a time when I devoured absolutely any book I could find on horror films (there wasn't many). It stretches back to *The Haunted Screen*, a volume in which Lotte H Eisner discusses the evolution of German Expressionist cinema. It would be years before I'd get the chance to watch the likes of *The Cabinet of Dr Caligari*, but the impact the stills had on me — impossible perspectives created by the set designers — was almost palpable: buildings and alleyways were all 'wrong', but in these unlikely shapes was created a new (psychological) reality. Not forgetting the shadows which I learned were not actually cast by any light source — natural or otherwise — but were instead *painted* onto the floors and walls of the set.

David Pirie's *The Vampire Cinema* was another landmark work, in that it helped to feed my interest in Euro horror, discussing films by such directors as Jean Rollin, Jorge Grau and Jesus Franco. That these films were being discussed at all was something revelatory back then; not many critics were acknowledging these films, let alone analysing them.

As the seventies slipped into the eighties, books on fantasy and horror cinema became more common place, and a whole new fan base exploded around the more visceral horror films that were emerging. This was the decade that saw the cult of the makeup and special effects artists, bringing celebrity status to the likes of Tom Savini and Giannetto di Rossi. Fans in Britain and the US were galvanised by *Fangoria* magazine, small press zines, and a sense of solidarity in the face of censorial bodies (like the BBFC) and increasing media backlash.

The wealth of fanzines devoted to horror cinema which appeared in the eighties is enough of a subject to warrant a book unto itself. These were energetic times for fans and the thirst for knowledge pertaining to non-mainstream, obscure and banned films helped to create an underground network which equalled — perhaps overshadowed — that of the punk music press several years prior. Titles like *Gore Gazette*, *Sleazoid Express*,

Slimetime, *Shock Xpress*, *Hi-Tech Terror*, *Video Drive-In*, *Cold Sweat*, *Sub-Human*, *European Trash Cinema*, *Demonique* and *The Splatter Times*, were a success in as much they lasted for a little while (three issues or more) and managed to etch out a niche in a market quickly being saturated by product of varying degrees of competence and quality. Many more titles were simply one-offs.

It is to the passion and energy of the best of the horror small press that we turn to for *Creeping Flesh*, combining it with fresh information on obscure, forgotten or ignored genre efforts.

(I will add here that any typos, glitches or lapses in quality you may encounter in *Creeping Flesh* are my responsibiliy, are deliberate, and in keeping with the spirit of the original zines!)

Having discussed the indirect inspirations behind the book you hold now in your hands, it was the recent availability of some archive telefantasy that ultimately pushed the idea of *Creeping Flesh* into a reality. It seemed a crying shame to allow the material covered herein to remain unchecked for much longer. Despite sterling efforts by the likes of the BFI — who are responsible for releasing several films under review — too much of the material in *Creeping Flesh* is superseded by the words 'Not presently available in any format'. Consequently, *Creeping Flesh* is intended as an ongoing series, with preparations already underway for volume two, scheduled for Winter next year.

But let's not get too ahead of ourselves. Dim the lights, sit back and — to paraphrase a character from *The Signalman*, one of the BBC's ghost stories for Christmas — "Take comfort in the discharge of your duties." Or was that Steve Coogan in *Dr Terrible's House of Horrible*...?

Because *Creeping Flesh* is an ongoing project, feedback and suggestions are particularly welcome. Contact details can be found at the beginning of this book.

David Kerekes
Manchester, Nov 20, 2003

THE FOLLOWING PROGRAMME IS NOT SUITABLE FOR THOSE OF A NERVOUS DISPOSITION…

by Phil Tonge

No doubt there will be many readers who are unfamiliar with the insular world of television fandom, so I thought it wise to first raise the question:

What Qualifies As Television Horror?

We could say that anything scary on the telly would count as <u>television horror</u>. That definition however would end up including BOOMPH WITH BECKER so we'll have to narrow it down. On a serious point, if we only include television series, serials and one-off plays that use <u>only</u> classic "gothic horror" trappings, we lose SF tinged productions like THE STONE TAPE. This also gives us problems with "crossover" stories that are science fiction foremost but rely on their horror elements for their impact. For example, do the QUATERMASS STORIES count as SF or horror or both? Is Rudolph Cartier's 1954 production of NINETEEN EIGHTY-FOUR SF/horror or political allegory with horror elements? This is probably why the term "telefantasy" was coined. In the end we have to follow our gut instincts.

An introduction to the GOLDEN YEARS OF BBC TELEVISION HORROR, which is followed by some of the outstanding examples of this small screen genre.

What is Telefantasy?

Telefantasy is a term originally coined by French writers who wanted to avoid long-winded sub-categories for programmes such as say *The Avengers*. It's much handier to term it a "Telefantasy" show than forever listing it as "One Time Trenchcoat Gritty, Surreal, SF-tinged, Action-Adventure, Comedy, Secret Agent, Leather Sex-Cop Show". Basically, if a programme contains elements of SF, horror, the supernatural, mythology and/or surrealism, then it can be deemed to be "telefantasy".

This of course leads to all manner of rows about which shows count as such, but this is all part of the fun of telly-fandom.

Why the BBC?

For a variety of reasons, this article looks solely at the TV horror output of the BBC. Not that the ITV companies didn't produce their own Horror and horror-tinged productions, HTV's *Children of the Stones* leaps to mind for one. It's just that the BBC has (or had) a more continuous run of horror projects, produced with, dare I say it, a lot more *conviction*.

The Great Archive Purge

What was once forbidden knowledge, then an open secret and nowadays a throwaway fact is that during the 1970s a great deal of the BBC archive went to the great electro-magnet in the sky.

There are many reasons for this, the first and foremost being that television is *still* not seen as a serious medium in Britain and all the websites and magazine articles in the world will not change that. Problems with repeat fees, clear-ances, copyright, the re-use of expensive videotape, the upgrade to 625-line colour telly and above all *storage...*

The BBC, to give them credit were saving as much stuff as they could on 16mm telerecordings, 35mm film and videotape, but of course they only had one place to put it in, the BBC Film and Video library. Imagine the BBC's dismay when their fire insurance certificate came up for renewal at the start of the seventies, only to have the insurance agents take one look at the bulging library and threaten to refuse renewal.

So, the Beeb started pruning back its collection, starting off with an alphabetical grading system (A=Save F=Skip) to eventually having to save just a few "examples" of series'. That's why we're missing all of *Late Night Horror* and choice episodes of *Out of the Unknown*. A great cultural tragedy that the BBC have finally admitted and apologised for. In fact they're starting to get a little annoyed when people bring this subject up. So, in the interests of balance it should be pointed out that the BBC was not alone in the junking of episodes.

ITV companies were up to the same thing at the same time, which is why we're missing episodes of, for instance, *The Georgian House* or most of the first season of *The Avengers*. Also, it wasn't just a British problem, with countless hours of television being torched or wiped in the US, to pick a country at random.

At least the Beeb can take a perverse pleasure in the fact that the seventies culture of "nick anything that ain't nailed down" which existed at the Corporation saved quite a few episodes from the chop. After all, a pile of 16mm film cans labelled up to be junked, they'll never miss them will they?

Although rumours that one-time Director-General Hugh Carleton-Greene was once seen trying to flog the cast of *The Woodentops* in a pub on the Edgware

Titles in bold are reviewed in detail elsewhere in *Creeping Flesh*.

Not Suitable for Those of a Nervous Disposition

Road are of course a wicked lie. The BBC's account of the events can be found on their website.

In The Beginning

The first BBC television horror story (in fact the first ever television horror production) was an adaptation of Edgar Allen Poe's *The Tell-Tale Heart* back in the gas-fired Baird 25-line (or so) days of 1939. This of course was in the days before any real form of television recording existed, unless they had a film camera operating next to the TV cameras that is. So the programme is non-existent and was watched by so few people that, for all we know, it could well have been an old woman banging a bucket with a spoon for an hour.

With British television off-air for the duration of WWII, there wasn't much to report until the 1950 production of *The Strange Case of Dr Jekyll and Mr Hyde*, and that quickly fell below cultural radar. It took the singular talents of an up and coming young writer, one Nigel Kneale, to change all that. Linking up with producer Rudolph Cartier he produced the first trouser-filling BBC TV series with *The Quatermass Experiment* (1953).

Ambitious, innovative and daring, *The Quatermass Experiment* told in six thirty-minute episodes the tale of Professor Bernard Quatermass and his involvement with an abortive British space mission. An astronaut has returned, but something is *horribly* wrong with him.

It's hard to describe the impact that this series had on the viewing public at the time, but it really did empty the pubs with people rushing home to see that particular night's episode.

(To relate a family anecdote from the time: My dad wasn't allowed to watch any of *Quatermass* at home so had to walk to his mate's house to watch it. Of course this was in the Forest of Dean, so my father had to walk back home through the woods, scared witless.)

Kneale later played down the horror element of the show, saying that it only made up "one percent" of the content, but that's not how the public remembers it. He then went on to adapt Orwell for Cartier's controversial *Nineteen Eighty-Four*, which featured a powerhouse performance by Peter Cushing as Winston Smith, before returning again to *Quatermass II* (1955) and *Quatermass and the Pit* (1958).

Apart from a 1954 adaptation of *The Monkey's Paw*, fifties horror on the BBC meant Nigel Kneale.

The Swinging Sixties

The Sixties brought a new wind of change for BBC television, due in part to the distinctly hands-off approach of Director-General Hugh Carleton-Greene. Carleton-Greene was a man with a background in journalism (he'd been the *Daily Telegraph*'s Berlin correspondent at the time of the "Night of the Long Knives") and realised that his staff of young-buck producers probably knew more about what was good for television than he did.

Horror themed productions came thick and fast, these included *The Tourelle Skull* (1962), part of the anthology series *Suspense*, and a 1965 version of *Sweeney Todd* (part of the *Gaslight Theatre* thread). 1965 also saw the debut of *Out of the Unknown*, but more of that later.

Also re-emerging to regain his crown was Nigel Kneale with his 1963 ghost story *The Road*. Starring James Maxwell and likely lad Rodney Bewes, *Road* was set in 1770s rural Britain where a haunting of a wood turns out to be a future echo of some nuclear catastrophe.

Popping up in the *Wednesday Play* slot came *Horror of Darkness* (by John Hopkins) and shoved away on late-nights came the stand alone *The Five-Nineteen*, whilst forgotten on BBC2 lurked the series *Witch-Hunt*.

A huge boost for TV horror came with the 1968 *Omnibus* production of **Whistle and I'll Come To You**. Based on an MR James story, directed by Jonathan Miller and starring the superb Michael Horden (with sterling support from the likes of Ambrose Coghill), *Whistle* richly deserves its reputation as the most frightening thing ever broadcast on television.

Unscathed by the archive purge, it surfaced again in 1986 as part of the BBC TV50 anniversary celebrations (it is now available on DVD). Masterful use of photography, editing and *sound* made this the obvious template for the A Ghost Story For Christmas dramas that were to come in the seventies.

Whistle contains so much that is frightening (a bit of rag dangling off a fishing line!) or downright bizarre (the scene between Horden and the concierge is like something out of Buñuel) that it deserves a book to itself.

Also in 1968 came BBC2's colour anthology series *Late Night Horror*. Alas this series was consigned to the flames, and all we have are some publicity shots and some viewers' fond memories of the Paddy Russell directed episode *No Such Thing As A Vampire* (based on a little known short story by Richard "I Am Legend" Matheson and starring Andrew Keir).

Those Seventies

If there was a golden age of horror for BBC television then the 1970s were it. In fact it seemed there was a time in the mid seventies where that most British of genres, the Gothic Horror story infested Auntie's output like a plague. From the sublime, *Doctor Who* (stories such as *Pyramids of Mars*, *Horror of Fang Rock* and *The Talons of Weng-Chiang*) to the ridiculous, *The Phantom Raspberry Blower of Old London Town* and *Dave Allen at Large* for example.

As for hardcore horror, we have to start in 1971, which not only saw the debut of A Ghost Story for Christmas: **The Stalls of Barchester** but also the fourth and final season of *Out of the Unknown*.

OOTU had kicked off in the sixties as a pretty much straight down the line SF anthology show. It featured adaptations of stories by "classic" science fiction

Not Suitable for Those of a Nervous Disposition

authors such as Isaac Asimov and John Wyndham. However, by 1971 it had gone full belt for out and out supernatural/ horror.

Amongst such lurid tales as *The Shattered Eye* and *Deathday* came *The Chopper*, penned by our old chum Nigel Kneale. *Chopper* sticks in peoples memories as the one where a female journalist is haunted by the revving of a dead biker's Harley (or knowing the Beeb, Suzuki 250). Also present is Patrick Troughton as a rather seedy garage owner.

Sad to relate, especially as this is the only *OOTU* I can vaguely recall, this episode no longer exists in the BBC archive.

No matter, as for winter 1972 we have BBC2's anthology offering *Dead of Night*. This series was produced by the legendary Innes Lloyd, and featured seven stories of general spookiness. The episode *The Exorcism* by Don Taylor seems to be the one best remembered, though this could have something to do with a popular American film doing the rounds at the same time…

The same production team joined up with Nigel Kneale (him again) to present the Christmas Day '72 opus *The Stone Tape*. In fact there seems to be some debate as to whether this story was meant to be part of *Dead of Night* or that year's Christmas ghost story.

As Lawrence Gordon Clark's team had already produced **A Warning to the Curious** for Christmas Eve, we can make our minds up accordingly.

The Stone Tape remains one of the oddest things ever broadcast by the Beeb. In which Jane Asher stumbles across a haunted room in a research facility and that the haunting may actually be a recording held by its stone walls. A mix of the occult, science and occasional washing machines for ninety minutes, leading up some stone stairs to some bizarre electronic effects.

Almost lost in 1972's horror fest was Terry Nation's *The Incredible Robert Baldick: Never Come Night*. A proposed pilot for a long abandoned series featuring Robert Hardy as the eponymous investigator/inventor and all round clever-dick, Mr Baldick.

Chugging off in his private train to sort out nasty occultish goings-on in rural England, Baldick discovers an ancient evil that may in fact be something from the future. (What was that Mr Kneale? You can't sue him, he's dead.)

1973 brought the anthology series *Menace*, which included a well-remembered episode *Boys and Girls Come Out to Play* (starring Peter Jeffrey and Sarah Sutton). A creepy story featuring kids in a suburban cul-de-sac who meet at night to play…and eventually murder. Alas, that didn't survive the archive purge either. With *Menace* out of the way, there was a lull in which only Clark's Christmas ghost stories held sway. These being the low-key but creepy **Lost Hearts** (1973) and the "tramp's hot breath on your nape" that was 1974's offering **The Treasure of Abbot Thomas**.

Some effort was put into the *Play for Today: Penda's Fen* (as well as the later *PFT: Vampires*) but it was all a big run-up for that year's ghost story **The Ash Tree** (1975, with Lalla Ward).

1976 saw the BBC have a crack at Oscar Wilde's *The Picture of Dorian Grey*. Featuring such big names as John Geilgud and the boyish Peter Firth as Dorian Grey. (Why the recent DVD release featured a photo of Jeremy Brett — who played supporting character Basil Hallward — on the cover I don't know.)

A Ghost Story for Christmas came back with a steam-whistle wallop with **The Signalman**. The first Ghost Story not to be based on a MR James tale, instead the production team went with a little known Charles Dickens spooker. Incidentally, there is evidence to show Dickens wrote the story as a way of coping with the post-traumatic stress of being in one of England's worst rail crashes (with his mistress, natch).

A seriously upsetting programme held together by Denholm Elliot's stalwart performance of a man shattering under stress and the mental electronic soundtrack of Stephen Deutsch.

The images of the figure by the rails, a bride falling from a speeding train, smoke from a tunnel pile-up billowing silently from the tunnel mouth and our Victorian gentleman (Bernard Lloyd) alone in a fog-shrouded field, haunt the mind long after their transmission.

Coming into that heady punk rock and Jubilee year of 1977, the BBC had another series for our perusal. Unfortunately, it turned out to be *Supernatural*.

The series was set in Victorian times at the fictional *Club of the Damned*, where prospective members would gain entry by telling a true horror story of their life. If they convinced the members, they would gain entry, if not, then they would be put to death.

Why did *Supernatural* fail? Was it the garish video it was recorded on? Was it the fact that the club members looked more like Mycroft Holmes' bridge partners than bent Hellfire types? Was it the fact the series was broadcast in high summer? Or was it due to the fact that it wasn't scary? Gentlemen, the vote!

With a competent production crew and an all star cast, the blame has to lie with writer Robert Muller (who wrote all the episodes apart from *Viktoria*, which was by Sue Lake). The only episode of note being *Dorabella* starring Jeremy Clyde, though *Night of the Marrionettes* has its fans. However, it's a bit of a bum note.

Much better was the December premiere of *Count Dracula* (adapted by Gerald Savory).

Sticking closely to Bram Stoker's novel, but cleverly giving the title role some *EuroThrust* with the casting of Louis Jourdan as well as presenting us with the screen's wettest Jonathan Harker (as he should be) in Bosco Hogan.

Although some elements jar to the modern audience, that noisy gear change of going from

> The programme is non-existent and was watched by so few people that, for all we know, it could well have been an old woman banging a bucket with a spoon for an hour

filmed exteriors to VT interiors being the main culprit, the adaptation still works well. Even with Frank Finlay making a meal of his role as Van Helsing. However, even he pales in comparison with the haunted visage that is Jack Shepherd's Renfield. A class act and no mistake.

That year's Christmas ghost story being the misjudged (in my opinion) **Stigma**, led to Lawrence Gordon Clark loping off to ITV (where he'd turn out a version of *The Casting of the Runes* and bother Stephen Gallagher for a while before returning to the beeb to direct *Casualty*, where he occasionally slips in a sly nod to Ghost Stories).

As the decade grinded to a halt so too did the Christmas ghost stories with 1978's totally forgotten **The Ice House**. The BBC did have the good sense to transmit during Christmas week 1978 the series *Late Night Story*. Using the el cheapo *Jackanory* approach of a story-teller in one set, this featured the talents of Tom Baker. Uncle Tom attacked each story with some relish, the best being *The Photograph* by none other than Nigel Kneale. A story of boy meets demonic photographer, with some delicious lines about "fingernails being cracked and open from chemicals" for Mr Baker to roar around.

However, our old friends at *Omnibus* saved the best till last with the 1979 Leslie Megahey masterpiece *Schalcken the Painter*. Based on the story by Sheridan Le Fanu (who is heard as Charles Gray's voiceover) this was a rare and exquisite creature indeed.

Transmitted just before Christmas (December 23, 1979), *Schalcken* intertwined expertly LeFanu's Horror story and the lifestyles, careers and techniques of the Flemish school of painting. From Jeremy Clyde's turn as the tortured Schalcken to the late, great Maurice Denham as the perpetually money counting Gerritt Dou, the acting is first

This article would not have been possible without the kind assistance of Andrew Pixley, Britain's most knowledgeable (and best-dressed) television historian. Thanks also to Mr Wolf and the members of the Mausoleum Club [w] www.the-mausoleum-club.org.uk

Not Suitable for Those of a Nervous Disposition

rate and the work of (proper) Lighting Cameraman John Hooper is enough to make you weep.

Why this production isn't slated for a DVD release should be a national scandal, it is just too damned good to be left rotting on the shelf.

I for one would have repeated it the same week that David Hockney broadcast his documentary on his theory about how painters of the period were all using camera obscuras and lenses. Oh yes David, what about Schalcken's use of pitch-black emptiness lit only by candlelight? Puts the mockers on your theory a bit, don't it?

Eighties, I'm living in the Eighties

That was it for the golden age of BBC telly horror. Public anxiety about the "Big One" led to more in-your-face offerings such as (the superb) *Edge of Darkness*. In 1981 we did have the sprawling *three-hour* long *Artemis 81*. A mish-mash of mythology, apocalyptic horror and Sting. Not really what we were after.

The final fling for BBC horror came with Stephen Volk's "wrath of the Tabloids" **Ghostwatch**. Times had obviously changed, as the BBC visibly shat itself with the media fallout following transmission and has kept well away from out and out horror ever since. Social realism yes, supernatural shockers, no.

Even the 1994 series *Ghosts* shunned scariness and replaced it with bafflement. Not the rewarding bafflement of say, *Twin Peaks*, but with the feeling of "so what?" that you get after sitting through an episode of *Jonathan Creek*.

So come on BBC, remember your legacy and scare us. Only don't repeat *Boomph with Becker* that's going too far. CF

A GHOST STORY FOR CHRISTMAS

THE STALLS OF BARCHESTER

by Phil Tonge

Each Christmas from 1971 to 1978, the BBC treated viewers to a late night ghost story — self-contained, specially commissioned programmes of between thirty-five to fifty minutes duration.
In the pages that follow, CREEPING FLESH takes a look at each of the eight A GHOST STORY FOR CHRISTMAS.

Synopsis

1932. Travelling archivist Dr Black is cataloguing the library of Barchester Cathedral.[3] Deeply disappointed with the overweening blandness of its archive, Black is offered access to the manuscript collection. However the good doctor is again unimpressed by mathematical tracts or "Cyrus, an epic poem in eight cantos". Then, newly remembered by the librarian is a dusty chest, containing the private papers of a former archdeacon, a certain Dr Haynes. Apparently, the former Dean of the library had vowed that the chest would never be opened during his tenure. Spurred on by the librarian's curiosity, and the fact that Black had seen Haynes' obituary in a back issue of the *Gentleman's Magazine* ("his death was most unbecoming of a man of the cloth"), the box is duly opened.

Inside are a dusty gathering of papers and the private journal of the unfortunate Archdeacon Haynes.

Back to 1872. Junior Deacon Haynes has taken up his newly appointed position at Barchester under the incumbent Archdeacon Pulteney — a man who, it appears, was going for Methuselah's coffin dodging record with some style. This leads to Haynes complaining rather sarcastically to his sister Letitia about the good Archdeacon's lack of death.

However, due to a missing stair-rod at his official abode, Pulteney falls foul of the laws of gravity and tumbles to his death.

Letitia Haynes blames the maid, Jane Lee for shoddy housework, while Dr Haynes makes a big song and dance about her lack of taste when it comes to discussing Pulteney's replacement.

Of course, Haynes gets the archdeacon's position.

1932. Dr Black points out to the librarian that Haynes' diary suggests a man keeping himself unnaturally busy, as though if he ceases activity at any time, certain things might come forth to prey on his mind.

What exactly these "things" could be become plainer when a blackmail letter (of sorts) is discovered — written from Jane Lee to Archdeacon Haynes for the sum of forty pounds to keep silent on certain matters. Reading between the lines, the note would point to the late Dr Pulteney's demise being rather less than the accident it first appeared.

1875. Left alone in his dwelling (Letitia has gone to visit relatives), Haynes becomes aware of "certain presences" in the house.

During evensong, the not-so-good Archdeacon is "struck by the character" of the carvings in his stall.

While absent-mindedly rubbing the carving of a cat, it turns into the fur of a real-life feline.

Haynes lets out a gasp, which he quickly masks with a polite cough. It's about now that his catchphrase "I must be firm" appears in his journal. The firmness relating to his mind, which he thinks he's losing due to cabin fever, overwork and the death of Pulteney on his conscience.

Haynes decides to research the carvings in the cathedral. Firstly by taking a tour with the verger, noting how most of the carvings seem to date from the fourteenth-century *apart* from the ones on his stall. According to the verger, these were made around two hundred years earlier, carved by a local artisan John Austin (nicknamed "Austin The Twice-born — they say he was blessed with second sight") from the oaks in "the Holywood".

Seeking the local historical knowledge of a priest, Haynes visits the woods and finds the stump of the oak from which his stall carvings (the Devil, Death and the Cat) came. It's the "Hanging Oak" of the wood, connected with executions, pagan worship, sacrifice and the like.

Coming home that night, the archdeacon is plagued by unholy whispers. On another occasion, leaving his bedroom to collect his watch from the study, he's confronted by the vision of a bog-eyed black cat whispering "take care" at him.

1932. Dr Black and the librarian are studying Haynes' diary. "I must be firm," written continuously. "See how it bites into the paper," Black observes.

1876. Again Haynes writes of the house outside his study plagued by "movement without sound". During evensong on October 22, during the singing of the 109th psalm[4] the archdeacon again has

Previous page Dr Black, archivist.
This page, top Archdeacons Haynes and (back) Pulteney.
Above Haynes is touched.

The Stalls of Barchester | BBC1 | 45mins | 11.05pm-11.50pm Dec 24 1971 | repeated Aug 16, 1972, as *An English Ghost Story* Adapted from *The Stalls of Barchester Cathedral* by M R James[1]

With: Robert Hardy (Junior Deacon Haynes), Clive Swift (Dr Black), Will Leighton (the librarian), Harold Bennett (Archdeacon Pulteney), Thelma Barlow (Letitia), Penny Service (Jane Lee), Martin Hoyle (the verger), Erik Chitty (priest), David Pugh (manservant), Ambrose Coghill (museum curator)

Costumes Verona Coleman; Makeup Marion Richards; Design Keith Harris; Camera John McGlashan; Sound Dick Manton; Dubbing Editor Ian Pitch; Dubbing Mixer Alan Dykes; Film Editor Roger Waugh; Action By Havoc[2]

Writer/Producer/Director
Lawrence Gordon Clark

trouble with the carvings.

This time it's death that takes physical form, with the cowl moving backwards to expose a skull. Next the archdeacon is followed around the cloisters after dark by mystery footsteps.

The verger thinks someone (Canon Arnold?) was with him, and swears to seeing a second figure following. But Haynes insists there was no-one there. "No-one!"

The poor fellow is going downhill rapidly: he has nightmares of the stump of the hanging oak and of Death itself playing "tag" with his shoulder.

1932. "It seems his firmness was giving out," surmises Dr Black. Although the doctor sees a supernatural element, the librarian can only see a man driving himself mentally ill.

1877. By now, Haynes' entries consist of a scrawl repeating "I must be firm". Then on Feb 21[5] it all goes pear-shaped. Finally unable to resist seeing who or what is making the scratching, banging, whispering noises, the doomed archdeacon makes the mistake of going to the top of the stairs in the darkness. In this case, Death, with big sharp claws…

1932. Dr Black agrees with the librarian not to publish Haynes' papers. Of course, our dear doctor is a most curious fellow, and visits the aforementioned stalls. The carvings have been removed.

Black decides to bother the curator of the town museum. He reveals that one of the carvings — though it's never said which one[6] or why they were removed — broke open, revealing a letter inside from John Austin:

When I grew in the Wood
I was water'd w(ith) Blood
Now in the Church I stand
Who that touches me with his Hand
If a bloody hand he bear
I councell him to be ware
Lest he be fetcht away
Whether by night or day,

But chiefly when the wind blows high
In a night of February.
This I drempt, 26 Febr. Ao 1699. JOHN AUSTIN.

Asking the curator what happened to the broken carving, Black finds that the old man who gave the letter to the museum had burnt it. "Because it frightened his children so much."

Wandering off, more bemused than before, Dr Black is wary of a large cat that sits on the local green…

Critique

The Stalls of Barchester is a textbook case of "Starting how you mean to go on". Clark for one should be congratulated on his adaptation, which sticks pretty rigidly to the original story, but not so rigidly as to stop him from providing us with visual treats. Sly uses of editing to provide us with sick sight gags, such as the wickedly evil cut from Pulteney's fatal fractured skull to a big close-up of Haynes' breakfast egg being caved in with a spoon. Or of Black's absent minded leaning gag in the museum. He leans on something before he looks at it, looks down, big skull in a glass case glares up at him.

Fantastically creepy is the scene where Hardy thinks his manservant John has come to his bedroom door to pick up a letter. There is a scratching of oak followed by a reverbed whispering of "Can I come in?" Haynes says yes, but after a tentative creaking of the door, there's no one actually there. Some lovely uses of sound, but without the more fanciful Radiophonic Workshop noodling of say *The Signalman*.[7]

Also, some clever Clark touches with the use of repeated, identically timed scenes. These being the old archdeacon's birthday celebrations (which cleverly have less old blokes hanging around as they go along), Haynes' morning walks with his sister past Pulteney's house and

The
Stalls of
Barchester

the interminable evensong service — towards the end of which, Haynes is openly giving it the "Hurry up and die you old bore" look.

Neither is Clark afraid to put in his own delicate dialogue dashes. When Haynes and the verger are discussing the cathedral's carvings and the verger points out the angels on one side and the damned on the other, Haynes cannot resist remarking: "There seems to be more conviction on the faces of the damned…"

John McGlashan's camerawork is of a very fine standard, too. *The Stalls of Barchester*, like all the Christmas ghost stories, is shot on film, and makes use of a lot of expensive (especially for the BBC) night shooting. Every penny well spent, as we can see from the results. Making great use of the locations (Norwich Cathedral and its surrounds), there is one spectacular shot roughly halfway through, with Hardy's character walking through a passageway at night. To the left of the frame, a typical early Victorian town house, the lights glowing orange through the curtains; to the right the imposing bulk of the cathedral, illuminated in a deathly blue. Centre frame, the figure of Haynes emerges from the pitch black of the alleyway — suggesting his moral darkness perhaps? A truly beautiful shot, worth looking out for in the middle of all these riches.

Clark has cast the story well. Swift exudes the correct amount of world-weariness in proportion to curiosity as Dr Black (and would go on to repeat his role in the following year's Ghost Story *A Warning To The Curious*), Harold Bennett *is* Archdeacon Pulteney and Hardy is a revelation as Haynes.

Robert Hardy's reputation as a slightly hammy character actor seems to be a rather short-sighted and somewhat malicious judgement by certain television reviewers. In fact his role as Haynes highlights Hardy's rather surprising (for myself, knowing him mainly as the one-note Siegfried Farnon in *All Creatures Great and Small*) range as an actor, coming over convincingly as a man driven bonkers by his demons.

Indeed, there's the rub. In James' story, we only have Haynes' journal, the blackmail note and the odd curse/precognitive rhyme to go on. At no time is the demise of the unfortunate Archdeacon Haynes attributed *directly by James* to the supernatural. That's left to the reader to decide in their spooked-up state. It would be equally reasonable to blame the man's own mental frailties, as the librarian does.

Clark of course takes us straight down the road of the supernatural, the long claws of Death seen raking open the side of Haynes' face.[8] Of course, that's if Clark is showing us what actually happened, but he might just be showing us what Dr Black is *imagining* happened. After all, the entire story is told by way of Black's voiceover, therefore we're only getting his version of the tale.

What a tale though… GF

Not presently available in any format

NOTES

1 *The Stalls of Barchester Cathedral* was first published in the *Contemporary Review*, *XCVII #35* (1910) pages 449–460. Originally subtitled "Materials for a Ghost Story". Original manuscript was sold at Sotheby's in November 1936 to writer (and friend of James) EG Bain.

2 "Action by Havoc." Havoc was a stunt team/agency that worked (mainly) for the BBC in the early to mid seventies, most notably on *Doctor Who*.

3 Barchester. Fictional town created by Anthony Trollope in series of novels, starting with *The Warden* (1855) and ending with *The Last Chronicle of Barset* (1867). The town and it's equally made-up county, Barsetshire, were also used as locations by the novelist Angela Thirkell. MR James created his own imaginary cathedral town Southminster in his story, *An Episode of Cathedral History*.

4 109th Psalm. Nice touch from James here, using the most unpleasant psalm in the bible as a plot point and one that Clark has gleefully gone with. See also its use by Thomas Hardy in *The Mayor of Casterbridge*.

5 It's the twenty-sixth in the original story.

6 Although we can probably assume it's the figure of death. This still leaves the mystery of why Erik Chitty's character refers to *three* carvings "the Devil, Death and the Cat" when the programme only shows us two. James refers to and describes three figures in his story, but has given death the *nom de plume* of "The King of Terrors".

7 The soundtrack of hummings, tape-loops and reversed bells etc is excellent by the way, I'm not having a go.

8 Certain fans of MR James point to the blatant gore in this scene as testament to the fact that Clark's adaptations were cheapening the "subtle horror" of James' stories. This, dear reader, is bollocks of the highest order. James was never shy of dropping in moments of physical disgust and entrails. See *Rats* or *Mr Humphreys and His Inheritance*, for example.

A WARNING TO THE CURIOUS

by David Kerekes

A Warning to the Curious | BBC1 | 50mins | broadcast 11:05pm–11.55pm Sunday December 24, 1972 | repeated Saturday May 25, 1974 and Saturday December 26, 1992

With: Mr Paxton (Peter Vaughan), Dr Black (Clive Swift), Archeologist (Julian Herington), Ager Ghost (Joun Kearney), Boots (David Cargill), Vicar (George Benson), Antique Shop Owner (Roger Millner), Girl (Gilly Fraser), Porter (David Pugh), Labourer (Cyril Appleton)

Costumes Joyce Hammond; Makeup Marion Richards; Design Geoffrey Winslow; Camera John McGlashan; Sound Dick Manton; Dubbing Editor Ian Pitch; Dubbing Mixer Ron Edmonds; Film Editor Roger Waugh

Writer/producer Lawrence Gordon Clark

**A Ghost
Story for
Christmas**

Synopsis

The Norfolk coast, East Anglia. Legend speaks of three Anglo Saxon crowns which were hidden in the ground to protect England from invasion. Two of the crowns have been disturbed, but as long as the third remains the shores will be safe.

Twelve years after the murder of an archaeologist searching for the last crown, an amateur treasure hunter by the name of Paxton arrives in Norfolk armed with a shovel. He takes board in a hotel which has only one other guest — Dr Black, a regular visitor who likes to paint landscapes.

A vicar at the parish church explains to Paxton that the locals still believe in the legend of the three royal crowns. He also tells the visitor of the late William Ager, buried in the cemetery, whose job it was to guard the crowns.

A porter at the hotel, suspicious of Paxton, is somewhat unconvincing when he informs the guest that he has never heard of William Ager nor indeed the Ager family, despite their strong links to the area.

Continuing his research, and on the heels of a shadowy figure who seems to mysteriously disappear, Paxton locates the cottage once belonging to William Ager. The new owner speaks of a "tramp" she sometimes sees in the nearby woods.

Later, back at the hotel, Paxton observes a distant figure on the beach watching him.

Telling the porter that he must go back to London on a business matter, Paxton instead takes the train and heads out to the woods with his shovel and a good idea of where the third crown might be buried. Whilst digging, he is overtaken by the sensation he is not alone. Night falls. Paxton's excavations turn up a human skull, a spearhead and finally the last remaining crown. Rattled by someone watching him, Paxton is then chased by the figure he saw on the beach, and perhaps earlier at Ager's old cottage.

He returns to the station and boards a train back to his hotel. The guard on the platform is mistaken in believing that a second man wishes to board the same carriage.

Hiding the crown in his hotel room, Paxton discovers pages from a book relating to Ager have been cut up and strewn about the floor — a discovery which is followed by a very disembodied wheezy cough from within the room.

"What a strange evening it is," deliberates Dr Black after Paxton stumbles across him later, painting a picture of the beach. The doctor points out to Paxton the figure in the distance. As suddenly as it has appeared the figure is gone again.

Paxton confines in the doctor his discovery, and that now — convinced he is being followed by the dead Ager — he is going to replace the crown. "Ever since I've touched this thing," he tells the doctor, "I've never been alone."

Dr Black agrees to accompany Paxton on his return to the woods. Shortly before they're about to leave, the doctor hears a wheezing cough from behind a door and inquires who the new guest might be. There is no new guest, responds the porter, and the door leads only to a storage cupboard. Moments later, Paxton gives out a scream when he catches a glimpse of a figure in his darkened room.

In the woods, the doctor keeps a look out with a lamp as Paxton sets to work returning the treasure to its rightful place. There is a distinct impression that the two men are not alone.

Having completed their task, the men return to the hotel. But Paxton is later lured away by someone he — and the porter — believes is the doctor. The real doctor hurriedly follows only to witness a shadowy figure chasing Paxton through the woods. The doctor catches up in time to see the treasure hunter being bludgeoned to death at the spot where the third crown lies.

Dr Black leaves on a train. The station guard opens the carriage door under the misapprehension that there is somebody else wishing to board the same carriage…

Previous page Having discovered the third royal crown, Paxton tries to outrun the ghost of William Ager.
This page, top "What a strange evening it is," comments Dr Black.
Above Paxton is pursued by Ager once again, this time through the woods to his death.

Critique

It's fair to say that Gordon Clark borrows somewhat from *Whistle and I'll Come To You*, Jonathan Miller's *Omnibus* adaptation of a MR James ghost story screened some years earlier. There is the same dreamy sense of space and isolation (and mysterious figures in middle distance!), which is key in the beach scenes of both productions. If either production was a season, Miller's *Whistle and I'll Come to You* would be a sprightly spring to the autumn of Gordon Clark's *A Warning to the Curious*. The horror element in Miller's earlier play is very much an introspective one, never clearly defined and something of an imposition on the central character who doesn't believe in non-scientific concepts like ghosts. On the other hand, from the opening shots of Gordon Clark's play, we see a beachy landscape that is muted brown and with it the immediate sense that nothing good is going to come out the other end. (The opening shots also appear to be running at the wrong speed, and as a consequence are grainy.) At one point in the play, Dr Black comments to Paxton that it's impossible to differentiate where the beach ends and the sky begins.

With or without its nod to Miller, *A Warning to the Curious* stands up enormously well to repeated viewings and takes a rightful place as one of the most enduring of the BBC's ghost story adaptations, not to mention a true classic of television fantasy.

> It's an image which predates the finale of The Blair Witch Project by close on thirty years

The spooky moments are understated and genuinely creepy. The viewer really does feel Paxton's sense of not-being-alone as he hunts for the treasure, constantly looking over his shoulder and catching sight of what may or may not be a man lurking within the trees. The sequence where his hotel room is suddenly thrown into darkness is a creepy highlight: Paxton shining the pencil beam of his torch around the pitch black room, illuminating the unexpected and fleeting figure of a man hunched over. It's an image which predates the finale of *The Blair Witch Project* by close on thirty years.

The long shots of Paxton being chased through the woods are also memorable, detached from reality and in some ways more akin to a drawing by Edward Gorey than anything quite as sober as a BBC production of an MR James story — like Gorey, not entirely serious but disturbing nonetheless.

Perhaps my own favourite moment is the one in which Paxton, having un-earthed the third royal crown, leaves the woods pursued by the spectre of William Ager. Reaching the open path back to the train station he is confronted by the menacing sight of a farmer holding a machete. The treasure hunter grips his shovel to his breast and marches past, preparing himself for the worse. But the farmer simply tells the stranger that there is no need to run for the train, there's plenty of time. Watching Paxton walk into the distance, the farmer suddenly witnesses a second figure calmly following the stranger (where there wasn't one before). It's a great sequence, subtly composed and executed but infinitesimally more effective than any lavish CGI extravaganza.

What of Paxton? What manner of person is he? He doesn't appear to be a greedy or arrogant man, and if anything comes over as simply 'misdirected' in his desire to find the treasure.

Paxton has joined the ranks of the unemployed — as insinuated early on by shoes in dire need of repair and a newspaper he carries whose headline is a comment on increasing job losses. Paxton confides in Dr Black that his interest in the royal crown lies in wanting to make a name for himself. Clearly a proud man desperate to regain his public standing, Paxton is sensitive to the social stigma attached to him, as evidenced in a scene where the hotel porter classes Dr Black as "a gentleman" — the inference being that Paxton isn't.

Paxton's only real crime is that he is something of a dreamer, which only serves to make his comeuppance all the more cruel. ⒸⒻ

Available on DVD through the BFI

A Warning to the Curious

LOST HEARTS

by David Kerekes

Synopsis

Master Stephen, an orphan, arrives at the grand estate of his "cousin twice removed", the rather eccentric Peregrine Abney.

Abney has agreed to take the boy into his care, and fusses somewhat over Stephen's age. "Twelve next birthday," he queries. "You're certain you're twelve next birthday?"

Of his curious manner, the servant Parkes explains that Abney is a scholar and likes to write everything down. Mrs Bunch, the cook, considers him kindness itself. Indeed, Stephen isn't the first orphan that Abney has given a home to.

Giovanni and Phoebe were two other children to have come into Abney's care. Both of Stephen's age and alas both gone now, Giovanni liked nothing more than to play his hurdy-gurdy around the place, and the general assumption is that he drowned; Phoebe was apparently of gypsy extraction and it is believed she simply ran away with the gypsies.

Stephen queries that if Giovanni was as attached to the hurdy-gurdy as everyone says he was, then why did he leave the instrument behind?

Stephen takes a walk around the grounds. He hears ghostly laughter and spies two children. About to tell Abney of his experience, he thinks better of it when the children appear at a window, fingers on lips.

Parkes accuses Master Stephen of having defaced one of the walls of the house, and reports the matter to Abney. Abney believes the boy's plea of innocence, however, later pondering to himself that no earthly child could have scored hard wood so deeply.

The ghosts of Giovanni and Phoebe watch over the mansion. They peer through the window of the study — which is full of old books and parchments pertaining to the supernatural. Abney sits writing and greets another day, another step closer to "everlasting life... in this world".

One night, Giovanni goes to Stephen's bedroom. He retrieves

Lost Hearts | BBC1 | 35mins | broadcast 11:35pm–12:10am Tuesday December 25, 1973 | repeated Saturday June 8, 1974

With: Simon Gipps-Kent (Stephen), Joseph O'Conor (Mr Abney), James Mellor (Mrs Bunch), Christopher Davis (boy), Michelle Foster (girl), Roger Milner (vicar)

Costume Velma Buckle; Script Editor Frank Hatherley; Sound Dick Manton and Ron Edmonds; Cameraman John McGlashan; Film Editor Dave King; Designer Don Taylor

Producer Rosemary Hill
Director Larence Gordon Clark

Master Stephen (left) and his "cousin, twice removed", Peregrine Abney.

Images of the ghost children,
Giovanni and Phoebe.

* My original notes on this sum up the
ghost-children better, if somewhat less
eloquently: 'creepy beyond belief.'

Lost Hearts

his hurdy-gurdy and starts to play, which has a mesmerising effect on Stephen who, half-asleep, follows the grinning ghost-boy down the hall to the bathroom. Phoebe sits smiling.

Giovanni suddenly casts aside the hurdy-gurdy to reveal a gaping cavity in his chest. Phoebe too has a similar wound, her ribs exposed.

The household is awoken by Stephen's screams. "They had no hearts!" he cries. Abney retrieves the broken hurdy-gurdy and catches sight of the children at a window, where they rap their long fingernails on the glass. Throwing the instrument in the fire, he analysis and writes of his experience in his notebook.

It's Stephen's birthday. While retrieving a bottle of port from the cellar, Parkes is spooked when he hears whispering.

Stephen inquires about the picture above the fire in the study. Abney explains that it is something very old, a sacred thing made "before the mechanical sciences cast their rude shadow over the world". He then tells the boy that he should come to his study at midnight to have his secret fortune told. "Our secret, mind."

Preparing for the appointment, mixing powder into a glass and placing a dagger on the table, Abney begins to read from a book: *"The heart must be removed from the living subject…"*

At midnight, Stephen arrives at the study and Abney quickly ushers him in. As the desired hour is almost upon them, and having had to wait twenty years for this moment, Abney is besides himself with excitement. He forces the boy to drink the drugged port, tears the shirt from his chest and lifts the dagger. "Here lies your fortune," he announces.

Before he is able to fulfil the deed, Giovanni and Phoebe edge their grinning way into the room.

"I am immortal!" Abney groans as the children take the dagger and turn it upon him.

At his funeral, the true nature of Abney is divulged to the scattered mourners. From a field nearby, Giovanni and Phoebe wave to Stephen before departing. It isn't just Stephen who sees them go.

Critique

This particular Ghost Story for Christmas boasts the most genuinely chilling segment of the entire series, courtesy of Giovanni and Phoebe — the two children who grin and peer through windows. Gleaned from James' original story, where the scratches found on a wall are described as having been made by a "Chinaman's fingernails" (drawing on the age-old fallacy that fingernails, like hair, continue to grow in death), the children need do nothing more than walk the corridors, their fingernails entwined, a ludicrous grin on their blue pallor faces, in order to evoke a palpable spine tingling dread.*

The manner of the children is very much a hybrid of classic

elements drawn from supernatural film and fiction, no less Carl Dreyer's *Vampyr*, as evidenced in *Lost Hearts'* oft repeated 'faces against glass' sequences.

Gordon Clark keeps things moving at a fairly decent, dialogue driven pace, not spending as much time on expositional shots as his other ghost story instalments. (Curious how the tales in this series differ so much in look and feel, appearing like the work of several directors rather than just the one.) It also contains the most graphic visceral imagery of the series — barring the infamous penultimate entry, *Stigma* (which is something of an anomaly anyway given its move from the classic tales and its contemporary setting). This is courtesy of the bloody exposed chest cavities of the ghost-children, a shot delivered quite unexpectedly and with some impact.

It's something of a shame that *Lost Hearts* doesn't carry the same kudos as, say, *The Signalman* or *A Warning to the Curious*. Though I suspect that this is more to do with the lack of actor-heavyweights as boasted by these other productions, more than it is the quality of the production itself. In *Lost Hearts* the characters are pretty perfunctory, lacking the depth and dimension of, say, Denholm Elliott's Signalman or Peter Vaughan's Paxton — Stephen is a boy, Parkes is a servant and Mrs Bunch is a cook, in the tried and tested tradition of all television period dramas. The one exception is Joseph O'Conor, who turns in a grand performance as Peregrine Abney, coming over as a bumbling eccentric whose mild mannered exuberance and blustering barely contains a sinister intent. Discounting the obvious Faustian element of the story, there is indeed a paedophiliac undertone which cannot be ignored — though I am curious as to whether this aspect of Abney's character is intentional or simply part and parcel of the tabloid-sensationalist baggage that surrounds us whilst viewing *Lost Hearts* today.

An adaptation of *Lost Hearts* had been brought to the small screen as early as 1966, as part of ABC Television's anthology series, *Mystery and Imagination*. ⑰

Not presently available in any format

M.R. JAMES A BIOGRAPHY

by Phil Tonge

The first five Christmas Ghost Stories are adaptations of works by MR James.

Montague Rhodes James was born in 1862 in the unremarkable (apart from its name) Goodnestone next to Wingham in Kent. The youngest of four children of one Herbert James, Clergyman and Mary Emily James, the daughter of a distinguished naval officer. Moving at a very early age to the Suffolk village of Great Livermere, the young "Monty" was never happier than face down in some dusty academic tome. Due to his Father's wish for his son to take holy orders (which he never did) and his Christian home life (of a very genial kind for the time), these books would usually be on Medieval art, architecture and Biblical studies (with a certain bending towards the Apocrypha).

When he was out and about, during what could easily be described as an idyllic childhood, he relished the visits to his grandmother, who lived at Aldeburgh, which became Seaburgh in *A Warning To The Curious* (other East Anglian locations from his youth would also appear in his ghost stories).

A gifted student with a razor-sharp memory, James soon attained a scholarship to that most privileged of schools, Eton. Moving there in 1876, his academic brilliance gained him a Newcastle Scholarship (the school's highest academic award) and in turn a scholarship to King's College, Cambridge.

It was at Eton where James indulged in his interest in the occult and the supernatural. He's known to have read de Plancy's

Cont on p.23

THE TREASURE OF ABBOT THOMAS

by Phil Tonge

Synopsis

The Treasure of Abbot Thomas | B B C 1 |
Broadcast 11.35pm–12.10am Dec 23, 1974 |
repeated BBC1 Dec 26, 1983 and BBC2 Dec
25, 1993
Based on the short story *The Treasure of Abbot
Thomas* by M R James[1]
Dramatised by John Bowen

With: Michael Bryant (Reverend Somerton),
Paul Lavers (Lord Peter Dattering), Virginia
Balfour (Lady Dattering), Sheila Dunn (Mrs
Tyson), Frank Mills (Mr Tyson), Anne Blake
("Local Lady"; referred to as Mrs Punch-
Hycliffe on-screen), Peggy Aitchison (landlady),
John Herrington (Abbot Thomas)

Production Assistant Terry Coles;
Makeup Rhian Meakin; Costume Janet
Tharby; Script Editor Matthew Waters;
Sound Dick Manton and Stanley Morcom;
Dubbing Editor Andrew Johnston; Camera John
McGlashan; Film Editor Roger Waugh;
Music Geoffrey Burgon; Design Stuart Walker

Producer Rosemary Hill
Director Lawrence Gordon Clark

A Ghost Story for Christmas

The English West Country in the mid 1880s. Young Lord Peter Dattering invites his friend and tutor, the Reverend Somerton to a séance at his recently widowed mother's house. Peter is suspicious of the two "mediums", Mr and Mrs Tyson, who have latched on to his mother's goodwill.

Somerton agrees, as he is "interested in all forms of the higher silliness". The good Rev is slightly more concerned with his research at the local abbey. These studies regard the legacy of a certain Abbot Thomas, late of the (unnamed) abbey in or around the year of 1429. According to Somerton's sources, Thomas was not only rumoured to have escaped burning at the stake by being whisked away by the devil, but also to have left clues to a stash of treasure.

A passage in an old Latin textbook gives some clues to the location, but is beyond the two men's understanding… for the time being.

Attending Lady Dattering's afternoon of tea and table tapping, the rationalist vicar spooks the Tysons by commenting casually that during the historical period covered in his studies, they would both be burned as witches.

During the séance, which features an unearthly whistling sound ("the spirits of the air"), the possessed Mrs Tyson speaks with the voice of a "Father Dominic". Apparently this is the spirit of a priest from the times of the War of the Roses, which gives Somerton his big chance.

Asking questions in Latin and Norman French, the Rev exposes the Tysons as charlatans. Although the clinch comes with the vigorous slapping of Mr Tyson's back, which ejects a tiny bird-whistle from his mouth.

Unnoticed during all this cheap mummery, Peter is transfixed by internal whisperings (although whether this is supernatural influence or merely deep thought is not made clear). Suddenly he exclaims that he realises where the church containing the clues to Thomas' treasure can be found.

With the Tysons booted out, the two investigators decamp to said church where the stained glass windows of "Bartholomew Jude,

Simon and Mattheius"[2] can be found.

While Peter takes photographs of the windows, Somerton prefers to use the time-honoured method of a detailed sketch. He doesn't yet regard photography an exact science: "I've seen too many blank plates."

The clues are as cryptic as the first, the Latin inscriptions reading in turn: "He looks down on high to see what is hidden", "They have on their vestments writing which no one knoweth" and "On one stone are seven eyes". During their ruminations a shape flaps noisily outside. A crow? Or something else?

Developing the plates, Peter shows Somerton what appears to be a blemish, but resembles a gargoyle on the abbey's roof. Taking to the roof, where the Rev reveals a fear of heights, Dattering finds that the sculpture seems to be staring down at a railed off culvert entrance in the graveyard. *"He looks down on high to see what is hidden."*

Heeding this clue, Somerton is attacked by a flapping shape. There is a suggestion that it's a startled murder of crows, or just an attack of vertigo, or not...

In Somerton's lodgings the two discuss their next move. Rev Somerton is appalled by Peter's assertion that they are "mere treasure hunters". He is worried what his hosts in the abbey would do if that were seen to be the case, and besides, alchemy is a foolish nonsense. There is *no gold*.

Anyway, the actual location of the "treasure" in the culvert is unknown. Looking again at their sketches and plates, the two notice there are unusually thick black bands on the clothing of the figures. *"They have on their vestments writing which no one knoweth."* Returning to the church, our heroes scrape off the paint to reveal a hidden code.

Upon deciphering the code, Peter and Justin have the location of the treasure and the amount — 2000 pieces of gold coin, a priceless amount. Hearing this, Somerton seems to take on the aspect of a man suddenly twitchy with greed. However, the last part of the code reads *"Gare a qui la touche" (I have set a guardian).*

Gripped by an unscholarly lust for the treasure, the Rev Somerton ventures out at night to break into the culvert. Armed with hammer and chisel he enters the slimy, slug infested underground

MR James cont from p.21

Dictionaire infernal and Walter Map's *De Nugis Curialium*. This tied in with his undying fascination with the "remorseless demons and gaping hell mouths"[1] of the Middle Ages and the works of his favourite ghost story writer, Joseph Sheridan LeFanu (1814–73) must have sown the seeds for his later fictional writings. Going up to Cambridge in 1882, James would have a glittering career at Kings, rising through the ranks from undergraduate to Provost. Indeed his list of academic achievement reads like a shopping list. From attaining his fellowship of the college with his dissertation *The Apocalypse of Saint Peter* in 1887, working as assistant in Classical Archaeology at the Fitzwilliam museum, gaining his Tutorship and lecturing in Divinity to starting the Herculean task of cataloguing *all* the Cambridge manuscript collections[2].

His election to the Provostship in 1905 seems like the cherry on an abundantly iced cake. In 1918 he left King's for Provost of Eton, a position he kept until his death on June 12, 1936. Looking at this purely scholarly record, of a man spending his life in the cosseted world of crusty old British academia, we could end up with a picture of a sour old git.

Quite the opposite. MRJ was a well-travelled man gifted with a finely developed sense of humour, was noted for his impersonations of various respected fellows and had a certain love of the theatrical (especially pantomime), of which his ghost stories were the main outlet. He also had a pathological dislike (hatred seems too harsh a word) of spiders, which explains the dénouement of *The Ash Tree*. These stories, for which he is now famous, were really designed as amusement for his friends. Chums of James[3] would recount the annual ritual at Christmas time where, following an invite back to Monty's abode and plied with sherry, the man himself would appear. In a deliberate manner he would circle his study, extinguishing the lights, until one solitary candle remained burning next to his chair. Then

Cont on p.25

Top Somerton and Dattering
— code breakers.
Above At least it seems to
be the doctor...

Notes

1 First published as the final story of *Ghost Stories of an Antiquary* (1904). Written by James in the summer of that year to fill up the volume. The manuscript was sold at Sotheby's in 1936 to MRJ's friend Owen Kent Smith.
2 In James' story these figures are John, Job and Zechariah.
3 Which I'm not going to reveal here. Go and read it.
4 "Mr Sludge – 'The Medium'" a poem by Robert Browning published in 1864. Another opponent of sprit-fakery, Browning wrote his poem about noted Victorian con-artist Daniel Duglas Home.

Treasure
of Abbot
Thomas

and finds the stone with seven "eyes" (in this case, the letter "I"). However, he is followed by *something*. In the darkness, Somerton removes the stone, where behind he finds an old leather bag. As he retrieves it, he is assaulted by some unmentionable wall of black slime, in the shadows the spirit of Abbot Thomas laughs.

Two days later, Peter finds his old tutor barricaded into his bedsit, under siege from a "thing of slime". In fact his landlady complains of clearing up after it.

Somerton describes the contents of the treasure bag to Peter as worthless "base metal", whereas he sees gold coin. The now unbalanced vicar implores Peter to replace Thomas' loot, which the young Lordling is seen to do.

Later, we see Somerton convalescing in a bathchair in the gardens of the Dattering's stately home. He is left alone to be with the local doctor who we see approaching up the driveway.

At least, it seems to be the doctor... at first glance...

Critique

When John Bowen took on the job of adapting James' short story, he had his work cut out. James' story is essentially a tale of code breaking with one (deliciously creepy) sentence of horror in the last few pages[3]. The original *Treasure* suffers from James' only real fault as a writer and that was showing off how clever he was. Although to be fair, when you're essentially writing for an audience of Fellows of King's College, Cambridge, you can get away with it.

Bowen instead had to add a framing device featuring Peter Dattering, his mother and the charlatan Tysons. This sub-plot of bogus mediums is a nice nod to James (and his hero Sheridan LeFanu) who, although interested in the supernatural, held no truck with what he called "spirit-rapping". Bowen gets in a nice clever touch (or two) of his own with his reference to "there is your Mr Sludge"[4]. Also the fact that the doomed Somerton is a fellow of Oriel College, Oxford, which would make MRJ (King's College, Cambridge) stifle a chuckle.

Plus his script has a certain fascination with mid Victorian manners and catering. With all its references to "grilled chops" and the light comedy of "slab-cake". In fact, the humorous pantomime of middle class teatime, act as a subtle juxtaposition to the slimy horrors that await us. When he does get to the core of the story, he remains faithful to the spirit of James' piece.

Instead of the usual Hollywood school of cryptography, where the hero takes ten seconds to decipher a clue, here our principal characters have to work at it. Indeed they spend a great deal of the running time doing so (and seem to be playing out Douglas Adams' old adage of "staring at a blank piece of paper till their foreheads bleed").

Clark's direction is of a more confined, claustrophobic kind than

A Warning to the Curious, even if the subject matter is very similar. Instead we're returned to the cloistered world of *The Stalls of Barchester*, but without that production's cinematic flamboyance. Not that this is a criticism; Clark seems to be going for a deliberately different style to the former ghost stories, one in which details are important. This might make the story seem rather bland compared to a *tour de force* like *Warning*, but it's well worth the effort.

Again, like *Stalls*, *Treasure* doesn't at first make any supernatural elements plain. During the séance, the voices in Peter's head may just be the sound of logic at work; the shape at the church window may simply be a well fed jackdaw; the cowled monk in the library may be just that. But then again…

Some subtle brush-strokes come with the scene of Somerton's barricaded room, where the camera goes to a shot of a plaster cast of a brain lying broken on the carpet — nicely alluding to the post-slime mental state of the good Reverend.

Gordon Clark's direction of his actors is of note: the story has been cast well, with his central players erring on the side of "under-acting". Paul Lavers plays Lord Peter Dattering with the right level of aristocratic enthusiasm, while Michael Bryant's Justin Somerton conveys quiet rationalism with some aplomb. The fact that he plays Somerton with a quiet devotion to facts, research and science, makes his slide into greed, recklessness and shock-based infirmity all the more disturbing.

McGlashan's camerawork emphasises the tranquillity of the English countryside with the emphasis on the lush greens of late summer, contrasting with the grey stone of the abbey and the black slime of the culvert.

In some ways this ghost story marked a step back, in other ways a step forward, but it showed that A Ghost Story For Christmas was continuing to hit it's stride. The production does leave some questions in the viewer's mind. Did Peter *really* put the gold back? If he did and the "Guardian" still comes after Somerton, does that mean he's next? Brrr… ⒼⒻ

Not presently available in any format

MR James cont from p.23

he would start reading his latest composition… What stories they were. The horror was always on the level of (to steal a phrase from Mick Mercer) "the madness of a warm lavatory seat"[4]. Or to really work your minds, imagine Hinge and Brackett doing a cover of the Ramones' I Don't Wanna Go Down To The Basement. Most stories come with a travel guide feel of its setting, similar to that which creeps up in H P Lovecraft's scribblings. His writing style has aged remarkably well, which is why they handle well for adaptation to radio, tube and cinema. His stories still have the power to make you feel uneasy (and this writer recommends reading them at night, by candlelight and with a glass of "something").

James also invented the use of quoting (fictional) official reports or providing footnotes to his stories to add a *faux* authenticity to his tales and a boost to the reader's suspension of disbelief. A technique that influenced many later horror writers e.g. Stephen King and *Carrie*. Egged on by his mates and members of the Chitchat Society[5], James started submitting his stories to be published. First by magazines such as the *National Review* and *Pall Mall Magazine*, then in book form.

Ghost Stories of an Antiquary appeared in 1904 and sealed our man's fate to be forever remembered as a "writer of ghost stories". "Monty" James summed up his reasons for writing the stories in the preface:

If any of them succeed in causing their readers to feel pleasantly uncomfortable when walking along a solitary road at nightfall, or sitting over a dying fire in the small hours, my purpose in writing them will have been attained.

MR JAMES SELECTED BIBLIOGRAPHY

Fiction

Ghost Stories of an Antiquary (1904)
More Ghost Stories of an Antiquary (1911)

Cont on p.27

THE ASH TREE

by Roy Gill

The Ash Tree | BBC1 | Broadcast 11.25pm Dec 23 1975
The Ash Tree by M.R James; A Television version by David Rudkin

With: Edward Petherbridge (Sir Richard Fell), Preston Lockwood (Dr Croome), Barbara Ewing (Mistress Mothersole), Lalla Ward (Lady Augusta), Lucy Griffiths (Mrs Chiddock), Oliver Maguire (William Beresford), Clifford Kershaw (Witchfinder General), Cyril Appleton (Master Procathro), David Pugh (Herdsman), David Sweet (priest)

Production Assistant Terry Coles; Makeup Jackie Fitzmaurice; Costumes Sue Cable; Sound Recordist Dick Manton; Dubbing Mixer Ron Edmonds; Film Editor Roger Waugh; Visual Effects John Friedlander; Designer Allan Anson; Cameraman John McGlashan

Producer Rosemary Hill
Director Lawrence Gordon Clark

**A Ghost
Story for
Christmas**

Synopsis

England, mid eighteenth century. Sir Richard Fell rides across a pastoral landscape to take charge of the estate he has inherited, his tenants and workers commenting on his arrival as he passes. At the hall, housekeeper Mrs Chiddock points out the portraits of his predecessors, the estate having passed from uncle to uncle. Sir Richard vows his line of descent shall be more direct, telling Mrs Chiddock she shall soon be taking instructions from the Lady Augusta. "Aye sir, a new mistress — please God," she responds quietly.

Sir Richard writes to Lady Augusta that evening. By the window, a silhouetted form can be heard to beg, "Sir Matthew, in this dread matter we entreat thee…"

Sir Richard goes about surveying his new estate. He notices a dead animal, and discovers to his surprise that the farmers must keep their sheep indoors at night in order to protect them from "the sickness". Whilst sketching a design for a new Italian-style front for the hall he encounters Dr Croome, and accompanies the priest to Castringham church. Fell explains that he also intends that a new pew should be built for his family. When Croome responds that this will involve disturbing one particular grave, Richard experiences a flashback to the past: in the form of Sir Matthew Fell he denies a request for leniency for a woman who has been found to be a witch and is to be put to death. Returning to the present Richard surveys the grave that is to be exhumed — it contains a Mistress Mothersole whose stone was paid for by the farmers so "she would not lie nameless in the earth" — and resolves to go ahead with his plans.

Lady Augusta visits Richard at the hall. She is to visit Paris to buy her trousseau and then return to him. As she rides away, Richard looks up to the great ash tree that stands by the hall — a baby's cries can be heard.

Walking his land Richard experiences another flashback. As Matthew Fell he watches a young flaxen haired woman gather plants by the river; this is Mistress Mothersole. Meanwhile, the Witchfinder

General traverses the land, his lackeys ominously beating a drum. Matthew assures them their search shall be in vain in Castringham.

At night, Richard is unable to sleep as the branches of the ash tree rustle and scratch outside. He crosses to his window and spies Mothersole cutting plants. "Now we have ye, now we see ye, Mistress Mothersole," he whispers. Richard/Matthew pursues a hare — who he believes to be Mothersole's "night shape" — to her dwelling, but Mothersole is apparently inside and surprised to be disturbed. In the present day, Richard's meeting with William Beresford to discuss the building work on the hall is similarly effected: he has a vision of a dirty and semi-naked Mothersole under interrogation by the Witchfinders.

Outside the hall, Beresford expresses surprise that Sir Richard has not had the ash cut down. He comments that some believe an ash so close to a house "drains the goodness from it". Sir Richard expresses discontent with his current bedchamber — he spies a room that might suit him better. Inside, Mrs Chiddock explains that particular room has been shut up since Sir Matthew died.

Another flashback occurs: Richard sees Mothersole and two other woman being taken to be hung. Richard/Matthew re-iterates his testimony against Mothersole, who declares before she dies, "mine shall inherit — and no sweet babes shall now mine be."

Richards speaks with Cromer. Mothersole's grave has been opened but no body has been found. Richard asks Cromer what Sir Matthew died of. The priest explains that the cause of death was unknown, but the body was found black and disordered as if from poison and those who touched it experienced some form of smarting shock. The death of Anne Mothersole and the other "unfortunates" had apparently prayed on Matthew's mind and he had sought counsel through sortilege — opening the Bible at random and reading the passage revealed. The verses Matthew picked told him "Cut it down", "It shall never be inhabited" and "Her young ones also suck up blood". Sir Richard resolves to have the ash tree cut down, and retires for the night to the room that was once Sir Matthew's. Before going to sleep Richard consults his Bible in similar

MR James cont from p.25

A Thin Ghost and Others (1919)
The Five Jars (children's fantasy) (1922)
A Warning to the Curious (1925)
Collected Ghost Stories (1931)

Non-Fiction

Abbeys (guidebook) (1925)
Eton and King's (autobiography) (1926)
Suffolk and Norfolk (guidebook) (1930)

MR James' ghost stories are rarely, if ever, out of print. Current collections available include:

Casting The Runes and other Ghost Stories (1999) Oxford University Press Paperback (This edition contains an Introduction and detailed notes on the stories by Michael Cox — from which I've pilfered heavily for this article. If you buy one book of James' ghost stories, select this one. *Avoid the 2003 US edition, however!*)

A Warning To The Curious and other stories (1998) Phoenix Paperback (With an introduction by Philip Gooden. Worth picking up as it has five stories not included in the Oxford edition, and it is somewhat cheaper.)

If you want to know more about "Monty" and other similar writers, I can heartily recommend the Ghosts And Scholars site [w] www.users.globalnet.co.uk/~pardos/GS.html ⒼⒻ

Notes
1 Michael Cox, from his Introduction to *Casting The Runes and Other Ghost Stories. Oxford World's Classics edition 1987/1999.*
2 Started by James, finished eventually in 1926.
3 Such as fellow ghost writer EG Swain.
4 My favourite analogy: You're alone in an isolated cottage on the moors in the middle of winter. One night you skip upstairs in the freezing cold by torchlight to go to the toilet. You sit down and the seat's warm.
5 One of those odd little clubs that spring up in esteemed institutions like Oxbridge.

Top Lady Augusta.
Middle Mistress Mothersole.
Above The work of the
Witchfinder General.

The
Ash Tree

fashion. The text reads: "Thou shalt seek me in the morning, and I shall not be."

In the night, baby cries can be heard from the ash. Strange, scurrying movement can be seen, and dark shapes crawl in through the window and cover Sir Richard. Concerned, Mrs Chiddock knocks at the chamber door and enters. Looking through the window she sees a cluster of monstrous spiders clinging to the ash. She throws her candlestick onto the tree, and it bursts into flame. The fire awakens the hall's tenants, and the men seek to douse the flames. The baby-like cries become harsher and the spiders attempt to flee but they are swatted by the men.

The next day, Lady Augusta returns to the hall. Passing by the smoking ruins of the ash tree, two locals can be seen staring at a charred human corpse. Augusta ascends to Richard's bedchamber. She reaches out to touch his blackened body and recoils in pain.

Critique

"Watch this," said a friend at the tail end of one year, passing me a VHS copy of *The Ash Tree*. So my partner and I settled down for some supposedly ideal Christmas viewing. I think what we both naively expected from a BBC Christmas ghost story was some hokey slice of Victoriana, melodramatic thespians being confronted by mutton-chop'd ghouls appearing courtesy of dodgy chromakey. Something that would be for two kids born into the fag end of television's supposed 'golden era' as homely and familiar as our vestigial memories of festive *Morecambe and Wise*, or the low budget chill of an episode of *Doctor Who*. Thirty four increasingly unsettling minutes later we emerged, dazed.

Returning to *The Ash Tree*, then — nerves suitably fortified by a medicinal tot of brandy — I'd like to try and root out where some of its malignant power lies. The first blow for cosy familiarity stems from the production itself. At a time when much television output and genre works in particular were still an uneven mix of multi-camera studio work and location filming, this is an all-film affair. Sympathetic use of lighting allows Sir Richard's metaphorical descent into darkness to be developed and explored onscreen. Contrast for example the idyllic rural scene in which Fell observes Mothersole picking flowers by the river bank, her blonde buxom figure suffused with warm light, to the interrogation sequence in which he once more regards the now captive woman, his features half-eclipsed in shadow. The surprise use of female nudity in this scene — surely still a relative oddity at time of transmission — provides a further jolt to shake viewers from their festive reverie and, more importantly, confirms the distinct undertones of male voyeurism that underscore this tale of persecution and revenge: "Now we have ye, now we see ye, Mistress Mothersole," indeed. There's inventive and effective use of sound on offer too. There's no incidental music — no cosy radiophonic trills to tell us when to jump or relax — the atmosphere instead being developed through landscape sounds, disturbing baby cries, and the occasional mournful refrain of Mothersole singing (which also plays out over the closing credits). Dialogue is often freed up from the requirements of naturalism: Fell's arrival at the hall is accompanied by a montage of commentary from the locals, and certain lines of dialogue are on occasion re-iterated for effect, i.e. "None shall inherit!" Fell's final journey reprises the above techniques. His short conversation prior to dying is stretched over a journey from day to night across country landscapes — including a stunning shot of the two silhouetted against a rolling river that appears to reach up to the sky — ending finally beneath the darkened boughs of the ash tree. Mention too should be made of the monster element. Assisted by low key lighting and rapid editing, Gordon Clark successfully avoids what in the hands of a lesser director could so easily have been an anticlimax due to poor special effects.

Praise for the production's success should also be attributed to David Rudkin, a writer whose other credits include a number of works with transgressive and supernatural themes (notably *Penda's Fen* and *Artemis 81*). Here, Rudkin does an admirable job of invigorating MR James' arguably rather dry prose. A nested series of narrators in the original text is dispensed with in favour of point-of-view character Richard Fell who must now experience first hand the sins of his ancestors; the eerie link across time pre-figured by the locals at the start of the piece who refer to him as "the new Sir Matthew". Playful use of death imagery abounds in the dialogue — the task of unpacking Sir Richard's library becomes one of "laying to rest the great unread" for example, and Fell jokingly tells Croome when illustrating his

planned renovations to the hall that he intends to make himself a "pestilent innovator". "Pestilence, Sir Richard? Please God not," responds the priest, Fell little realising that it is not his architectural aspirations that provoke such apprehension.

More notably still, Rudkin adds to the story a theme of the loss of fertility, perhaps inspired by the accused woman's name *"Mother sole"* or even her supposed "nightshape" of a hare. In the original short story her before-death pronouncement is simply, "There will be guests at the hall." Here, her curse of "mine shall inherit" is part of the harrowing cry of a woman that is to be taken from the only world she believes in and deprived of her own chance to raise "sweet babes" — the Fells' are correspondingly denied a direct line of succession. Gordon Clark's use of baby cries for the spiders further cements this idea of a perverted line of progeny.

The cast offer good, solid performances — Edward Petherbridge in particular impresses, underplaying rather than exaggerating his role of a man caught up in a pre-determined fate. While the SF fan in me yearns for slightly more screen time for *Doctor Who* girl Lalla Ward, her appearance here is actually perfectly judged. We see just enough to learn that Richard is to be denied a loving relationship with a beautiful woman. Her reappearance in time for the date "burned on [her] heart" only to discover Fell's blackened corpse and confirm by touch the unearthly nature of his inherited fate provides a suitably creepy closing shot to the tale.

The Ash Tree, then, is somewhat of a *tour-de-force*. Certainly in execution it stands apart from the majority of telefantasy product of a similar vintage. Perfect viewing, albeit not for the faint hearted. ⒼⒻ

> Female nudity in this scene — surely still a relative oddity at time of transmission — provides a further jolt

Not presently available in any format

THE SIGNALMAN

by David Kerekes

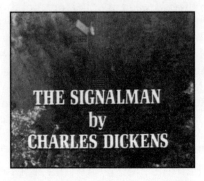

THE SIGNALMAN by CHARLES DICKENS

The Signalman by Charles Dickens | BBC1 39mins | broadcast 10:40pm–11:20pm Wednesday Dec 22, 1976 | repeated Wed May 25, 1977; Sat Dec 25, 1982; Sat Dec 21, 1991; Tues Dec 2, 1997; Thurs Dec 3, 1998; Mon Oct 23, 2000; Tues Jun 4, 2002 | A television version by Andrew Davies

With: Denhom Elliott (The Signalman), Bernard Lloyd (The Traveller), Jessup (The Engine Drive), Carina Wyeth (The Bride)

Production Assitant Vee Openshaw-Taylor; Makeup Toni Chapman; Costumes Christine Rawlins; Music Stephen Deutsch; Sound Recordist Colin March; Dubbing Mixer Brian Watkins; Film Editor Peter Evans; Designer Don Taylor; Cameraman David Whitson

Producer Rosemary Hill Director Larence Gordon Clark

A Ghost Story for Christmas

Synopsis

A man out walking is drawn to the sight of a passing steam train. He ends up on an embankment overlooking a rail track, where he spies a signalman.

"Hello!" calls the man, slowly waving his arm to attract attention. "Below there!"

The signalman, stood by the side of the track, seems startled — a little fearful — of the cry.

"Hello! Hello!" the man calls again and makes his way down the embankment.

"You look at me as if you have some dread of me," he tells the signalman. "I am simply a man."

The signalman is at first a little hostile, but soon warms to the stranger and invites him into the signal box to share the fire and a hot drink.

When his host becomes distracted, the traveller asks, "Is everything as it should be?"

"What brought you here," responds the signalman.

"I was drawn here."

The signalman rounds off the evening with the graphic and gruesome details behind the worse kind of rail accident, the catastrophe that is the tunnel accident.

The traveller bids his good night, arranging to visit again the following day. On his return, and at the request of the signalman, he agrees not to call out in the manner that he did earlier.

The traveller has a room at an inn. That night he peers from his window into the darkness, listening to the sound of a passing train. He sleeps uneasily, dreaming about a tunnel collision and the signalman requesting that he doesn't call out.

The following evening, the traveller meets again with the signalman who reveals what it is that is troubling him. He is troubled by the spectral figure of a man who stands by the mouth of the tunnel, covering his face with one hand and waving the other as in warning. The same cry always heralds the appearance of the figure: "Hello! Below there!"

The first sighting happened about a year ago, and within six hours "a memorable accident on this line occurred" — a collision in the tunnel.

The traveller, evidently a man of some learning, regards the spectre as a trick of the mind, a deception. "We are men of good sense —"

But the signalman hasn't finished. Six or seven months later, the figure reappeared, again at the mouth of the tunnel beneath the red warning light. The signalman implored of the figure, "Where is the danger? What can I do?!"

The spectre said nothing but dropped the arm from its face to reveal a mask frozen in an empty scream. The train that emerged from the tunnel saw a young bride being thrown to her death.

The signalman concludes his story with the revelation that the spectre last showed itself only a week ago. "I have no rest or peace for it." This third appearance will bring yet another calamity, but the signalman is powerless to do anything. He cannot notify anyone because they would consider him mad.

"Take comfort in the discharge of your duties," consoles the traveller. "You cannot be to blame."

The fretful signalman takes the heed to heart, and considers that his new found friend has managed to put his mind to rest. They arrange another meeting and the traveller heads off back to the inn, where again he has troubled sleep. When he awakens with a start, the door to his room is ajar.

Top The traveller (left) offers the signalman a little peace of mind.
Above Ambivalent infinity.

The next day, with a sprint to his step, the traveller takes a walk but is stopped dead in his tracks upon hearing an ethereal whistle. It's clearly the whistle that the signalman has spoken of, a communication from the grave. The man bolts for the rail track, where the signalman has already heard the familiar refrain of "Hello! Below there!" Rooted to the mouth of the tunnel, the signalman is transfixed before the spectral figure and doesn't heed the oncoming train... The traveller arrives to see the signalman being run over and killed.

With the dead body face down on the track, the shocked train driver explains to the traveller how he called out but the signalman didn't seem to notice. "Hello! Below there!" were his words, waving his arm in warning. "Look out! Look out!"

The traveller is overcome — by realisation, by shock, by fear. His face is like a mask frozen in an empty scream.

Critique

The Signalman is a claustrophobic piece of work that is so isolated, so estranged that it seems to be taking place in a vacuum. It's very much a two-man piece, with the closing credits referring to Denholm Elliott as the "signalman" and Bernard Lloyd simply as the "traveller". But the play itself dispenses with even these most

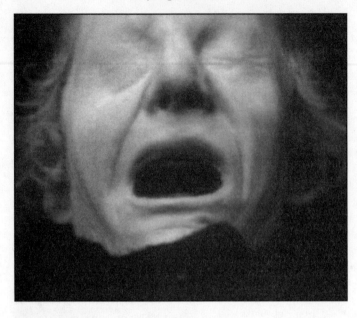

The spectre.

* The most obvious
thought would
be that the man
has recently been
released from jail,
but it could also mean
that he was once a
man of the cloth, or
is free from a stifling
marriage. Maybe
there is something
in the latter, given
that Charles Dickens
wrote *The Signalman*
following his own
escape from a bad
train wreck... in
the company of his
mistress.

The
Signalman

base of references and nowhere in the actual production is anybody referred to by any name at all.

The setting is perfect: a signal box locked on each side by a steep wall embankment, which has only one hazardous means of negotiation up or down. The rail track that cuts through this landscape is sucked into a black tunnel at the one end, while in the opposite direction it slips into ambivalent infinity. Both directions are foreboding and don't suggest the slightest hint of escape for the men caught between the two.

The claustrophobia and ambiguity of the piece is so pronounced that it takes on a surreal quality. When the traveller heads off to his board at the inn (described only as being "a fair walk" away), it is shrouded in fog. There are no guests or anyone else that the traveller encounters, and even the name of the place is veiled in the swirling mists.

The only other people in the whole production are perfunctory characters, who — save for the engine driver at the end — say not a word. They behave as though they belong in a completely differ-

ent time zone. Their actions (if they have any, most are static) are laboured. When the bride is thrown from the train, one of the mourners at the trackside clutches his face in such a precise way that the viewer is left in no doubt that the action must convey some significance. Well, it does and it doesn't — it really depends on how deeply you wish to interpret *The Signalman*'s odd denouement.

The actual framing of *The Signalman* is very considered and precise, with the camera lingering a couple of seconds more than it has to on many scenes, which only compounds the surreal quality of the production. A particularly masterful shot is that of the signalman walking from the tunnel after the first accident, standing in a near perfectly symmetrical landscape, smoke billowing out behind him.

Although the part of the traveller appears at first to be 'straight man' to the signalman's ramblings, the voice of reason, his exact role becomes less obvious with time. When he first introduces himself, he empathises with the signalman's solitude, stating somewhat cryptically that he himself is a man used to confinement, but now he is free.* But no man and nothing in this play has any true history or value; everything is in a limbo of the here and now. Or purgatory. Could it be that the traveller is a channel for the supernatural — as the signalman seems to think at one point, given his first words of greeting? And what of the creaking open door that the traveller discovers upon waking at the inn — what is implied in that? A visitation? It isn't clear. But the ending, in which the traveller's face takes on the attitude of the spectre, does appear to signify that the traveller himself is the unwitting harbinger of death. Indeed, in his description of the accident, the engine driver uses the same curious words uttered by the traveller days earlier: "Hello! Below there!" All told, not really the thing one would likely shout in desperation to clear the path of a fast approaching train.

There is never any doubt that the supernatural is playing a part in the whole play, which makes the traveller's attempts at rationalising what he considers a deception of the mind a little unnecessary. The signalman is only too aware that he has too much time on his hands; there is so little to do, he acknowledges, with so much depending on it. But at the same time he has to wonder what might be the purpose of trying to build knowledge (in the signalman's case, through books on mathematics) if he has no outlet for that knowledge? Here *The Signalman* skips around some deep philosophical concepts, and again it isn't clear to what end any of it might play in the grand scheme of it all. The spectre is clearly not a deception of a bored mind, and neither is it a reaction to scientific conceit — a direction in which we appear to be headed for at one point.

The Signalman has all the markings of an allegorical tale (the "signalman"! the "traveller"!), but then nothing is quite what it seems and there is no allegory. No pearl of wisdom on which the viewer may ruminate.

The whole episode works with its restrictive budget remarkably well. The spectral face is very simple but enormously effective. Points of action, such as the bride falling to her death and the signalman's own demise, are implied with editing. The only time the play does overreach itself is the catastrophic accident in the tunnel, which is simply a series of train wreck noises over a blank screen. (I'm sure I used to have that BBC sound effects record!) This scene brings with it an unintentional element of humour.

Outside of natural noises, the soundtrack uses no music or incidental sound beyond the ghostly warning, which takes the form of a low humming sound. Again, very effective. Denholm Elliott and Bernard Lloyd play their parts admirably; Elliott in particular bringing to his role his customary weight and dignity (there is a great moment when it does look like he might be cribbing his dialogue from notes on the palm of his hand!).

Of all the BBC ghost stories, this is the only one I have any recollection of having sat through on its original airing in the seventies. It impressed me a lot, and when I came to see it a second time, some twenty-odd years later, courtesy of its BFI DVD release, it impressed me over again. (I'm clearly not alone in being impressed, because this is the most commonly repeated of the ghost stories, having aired a total of eight times as of writing.) I was surprised at just how vivid and accurate my memories of it had remained. But then, every scene is precious without a wasted moment in the whole production.

The opening credits on *The Signalman* are preceded simply with the legend "A Ghost Story". Christmas doesn't enter into it.

Aavailable on DVD through the BFI

> The Signalman has all the markings of an allegorical tale (the "signalman"! the "traveller"!), but then nothing is quite what it seems and there is no allegory

STIGMA

by Phil Tonge

Synopsis

Stigma | BBC1 30mins | Wednesday Dec 28 1977 11pm–11.30pm | repeated Monday May 28 1978

With: Kate Binchy (Katherine Delgado), Peter Bowles (Peter Delgado), Maxine Gordon (Verity Delgado), Jon Laurimore (doctor), Christopher Blake, John Judd

Production Assistants Daphne Phipps and Val Sheppard; Production Unit Manager Elizabeth Small; Costume Designer Linda Woodfield; Makeup Madeleine Gaffney; Sound Recordist Mike Savage; Dubbing Mixer Peter Rann; Lighting Cameraman John Turner; Film Editor Dave King; Designer Stuart Walker; Writer Clive Exton

Producer Rosemary Hill
Director Lawrence Gordon Clark

**A Ghost
Story for
Christmas**

A red Citroen 2CV drives through the Wiltshire countryside, carrying Katherine Delgado and her daughter Verity. Newly moved to the countryside, Verity expresses a certain mardy-ness about the entire situation with a sullen "You can't get Capital[1] down here".

Pulling into their quaint little thatched cottage's driveway, we become aware of standing stones in the adjoining field. Two local workmen with a JCB are working around a large stone in the garden. Katherine's husband has ordered it moved, so as not to spoil his plans for a new lawn. As the workmen attach chains to the rock, a panning shot reveals more upright monoliths behind them.

As Katherine prepares dinner (a very red joint of beef), Verity jokes with the workmen outside and the kitchen radio reports on the (then current) news of the Voyager space probes. Sending Verity off to the shops for a bag of sugar, Mrs Delgado takes some tea out to the lads. They are in the process of trying to lift the huge lump of rock. The JCB strains against the weight, the stone begins to rise slightly, as it does there is a suggestion of a hole or somesuch under it. At this moment an "unearthly wind" picks up and envelops Katherine. The JCB gives out under the strain.

Coming over all trance-like, she wanders back to the kitchen. Verity returns with the sugar to find the workmen giving up for the day, unable to shift this monolith. "Some fell on stony ground," cracks one of the men. Mother is meanwhile "distant" in the house. Through the window — at which she vegetates — are more standing stones. She is oblivious to the ringing phone, which is answered by Verity.

After she takes the call from her husband, there is a mini-earthquake that rattles ornaments, cracks the plaster and breaks a mirror in the front room. Not that Verity seems to notice, as she trots into the room and straightens a picture frame.

Peeling runner beans for dinner, Katherine notices blood on a plate she's handling. Thinking she's cut her hand on the knife, she washes the blood off. There is no wound. She looks at the still raw and bloody joint and surmises she handled that. Whilst selecting a (red) dress for dinner, Katherine notices a red stain on her blouse. Running to the bathroom, she finds she's bleeding from under her left breast. In a silent panic she strips off and tries wiping away the blood, which is now covering her hands, face and most of the bathroom. There is no wound.

While this scene plays out, Verity is out wandering around the standing stones and looking at the distant Silbury Hill. Mother, meanwhile is cleaning up all the blood in the bathroom, as she does she notices fresh leakage coming from *somewhere*. In an unflinching close-up we see that her blood is actually seeping through the pores of her skin. She attaches what can only be described as a WWI field dressing to her afflicted area and hopes for the best. At this point her husband Peter arrives home in his white Volvo estate. He enters the cottage with Verity, whilst upstairs, Katherine exchanges her (red) dress for a horrible brown Laura Ashley number.

After dinner, Peter notices a red stain on Katherine's dress, which leads to a boorish remark about women being useless at uncorking wine. In a vaguely controlled panic, Katherine runs to the bathroom again. Peeling back the dressing... there is nothing. It really was a wine stain. She is relieved and laughs the incident away.

We cut straight to a shot of a blood-soaked sheet, dripping remorselessly onto the bedroom floor. Katherine is bleeding to death in her sleep. Peter wakes up next to her, disturbed by something downstairs (A woman singing? Laughing?). Coming down the stairs into the kitchen, Peter can hear a definite thumping. Turning on the light, an onion rolls on the kitchen floor. Putting it back on the worktop, a large vegetable knife moves by its own accord nearby. Remarkably undisturbed by this, Peter goes back to bed. He notices nothing at all amiss with his wife.

Dawn. A bigger crane turns up with the workmen. This time the stone is lifted. Underneath is a grave containing a skeleton. This is when Peter finds Katherine in a pool, well, lake of her own blood.

The local doctor turns up and is non-plussed by Mrs Delgado's condition. Again we are treated to more close-ups of oozing claret. The doctor and Peter load Katherine's limp body into the car, leaving Verity behind in the mad dash to the hospital.

Left alone with the workmen, Verity goes over to watch them dig out various artefacts from the grave. They find coins and four ceremonial looking daggers, one of which is found in the skeleton's ribcage. The doctor is giving Katherine CPR in the back of the car. The workmen show Verity the daggers. The doctor tells Peter to pull over... Katherine is dead. Verity tells the workmen, "The old religion. I read it in a book; they used to bury them under big stones. They thought they were witches..." She then pulls out an onion that she begins to peel with her long, red-painted fingernails. Katherine's dead face fills the screen. Cut to a helicopter shot of Peter's car in the lay-by, which merges with shots of a stone circle. The End.

Top Katherine oversees the workmen trying to remove the tree stump.
Middle and above Later she tries to stop the bleeding...

Notes

Thanks go to Mr
Dark-Season for his
help in producing this
review.

Critique

In 1977 the production team behind A Ghost Story For Christmas decided to ditch adaptations altogether and instead commission original teleplays. From this premise, the writer Clive Exton[2] provided the script for *Stigma*.

A massive departure from the stories that proceeded it, *Stigma* is based slapbang in the contemporary setting of the 1977 British countryside. It uses some touches to convey the contrast between the modern world (the Voyager space probes) with the ancient (the standing stones), and the acting (Binchy's silent panic in the bathroom is excellent) and direction are of a high standard.

However, the problem is that this is not a ghost story. *Stigma* is a straight down the line *horror* story. Although it's a perfectly competent television production, it just doesn't fit in with the *feel* of what a Christmas ghost story should be. The plot is simply about the horror of someone bleeding to death and it comes over as being just too cruel and *bad tempered* for it's Christmas slot.

I'm also sure that many female writers would have a field day pointing out that *Stigma* is a skit on the male fear of menstruation, and a nasty-minded one at that. It doesn't really help, that the first thing you see is an out of focus red blob that clumsily morphs into the Red 2CV. The gore and nudity (following on from the topless scene in *The Ash Tree*) are also signs that this story was "misjudged" for its slot.

Although, to be fair, the nudity is completely matter-of-fact and in no way salacious or puerile.

Exton tries to get some level of sophistication into his script, although with the programme length at a paltry thirty minutes he's somewhat handicapped.

1 London-based
independent radio
station.
2 Clive Exton (alias
MK Jeeves, a moniker
used by WC Fields)
has written for
many film and TV
productions including:
Armchair Theatre
(*Dumb Martian* being
of note), *Out of This
World* (the teleplays
Cold Equations and
Target Generation),
Doomwatch,
Survivors, *The Crezz*
and *Poirot*.
Also responsible for
the screenplays to
10 Rillington Place
(1971) and *Red Sonja*
(1985).
3 A peeled onion
carried in the hand
was also supposed
to ward off snakes.
If you dreamt of
peeling an onion
this would forecast
family troubles. Plus,
pagan/witchcraft
sources name the
onion as a symbol of
banishing, protection
and purifying.

Stigma

Deprived of the length to explore characters, Exton slips in references like the onion. Now, in English folklore, the onion was used as a way of attracting infection and illness in the house. The onion would be peeled, or in severe cases, cut into two four-pieces and placed around the sickbed. After a while the onion (peeled or sectioned) would be taken away from the house and buried. Thus removing the illness/infection.

Therefore, the scene where Peter is awakened to find a leaping onion and twitchy knife in the kitchen could have a deeper meaning. Could the sender of the curse be pointing to an obvious way to lift it? Is Verity's peeling of the onion be testament to a part two of the curse: "You daughter's a witch! Burn her!" Interesting, but very obscure.[3] In fact the more you study this production the more you wonder if Exton produced a longer script for, let's say, a fifty-minute teleplay.

Stigma seems largely forgotten by its viewers, although the *Daily Mail* gave it a favourable write-up ("...*worked on the imagination as well as the senses*") which the *Radio Times* used on it's listing blurb for the 1978 repeat.

All this may have had something to do with Lawrence Gordon Clark's decision to give up the ghost story strain and leg it to ITV. Mind you, the fact that he'd been doing them for the best part of a decade might have had a lot to do with it as well.

In the end *Stigma* comes over as a misjudgement, trying to update the "brand" but forgetting what made it a household favourite in the first place. Maybe even signalling the death-knell that would be next year's offering, *The Ice House*. ⒼⒻ

Not presently available in any format

THE ICE HOUSE

by Roy Gill

Synopsis

A health spa in a country house retreat, contemporary Britain. After his sauna, Paul goes for a massage but recoils from the masseur's cold hands. Bob explains that he has "a touch of the cools" — a condition that seems to affect most of the permanent staff, some more than others.

The Ice House | BBC1 35mins | Broadcast 11.35pm–12.10am Dec 25 1978 BBC1

With: John Stride (Paul), Elizabeth Romilly (Jessica), Geoffrey Burridge (Clovis), David Beames (Bob), Gladys Spencer (Diamond Lady), Eirene Beck (Rosetti Lady), Sam Avent (guest), Dennis Jennings (guest), Ronald Mayer (guest)

Production Assistants Brian Morgan, Terence Banks; Production Unit Manager Liz Small; Costume Designer Anna Downey; Makeup Magdalen Gaffney; Sound Dick Manton, Peter Rann; Photography Nigel Walters; Film Editor Tony Woollard; Designer Roger Murray-Leach

Producer Rosemary Hill
Director Derek Lister

Paul goes for a walk in the grounds, remarking to another resident — a silent older gentleman — on the comfort and warmth provided by the house. He encounters Jessica, one of the brother-sister team who runs the establishment. She claims looking after the guests comes easily to her as she has "always enjoyed people". Paul continues his walk, watched unseen by Jessica's brother, Clovis.

Later, on his way to dinner Paul passes an elegantly dressed elderly female resident. Realising he must dress more formally for meals, Paul returns to his room. As the old woman continues out of sight, a plaintive whimpering can be heard. In the drawing room, Paul converses with his hosts. They discuss ideas of human suffering, and Clovis suggests if life is "something merely to be got through, the only agreeable aspect of it might be its end". Paul is a little perturbed by the line of his host's argument, and assumes Clovis is joking. Jessica confirms that her brother has "very little sense of what is proper". Elsewhere in the room, the elderly lady that Paul encountered earlier can be seen to shiver and moan — despite the blazing fire in the drawing room grate.

The next day Paul goes for another massage, but it seems that Bob has an even icier touch than before. Bob begins to ask Paul for help to get away from the establishment but is interrupted by the arrival of Clovis, who takes over Bob's massage.

At night, Paul is awoken by a tapping sound. He opens his bedroom window, and is briefly disturbed by a mysterious cry. He dismisses it as "county noises" and returns to bed.

Walking in the garden the next day, Clovis reveals to Paul that Bob has left, suggesting that he was perhaps unhappy with the isolation of country life. They encounter Jessica, who enquires if Bob

Top Jessica and Clovis.
Middle Paul feels cold.
Above Jessica shows Paul
the "brother and sister" vine.

The
Ice House

has seen the ice house. They take him to see it. On the wall of the building grows an unusual vine with two large trumpet blossoms projecting from it. Jessica claims it was brought from overseas, and has been there as long as the ice house has. Bob asks for a cutting, but Jessica refuses. She insists that the vine is a "brother and sister" and does not need to bear fruit. Paul lingers by the ice house door, but does not enter. He comments that the pair should really think of a way of propagating the plant, as in time everything dies. "Ice preserves," responds Clovis.

Exercising in the gym, Paul talks with Clovis about his plans to move to a smaller house now that his wife has left him. Clovis comments that the advertisement for the establishment draws many isolated people to them. Later, taking tea in the garden with the pair, Paul is encouraged by Jessica to go visit the vine again. Paul inhales the plant's scent, but is disturbed by the door of the nearby ice house slamming shut. He goes to investigate but finds it is firmly locked. On his way back through the garden, he attempts to greet another guest. The woman appears at first to be frozen in place where she sits — she rocks rigidly to one side when touched by Paul — but later is seen to continue on her way as if nothing has happened.

In the evening, Paul comments to his hosts on the incredible "almost overpowering" scent of the vine. The pair exchange knowing glances. Later, Paul inhales the vine's scent from his bedroom window before closing it for the night. Meanwhile in the garden we see Clovis letting down his sister's hair and kissing her passionately. Above them, the twin trumpets of the vine inch apart. An orchard-shaped crack appears in Paul's bedroom window.

During his activities the next day Paul shivers abruptly — perhaps he too is getting "a touch of the cools"? He reports the crack in the window to Clovis, who says it must be fixed, but mentions this may take some time. Paul quizzes his hosts about the purpose of the ice house — they insist that even in this day and age it is used to store ice. Paul goes to investigate, but becomes flustered at the ice house door. He tells Jessica he is coming down with a cold, and must return to the house.

Paul wakes in the night, dresses and heads to the ice house. Pausing only to smell the vine blossoms, he enters the darkened storeroom. Lighting a piece of paper to see by, Paul discovers a number of shrouded shapes. He removes a tarpaulin, and to his horror sees Bob's face staring back at him from within the block of ice. Fleeing the building he runs into Clovis, and tells him that he plans to leave tomorrow. Clovis agrees, and ushers Paul back to his bedroom. Clovis talks soothingly to Paul, and enquires what he used to light his way inside the ice house. Paul reveals it was a letter from his wife. Clovis remains by Paul's side, comforting him, as he goes to sleep.

Jessica brings Paul breakfast the next day, and claims that he went sleepwalking last night and suffered from nightmares. She encourages him to re-inspect the ice house by day. They go together. Contrary to his recollection, the ice house interior is now illuminated by electric light — and there is no large free-standing block containing a deep frozen masseur! Paul slowly comes to the decision that he must have been mistaken, and agrees to spend the rest of his stay as planned.

Later in the sauna Paul cries out that he is cold and begs for help but the other residents simply look on impassively. Clovis and Jessica arrive. Jessica tells Paul that she and her brother do not approve of death — flesh returns not to dust or ashes but stench and slime. "Ice preserves," finishes Clovis. The pair lead the unprotesting Paul by the hand to the ice house. A waiter in a white shirt and black bow tie opens the door for him. Looking back only once, Paul goes quietly inside and the door is closed.

Critique #1   *by Roy Gill*

The Ice House provides a rather atypical conclusion to the Ghost Story For Christmas sequence. Directed not for once by Lawrence Gordon Clark, and offering for only the second time a contemporary tale rather than an MR James or Dickens adaptation, *The Ice House* is a strange, hallucinatory experience that offers more questions than it answers.

Director Derek Lister creates a hazy dream-like atmosphere for the health resort. An almost-silent cast of immaculately dressed older people are pictured arranged in opulent drawing rooms, taking tea, playing croquet or strolling on sun drenched lawns. Only one guest is ever heard to speak — the woman Paul encounters sitting rigidly in the garden — and even here Lister employs an abrupt edit between an image of the woman seated and one of her walking away bidding "good evening", leaving Paul (and the viewer) uncertain as to which event actually occurred. Does Paul notice that the other guests barely communicate? It seems unlikely, given that it takes him a good while even to realise that Clovis and Jessica pay attention mainly to him whilst the other guests seemingly go about their stately, disconnected

manoeuvres unassisted. He isn't genuinely perturbed by the strangeness of it all until his grisly discovery in the ice house, and even that passes swiftly as Clovis lulls him back into submission. The resulting scene in which Clovis offers to stay by Paul as he sleeps and cradles the troubled older man in his arms is, due to the mixed signals of nurture/love and threat it sends out, one of the text's most unsettling moments. All in all *The Ice House* is rather like a nightmare in which periods of lucidity and self-awareness are all too fleeting. As a viewer you find yourself wanting to shout and raise Paul from his torpor, his stupefied middle class delight at the comfort of his surroundings, but the narcotic influence of the vine is too strong — he's already been dragged under. Moments like these reach their apogee with the strange, quiet ending where Paul walks willingly into the ice house — surely an infinitely more disturbing fate than any gory coerced dispatch could offer.

Undoubtedly the programme's biggest enigma is Jessica and Clovis. What exactly are they? Despite the tale's billing as a ghost story there's nothing remotely ethereal about this pair — quite the opposite in fact. Costume and makeup designers Anna Downey and Magdalen Gaffney outfit Clovis and Jessica to emphasise both their physicality and their mysterious connection to the red and white vine: Jessica wears floral print dresses, her dark red lips and full auburn hair a contrast to her pale face, whilst her handsome blond brother favours elegant white linen suits and pastel shirts. There could be a suggestion of vampirism in Bowen's script. Do the pair somehow draw vitality from the lonely guests they lure to their establishment? Paul, who appears to be in robust middle age, is notably younger than the others who due to their passivity and silence could be deduced to be "processed goods": Jessica does assert — in one of many innuendo laden speeches — that the most recent guest gets the most care. There's certainly an element of seduction to the siblings' technique — Jessica enjoys "having people" (more knowing innuendo) and their "pleasure to please" Paul's every whim extends from forfeiting a game of croquet to instantly taking over his massage when Bob's touch proves too icy: "Mmm, delightful," groans Paul as Clovis' fingers caress him… However, if Clovis and Jessica are vampires, how do we reconcile this with the pair's stated disgust at the corruption of decaying flesh and delight in the possibilities of ice for preservation? Such aesthetic concerns seem distinctly at odds with the gory pursuit of vampirism, which after all comes down to animating a dead body through ingesting the life fluid of another.

Furthermore, how exactly are the pair connected to the vine? Do they make use of its power to lure people in, or are they subservient to it (perhaps even siren-like hallucinations created by its overpowering scent)? There's even an ambiguity to their relationships. Ostensibly a brother and sister, they are presented also as lovers, parent-comforters, seducers. I assume the writer and director's intention is for the couple to be both erotic and disturbing, but it has to be said that their over-determined dialogue and knowing glances do occasionally push the production into the realm of high camp. The fairly unsubtle psychoanalytic undertones of the script are an essay in themselves: it's as if Paul — who I assume from his comments to be if not a psychiatrist then at least in the medical profession — has conjured up a walking pair of Freudian nightmares to alternately comfort and torment him into his final ice house fugue…

It's this very lack of definition, of answers and explanations, that differentiates *The Ice House* from more traditional ghost tales and indeed from the areas explored in the rest of the Ghost Story For Christmas sequence, where supernatural events require an origin (usually a past traumatic event) and a catalyst to trigger them (a warning, retribution, a disturbed artefact etc). The existence and nature of the ghost is usually further legitimated through techniques like tales being told, multiple narrators, ancient documents (a tradition continued right up to current

supernatural series *Buffy the Vampire Slayer* in which there's usually at least a quick net reference to substantiate and explain the latest monster-of-the-week). Here, by contrast, there's no cause/effect chain, no dusty tome finally revealing what was going on and why. Instead, we are told only that the vine has been there as long as the ice house has. It came from overseas and will sustain until it is replaced (whatever that means). That is all. The overall success then of *The Ice House* depends entirely on your personal perspective. It might be an overheated mixture of half-formed and unexplained ideas, or it could be a daring transgression of genre conventions, a dream-like coda to the series.

Take a deep breath. The scent is… almost overpowering.

Critique #2   by Robin Davies

This is certainly the most enigmatic of the Christmas ghost stories and it has been dismissed by some viewers as pretentious; but repeated viewings reveal it to be perhaps the richest and most rewarding of the whole series. Written by John Bowen, it bears little relation to the Jamesian archetype, but its milieu of middle class characters caught up in inexplicable events and its elegant, subtly menacing dialogue is strongly reminiscent of the work of Robert Aickman (particularly his stories *The Hospice* and *Into the Wood*). Aickman actually preferred to label his tales as "strange stories" rather than "ghost stories". This is a much more accurate term for his hauntingly ambiguous and insidiously disturbing work which, like *The Ice House*, resists easy supernatural or psychological interpretation, and sometimes verges on surrealism.

The protagonist of *The Ice House*, Paul, is staying at a health farm run by Clovis and his sister Jessica. We soon

The Ice House

learn that the local villagers avoid the place and that the other residents are all solitary types, mostly old or middle aged. "Those who do come tend to stay," says Clovis.

The health farm attracts people of a particular type, people who are tired of life, and the place seems to offer them a strange sort of immortality. They are intoxicated by the perfume of the strange vine in the ice house (perhaps the holes in Paul's window are to allow the scent into his room) and suffer sudden chills until they somehow enter a zombie-like existence. They are preserved by the ice in some way, neither dead nor alive but immune to bodily decay and presumably also confined to the house and its grounds, trapped in an eternity of croquet games and afternoon tea. The presence of the other blocks of ice that Paul sees suggests that the guests re-freeze themselves periodically. On one occasion after Paul hears the door of the ice house closing he finds an old woman (credited as "diamond lady") sitting impassively in the garden apparently in a trance. Presumably she needs a little time to "thaw out" because within minutes she walks past him with a polite greeting.

A scene on the croquet lawn encapsulates the major theme of the play. When Clovis declines to knock Paul's ball off the lawn when he has the chance Paul expresses surprise that the game is played in so gentle a manner. Clovis asks "You find it lacks edge?" and Paul replies "No indeed. Surprisingly pleasant." Within seconds he shudders with an attack of "the cools". Paul seeks to avoid conflict, risk, commitment, vitality. The health farm is an entropic zone where he can enter his desired state of somnambulant stasis.

The Ice House is the only one of the series not to be directed by Lawrence Gordon Clark (around this time he filmed another MR James adaptation, *Casting the Runes* for Yorkshire Television which aired April 24, 1979) but Derek Lister does a superb job in his stead. The restrained music, sensitivity to natural sound, extensive use of natural locations, the deliberate pace and careful avoidance of lurid shock tactics and special effects — all these combine to evoke a mood of strangeness and unease. Also, the visual design expresses the themes of the story. The decor of the health farm is predominantly white. There

are even two white peacocks in the garden. This not only echoes the white clothing of the man in charge (Clovis) but also points up the siblings' obsessive revulsion of bodily decay. Of course it also represents the whiteness of ice itself. The mysterious, whimpering "diamond lady" is always seen wearing a white dress and diamonds (colloquially "ice").

But who are Clovis and Jessica, and where do they come from? This is not clear at all but, because they are symbolically echoed in the film by the flowers on the vine, perhaps their comments about the plant may shed light on their own nature. The plant was brought to England from abroad and Paul is surprised by how hardy it is. His request for a cutting is firmly refused, which suggests that damage to the plant might also damage Clovis and Jessica. The vine is not self-pollinating and it "does not die". The flowers are brother and sister and do not bear fruit. Clovis says, "They persist until they are replaced." This suggests that Clovis and Jessica cannot reproduce themselves (though they seem to be lovers). It's tempting to speculate that the two of them actually grew from the plant (like the pod-people in *Invasion of the Body Snatchers*) and that they will eventually be replaced by fresh blooms. All this is fairly tenuous speculation but there is no denying that Clovis and Jessica are not normal human beings. Their unctuous politeness and excessively crisp diction are distinctly sinister, and perhaps they are best viewed as metaphors for middle class ennui. They represent the world of genteel English good taste taken to an extreme, a fossilised state where emotions are suppressed beneath a veneer of etiquette and routine, where life (as Paul implies at one point) is something to be "got through" rather than lived, and where the inevitable horrors of death are swept under the carpet. All health farms are devoted to the battle against death but this one seems to be against any kind of meaningful life as well.

If *The Ice House* contains a message, perhaps it is that we must engage wholeheartedly and realistically with life and its risks. Failure to do so means that we are never really alive at all... 𝒢𝓕

Not presently available in any format

BBC HORROR: A MISCELLANY

WHISTLE AND I'LL COME TO YOU

by Darren Arnold

WHISTLE AND I'LL COME TO YOU is a fairly astonishing work. While viewing the film, it is difficult to comprehend that it debuted on UK TV way back in 1968 — not, you understand, because it possesses anything in the way of risqué content, but rather due to the highly ambitious nature of the piece. WHISTLE AND I'LL COME TO YOU is a clever and daring take on what was even in its time a well-established genre.

Dir: Jonathan Miller
1968

Before we even get to the actual film, there's an audacity present in the circumstances of the film's initial screening — *Whistle and I'll Come To You* played as part of the BBC's *Omnibus* strand, an arts documentary slot not entirely dissimilar to the same station's *Monitor* or ITV's arts ghetto *The South Bank Show*. It seems a rather odd place to put what is essentially a ghost story, and almost as if to justify the film's inclusion in the series there's an opening voiceover by the director (Jonathan Miller), who makes reference to the work of *Whistle*'s author MR James. It's as if the film was ostensibly being screened as an essay on James, when in reality it's little more than a dramatisation of one of the author's best-known stories.

On first viewing, *Whistle and I'll Come To You* turns viewer expectations firmly on their head. A late 1960s b&w BBC ghost story that opens with a somewhat stilted voiceover would, you'd have thought, normally play as a garden-variety haunted house tale (or a slight variation on that theme). And at the beginning of *Whistle and I'll Come To You*, we have no reason to expect anything as radically different as what eventually unfolds.

While the above would seem to suggest that the film is a very different beast to what was doing the rounds at that time, *Whistle...* isn't some sort of experimental, inaccessible avant garde exercise. Miller doesn't dispense with orthodox storytelling techniques, but weaves his narrative in a way that's instantly recognisable to anyone with the slightest knowledge of how ghost stories are structured. That said, the film tends to end with the climax, leaving no time or space for the often comforting dénouement that usually wraps up such stories.

Arguably the most daring and innovative aspect of *Whistle and I'll Come To You* is that, at first glance, it doesn't really appear to be about anything much at all: an eccentric academic takes a holiday in an isolated, windswept part of East Anglia; whilst out walking he finds an old whistle; he experiences strange dreams; and finally, he witnesses an alarming incident in which the sheets on an unoccupied bed appear to be moving. Not a great deal happens on the surface, and much is left for the viewer to figure out. Even nowadays it's a work that takes more than one viewing to "get", and, as already mentioned, in its time it must have left many of its audience thoroughly confused and unsatisfied; this wasn't entertainment on a plate, and even for those sufficiently interested in taking a second look at the film there obviously wasn't the benefit of the video recorder (how video and DVD has transformed film/media criticism...).

In addition to the film being a subtle, suggestive work, there's an astonishing performance from Michael Hordern. Not necessarily astonishing in terms of how we generally judge actors' performances, but rather in how Hordern (and no doubt Miller) interpret the part of Professor Parkins. As with the general feel of the film, what is noteworthy about the performance seems especially daring for its day — Hordern plays the Professor as a predictably stuffy and inward-looking academic, yet manages to neatly sidestep mere caricature. This is mainly achieved through his near ceaseless breathy mutterings, autistically latching onto throwaway phrases that he hears from the other guests in the hotel, or chuckling to himself as he utters self-originating banalities — the scene in which he takes a pencil rubbing from the whistle being a prime example. His body language is also completely strange — just look at how he bends and twists in the after-dinner scene where several other guests walk past him in the hall.

Parkins appears virtually incapable of holding anything like a typical conversation — when fellow guest the Colonel (Ambrose Coghill), by way of polite conversation, enquires as to whether or not the Professor believes in ghosts, it leads to such a frankly painful dissection of the question that it's a wonder that the Colonel

Previous page Whether he likes it or not, the child-like Prof Parkins is given his own dinner table, away from the rest of the guests.
This page, from top Parkins discovers the flute and is immediately struck by a sense of being watched. He spies a static figure on the beach behind him.

Top and middle Parkins cleans the flute and blows into it, a strange feeling overtakes him. ***Above*** Parkins has no explanation as to why the other bed in his room looks like it has been slept in.

Whistle and I'll Come To You

remains reasonably good-humoured throughout. Not only does the Professor rather condescendingly indicate the Colonel's initial question (and half-hearted follow-ups) to be rather childish, but he also can't really engage in eye contact or any other form of meaningful interaction with his fellow diner (the whole "conversation" takes place over breakfast). It is obvious that, in Parkins' eyes, the question is more of a presence than the actual enquirer, which provides further evidence of the Professor's preference for the academic over the personal. A rather uninspired question it may have been, but Parkins is completely oblivious to the purpose of such an enquiry — simply to fill the kind of dead air that can be uncomfortable when in close proximity to strangers. If the Colonel could have his time over again, I'm sure he'd plump for the dead air.

Interestingly, this scene is arguably one of the most important in the film. While the Professor's ideas on ghosts are not to be paid too much attention, his arrogance in the face of such an innocuous question is undoubtedly linked to the end of the story (that said, the film doesn't descend to a clumsiness where the Professor clearly rubbishes the idea of ghosts, which would have telegraphed what was to come in very plain terms). In the middle of the night the Professor sees the sheets on the other (unoccupied) bed in his room moving around as if something (or someone) is inside them, and his hysterical reaction is only quelled somewhat when the Colonel comes into the room, switches on the light, sits the Professor down, and tries to restore some order by making up the rumpled bed sheets. The payback seems obvious: Professor Parkins' clever-clever answer(s) to the Colonel's throwaway question have just earned him a visit from a ghost. And to compound matters, the saviour of this episode just so happens to be the Colonel. Further still, Parkins' humiliation is well and truly complete by the visiting spirit taking the form of an animated white sheet at face value, it's harder to think of a more infantile, hackneyed representation of a ghost (although that said, the moving sheet does look pretty creepy). It's quite an answer to academic musings regarding just exactly what is meant by the term "ghost".

It's never clear whether the visitation is for real, or a result of Parkins' seemingly unhinged mental state, or simply a bad dream. The sheets on the bed have certainly been moved, but that could quite easily be the sort of thing someone might do in their sleep, especially considering the skewed mindset of the room's inhabitant. Jonathan Miller's opening voiceover refers to the story as being about "the dangers of intellectual pride", and the conclusion seems to strongly hint that there may be a price to pay for an overtly academic, unworldly existence such as that of the Professor's. ℭℱ

Available on BFI DVD

THE WITHERED ARM

by Martin Jones

Southern England, in the midst of the nineteenth-century. When farmer John Lodge returns home with his new bride Gertrude, milkmaid Rhoda Brook becomes strangely agitated by her presence. It transpires that Rhoda's son Jamie is the illegitimate spawn of Lodge. One night Rhoda has a dream in which Gertrude, appearing as a dishevelled, grinning grotesque, taunts her with the wedding ring on her finger. Angry, Rhoda grabs the bride's arm and then wakes. The next morning, Gertrude discovers four welts on her left arm. The ailment baffles the local doctor, and soon becomes not just a burden to the bride, but also a tarnish on Lodge's reputation. Trapped and alone on the farm, Gertrude turns to Rhoda as the only person who can help her. Reluctantly, Rhoda takes her to Conjurer Trendle, the healer of the district. He recognises the marks to be the work of an enemy, but he can only bring to light the image of that enemy. In a glass filled with water and egg yolk, Gertrude sees her antagonist's face: Rhoda.

After Rhoda and Jamie are forced to leave the farm, Gertrude becomes more solitary and her arm increasingly withered. In desperation she returns to Trendle. He tells her there is only one sure cure: "You must touch with a limb the neck of a man who's just been hanged." Gertrude travels to the town of Casterbridge and bribes the hangman so that she might do such a thing directly after a hanging the next day. The hangman tells her that the accused, a young boy caught setting fire to hay bales, is most likely innocent. After the hanging, the corpse is brought down and Gertrude hurries to touch it, only to see that it is in fact Jamie. When Lodge and Rhoda appear, she sees Gertrude holding her arm above the corpse just as she did in her hideous dream: "You're like her at last!" Gertrude collapses and soon after dies. Without an heir, Lodge sells the farm but makes sure that Rhoda is reinstated back in her old cottage.

Dir: Desmond Davis
1973

Rhoda has bad dreams...

The Withered Arm

Part of a BBC series entitled Wessex Tales — presumably all adaptations from Thomas Hardy's 1888 short story collection of the same name — *The Withered Arm* is a fifty-minute tale of loss, jealousy and revenge; all the complex emotions that Hardy dealt with in his writing. It's also about how resolutely unfair and rigid nineteenth-century social conventions could be. Pretty young Gertrude (Yvonne Antrobus) marries into an unfamiliar world, and soon finds her status slipping when she cannot bear Lodge (Edward Hardwicke) a child. Work-weathered Rhoda (Billie Whitelaw)

is stuck with her ghosts of the past in the form of Lodge's unacknowledged son, a constant reminder that her meagre way of life will never change. Such loss makes her want to take it out on an innocent: Gertrude.

Rhys Adrian's dramatisation takes a few pointers from period-set British horror films of the time, such as *Witchfinder General* and *Blood On Satan's Claw*. Wessex was Hardy's name for the county of Dorset, and director Desmond Davis (who went on to direct the 1981 star-bloated clunker *Clash of the Titans*) captures the bleak beauty of it all. Like Piers Haggard and Michael Reeves, he fills the screen with more sky than land, and has his solitary characters wander through dry, brown fields of bracken and ploughed earth. These sinister rural landscapes give *The Withered Arm* a connection to *Witchfinder*, whilst Gertrude's ugly physical affliction makes it a close relation to *Blood*. Davis also adds some seemingly slight but effective scenes to the story: a sequence in which Rhoda's cottage becomes more and more derelict in order to show the passing of time; the locals of Casterbridge clambering to see the noose being made; the silhouette of the gallows against the day-for-night sky; and an old man outside Gertrude's window selling little wooden hanging figures (Hardy himself was an enthusiastic spectator of public hangings). Top acting honours go to the eternally creepy Billie Whitelaw. Only she could make milking a cow look unnaturally sinister. **CF**

THE YEAR OF THE SEX OLYMPICS

by Andy Murray

Thankfully, quality does seem to win out in the end. Copies of BIG BROTHER 3: UNSEEN AND UNCUT! can be picked up for a song from your local bargain bins. But twenty-five years after its first broadcast, Nigel Kneale's extraordinary TV play THE YEAR OF THE SEX OLYMPICS (1968) has just been released on DVD. It's a tale of the near future — 'sooner than you think', according to the opening titles — where almighty television has become a vacuous social placebo, awash with sexual content expressly designed to suppress physical desire in viewers, and thereby keep the population explosion down. A spirited dissenter manages to get on screen, but is accidentally killed. The viewers respond well to this, though, and canny executives promptly launch The Live-Life Show, in which a young family is filmed twenty-four hours a day struggling to survive on a weather-beaten island. And to keep proceedings on the boil, they're unwittingly sharing the place with a psychotic killer. It's dark, satirical stuff, a rich and compelling work from one of television's great unsung directors.

Kneale's unparalleled TV writing career kicked off fifty years ago, when his groundbreaking BBC serial *The Quatermass Experiment* (1953; intended merely to plug a gap in the summer schedules) became a national phenomenon, spawning three follow-ups and a memorable set of big screen adaptations from the then-unknown Hammer Studios. Today, Kneale is increasingly regarded as the forefather of British television drama, worshipped as a genius by modern TV writers such as Russell T Davies and The League of Gentlemen. Although he's been lauded for predicting the coming of Reality TV thirty years in advance with *The Year of the Sex Olympics*, Kneale is wary of this oversimplified comparison (and who can

"This must not be put on! I will have the producer sacked!" So said Mary Whitehouse about NIGEL KNEALE's 1968 play, THE YEAR OF THE SEX OLYMPICS, oblivious to the fact that it might just predict the shape of entertainment to come.

Dir Michael Elliott
1968

This page Contenders in the Sex Olympics.

Year of
the Sex
Olympics

blame him: would you like to be held responsible for *I'm a Celebrity, Get Me Out of Here?*). Kneale's piece has a wider point to make about the nature of television, and what society needs from it. The play seems to be saying that, if allowed, television will quickly be sapped of any worth or intelligence, and will pander to the very lowest common denominator. Although capable of stirring and challenging the viewer in his own home, it's more likely to turn into an armchair-friendly version of throwing Christians to the lions.

Kneale had, in fact, left television to write for film some years previously. On the recommendation of Kenneth Tynan, he adapted John Osbourne's *Look Back In Anger* (1959) and *The Entertainer* (1960) for director Tony Richardson. Other adaptation work followed, but two cinema projects that fell by the wayside were a version of *Lord of the Flies* for the fading Ealing Studios, and a film of Aldous Huxley's *Brave New World*, which was to have been directed by Jack Cardiff.

The Year of the Sex Olympics therefore marked Kneale's first TV work for four years, the BBC having effected a tenuous reconciliation with the writer. Looking back today, Kneale is clearly proud of it, but remembers a production beset by problems. "It was a funny piece. It was a nightmare to even contemplate doing it, and we had every possible trouble." Indeed, there had been initial doubts as to whether it would go ahead at all. "Mary Whitehouse somehow got hold of the script," Kneale says. "There was always some little spy around to slip her things. She read little more than the title before announcing 'This must not be put on! I will have the producer sacked!'" Thankfully, her demands fell on deaf ears and the BBC brazened it out. This was to be an unusual piece, part of a season of new dramas and made entirely in colour; it made extensive, early use of the 'chromakey' process, electronically patching studio performances over artificial scenery. The designers promptly went to town on an elaborate, gaudy vision of the future, not stopping short of gold face make-up (causing Nancy Banks-Smith, in a contemporary review, to exclaim "If you didn't see it in colour, you didn't really see it").

Director Michael Elliott, a regular collaborator with Kneale during the period, knew a thing or two about actors: at the time, he was busy putting Manchester's Royal Exchange Theatre on the map. Leonard Rossiter, then a staple of TV drama (before his seventies sitcom heyday), was cast as cynical TV producer Ugo Priest. The role of ambitious young TV executive Lasar Opie was actually earmarked for Tom Courtenay, who elected late in the day to star in a production of *Hamlet* instead (and received as a result some of the poorest notices of his career). The part went instead to a TV newcomer — one Brian Cox, today a staple of Hollywood fare such as *X Men 2* (2003) and *The Ring* (2002). Kneale retains much fondness for Cox' "outstandingly good" performance. Likewise, Cox clearly holds his debut in some regard, as he provides a commentary track for this DVD release. Production was further blighted by a BBC electricians' strike, as Kneale recalls. "We lost days. Meanwhile they all came back here [to Kneale's family home in South London] — Leonard Rossiter, Brian Cox and the others. They all just sat about in acute gloom, wondering if they'd ever finish the thing."

Nevertheless, finish it they did. Kneale remembers the result as "a very splendid show — it looked marvellous on the screen". Sadly, the transmitted colour version no longer exists. Much archive TV material was, of course, wiped prior to the coming of home video and DVD, as the costs of storing it vastly outweighed the seemingly negligible advantages of keeping it for posterity. Many of Kneale's key works were lost in this manner, not least his unsettling 1963 nuclear catastrophe warning *The Road*. *The Year of the Sex Olympics* was thought to have suffered the same fate, but a telecine copy was located in recent years. Regrettably, it's in b&w, which robs the result of the impact of an overwhelming barrage of colour.

Nevertheless, what ultimately gives the piece its power is the clarity of its vision. One of the pioneers of television drama is allowed to predict a very unappealing future for the medium, creating a whole future world with its own attitudes and even speech patterns. With its notions of widespread social control and a sterile, state-controlled future, it's in much the same vein as Huxley's *Brave New World*, suggesting the unmade film project left its mark on Kneale. And it bears some comparison to Orwell's dystopian *Nineteen Eighty-Four*, which Kneale had previously adapted for television in 1954 to extremely powerful effect (questions were raised in Parliament about the impact of the serial, and high-level discussions almost scuppered a repeat performance days later). Most importantly, however, *The Year of the Sex Olympics* is the work of a remarkable TV writer creating something entirely unique to television, and it stands, rather ironically, as a testament — perhaps even an inspiration — to the idea that television can have a vision, and be truly original and powerful in the process. ◑

This review first appeared on [w] www.kamera.co.uk
The Year of the Sex Olympics is available on BFI DVD

Top Brian Cox as Lasar Opie and Leonard Rossiter as Ugo Priest, discussing the finer points of television.
Middle Opie finds himself on a lonely island, one of the unwitting participants in The Live-Life Show.
Above When it all ends tragically for Opie, the studio is overjoyed.

Andy Murray is the author of *Nigel Kneale: Into The Unknown*, to be published in 2004 by Headpress. Truly a key figure in British popular culture, yet a vastly underrated one, *Into The Unknown* draws on Kneale's work and assesses its pioneering nature and subsequent massive influence. Drawing on interviews with major collaborators and high-profile fans — including John Carpenter, Dan O'Bannon, Ramsey Campbell, Grant Morrison and Mark Gatiss, to name but a few — *Into The Unknown* has the full support of Kneale himself, whose conversations and anecdotes feature throughout.

THE MAKING OF
THE WAR GAME

by Andrew Screen

It was a bleak and unconventional drama concerning a nuclear strike on Britain. Made in 1965 by PETER WATKINS, THE WAR GAME frightened the government and resulted in a ban spanning twenty years.

Peter Watkins spent his childhood experiencing the Blitz in London during the Second World War. These early years of life would form part of the inspiration behind his most widely known work, the controversial 1965 BBC drama documentary THE WAR GAME. Considered at the time by both the BBC and the government to be too controversial for transmission the programme was banned for twenty years. Born in Norbiton, Surrey, on October 29, 1935, Watkins originally studied drama at RADA before undertaking his National Service with the East Surrey Regiment in Canterbury. It was during this period that Watkins made his short film, THE FORGOTTEN FACES (1959), which recreated the 1956 Budapest uprising on the streets of Canterbury. This was a companion piece of work to the equally remarkable DIARY OF AN UNKNOWN SOLDIER (1960), which recreated the gruesome conditions of WWI in a field in Southern England.

The strength of these short films was enough for Watkins to land a job at the BBC in 1963, working as production assistant on various documentaries for the new channel BBC2. His first directing credit for the BBC was *Culloden* in 1964. With positive reactions from both critics (a BAFTA award) and audience Watkins wanted to reactivate an idea for a film on atomic war that he had been planning since 1961. In fact, on entering the director's position at the BBC this had been his first pitch for production. In 1964, and after much debate and scrutiny at the highest levels within the BBC, Watkins was finally given the go ahead for the production. Even at this early stage the BBC warned Watkins that the production might never be finished.

Commissioned for the Wednesday Play strand, and originally called *After The Bomb*, Watkins' early script featured the stories of individual characters caught up in the apocalyptic events and was much more drama stylized. Some of these characters such as Dr David Thorley and Chief Fire Officer Charles Brookes are present in the finished programme in greatly reduced roles.

Watkins invested a great deal of time and energy in researching his script. As well as consulting many books, papers and pamphlets on nuclear war he also viewed newsreels and photographs from Germany concentrating on the bombing of Dresden, Hamburg and Darmstadt, and from Japan regarding the hydrogen bombing of Nagasaki and Hiroshima. Dresden inspired the scenes involving the firestorm, which was severely critisised by the Home Office who stated that this was a highly unlikely event after nuclear conflict. This is in fact now commonly accepted as a genuine fact and was a documented phenomena of the Dresden bombing, killing more people than the actual explosions.

> The BBC panicked on seeing the final cut and violated their Charter of Independence

Many of the rolling captions featured in the production carry facts and quotes derived from Watkins' meticulous studies. During the course of his research, Watkins was appalled at the lack of education and information on nuclear conflict available to the general public. With historical perspective and the declassifying of official documents we now know that from 1954 subsequent governments, both Labour and Tory, were deliberately suppressing information to "retain control of the manner in which the effect of nuclear weapons were made known to the public". Watkins also

consulted articles on the 1954 Nevada Desert nuclear tests as well as interviewing over fifty people including scientists, doctors and psychiatrists. Watkins later commented on his thorough research:

> I wanted to know the amount of force required to fling a brick three hundred yards in how many seconds, the amount of thermal heat required to melt an eyeball at this and that distance. I read reports from Hiroshima, Nagasaki and Dresden and found that, though there is plenty of technical material, the emotional effect of the atom bomb on people has been less thoroughly investigated.

Watkins submitted a list of questions to the Home Office as part of his research, which immediately alarmed the government department. Watkins asked about the preparations for war and what emergency actions the country would undertake. The Home Office contacted the BBC seeking clarification of what was being attempted by the broadcasters and shortly afterwards officially withdrew all support for the film. Watkins still managed to gleam such terrifying information as the placing of patients into three categories. Two categories were deemed treatable, whilst the third would be left without painkillers to die. The mercy killing of such patients and the execution of looters was also part of emergency procedures put in place by the Home Office.

Much of the rain of critical fire showered upon the production consisted of personal attacks on Watkins himself and his motivations. He was portrayed as a crude propagandist for the fledging CND and peace movements, though none of the contemporary critics attacked *The War Games'* technical depiction of a nuclear attack and its aftermath. The Fire Service did co-operate however, going against Home Office instructions. Senior Fire Officers who had seen the effects of small scale firebombing in WWII were very aware that there was absolutely no way their service could

Peter Watkins

**The Making
of The
War Game**

cope with nuclear attack and the resulting firestorms.

Shooting began in April 1965 on location in the Kent towns of Tonsbridge, Gravesend, Dover and Chattham. The mainly amateur cast was recruited via a series of public meetings throughout Kent held by Watkins months before photography began. Cinematographer Peter Bartlett had begun his career as a newsreel cameraman and his later credits included many BBC plays such as *The Adventures of Don Quixote* (1973) and *Brimstone and Treacle* (1976). Watkins and Bartlett utilized a lot of wide-angle shots with deep focus to emulate newsreel photography and to give *The War Game* a momentum and energy. To convey the intensity of the atomic blast wave instead of simply shaking the camera, which would have given sharp movements, Watkins and other crewmembers physically jostled Bartlett. This gave a less jerky and smoother impression. The effect of the heat flash was realised in camera by over exposing the 16mm film and then printing a portion in negative to convey the intensity of the flash.

The scenes set around the firestorm were shot at an abandoned military barracks near Dover. Stuntman Derek Ware instructed the extras in how to tumble and roll realistically to portray the effects

of the scorching inrush of wind. Ware had worked on *Culloden* coordinating the battle sequences and would also go on to work on the film *Privilege* with Watkins. During the sixties and seventies Ware provided the majority of the stunt work on *Doctor Who* and many other BBC productions with the stunt team simply known as Havoc. The deadly cloud of carbon monoxide gas was realised by using ordinary household flour that was then blown by large fans on location.

Film editor Michael Bradsell had also worked previously with Watkins on *Culloden*. His credits after *The War Game* include many major and important British films including *Women In Love* (1969), *Savage Messiah* (1972), *The Duelists* (1977), *Jabberwocky* (1977), *Local Hero* (1983), *Gothic* (1986) and more recently *Wilde* (1997). For events featured after the nuclear attack Watkins and Bradsell deliberately scuffed up and copied the film. This was to increase the contrast and grain and thus mimic WWII newsreel footage.

The use of non-actors extended to the many vox-pop scenes. Watkins asked extras unscripted questions and used their first replies in the final edit. Their views and lack of wider knowledge shocked Watkins, and their use in the finished film contrasted with images of

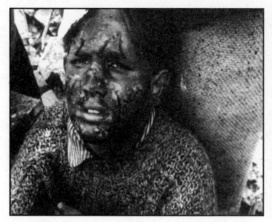

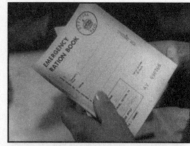

the horrific effects of nuclear war. Watkins' own voice is heard questioning various characters such as the man delivering Protect and Survive pamphlets and the battle weary Civil Defense worker after the attack. Other voice-overs were supplied by Michael Aspel who delivered all the factual items, whilst real life BBC newsreader Dick Graham narrated the unfolding story of the nuclear attack. This helps separate fact from fiction for the viewer and give the storyline grounding in the present. The diagrams used during the opening scenes to illustrate nuclear fallout would have also been familiar to the viewer at the time, as similar designs were used in documentary and news programmes. Thankfully, as proposed by the script, a nuclear war had not come to pass by 1980.

Preparation... and the bomb goes off. *Scenes from* The War Game.

The head of documentaries Dick Caulston and BBC controller Huw Wheldon pressured Watkins to delete the climatic execution scene. Watkins relented on other cuts, but remained steadfast on the execution. Together with a number of other objections that included the depiction of armed police mercy killing and scenes of civil defence workers criticing the inadequate government plans, it was the final nail in the coffin. Mary Whitehouse added her weight to the controversy before the programme had even been broadcast. She objected to the depiction of public violence in the programme and felt that the "Blitz spirit" would see the masses through any such emergency. She went on to claim that showing a panic stricken British public would have negative effects abroad and tarnish the view of the British population around the world.

The BBC panicked on seeing the final cut and violated their Charter of Independence (which stated that they would show no political alliance) and contacted the Government for advice. On September 24, 1965, the film was screened to representatives from the Home Office, Ministry of Defence, the Post Office, the Military Chiefs of Staff and Sir Burke Trend — Secretary to Harold Wilson's cabinet. This screening was officially denied for many years, but recent declassified papers have confirmed it went ahead. Unfortunately many

Wounded and the aftermath.
Scenes from *The War Game*.

The Making
of The
War Game

other papers pertaining to this event have gone missing in the intervening years, so a totally clear picture of events will ever be known. Six weeks after the unofficial screening the BBC announced they would not be airing *The War Game*. Even now the BBC still denies that there was any political intervention or that the film was ever officially banned. The banning of *The War Game* for twenty years was not just limited to UK screens, but also any TV broadcasters worldwide. The BBC would flatly reject any offers for transmission from abroad and it was only in 1985 that the film received a TV premiere. Ironically, and much to Watkins fury, the film was shown to help mark the fortieth anniversary of Hiroshima.

Questions about the depth of government involvement in the affair were tabled in Parliament and this, along with a flood of letters from the public urging the BBC to screen the film, prompted an open letter from the BBC to the public. The letter, dated December 23, 1965, implied *The War Game* had been dropped from transmission as it was deemed a failure:

> There was an element of experiment in this project, as in much broadcast production. Such programme experiments sometimes fail and have to be put to one side at some stage in production, even though money has been spent on them. They are, nevertheless, a necessary part of the development of broadcasting, and such failures as may occur are the price we must expect to pay if new forms and subjects are to be brought within the compass of television.

The public outcry continued to grow and so the BBC organized a week of screenings for the film at the National Film Theatre during February 1966.

With a limited cinema release it was enough for the film to be nominated for, and win, the 1966 Academy Award for Best Documentary Feature. In another snub to Watkins the director of BBC TV, Kenneth Adam, was selected to accept the award. Watkins was furious and side stepped the BBC by asking his friend Elizabeth Taylor, who had the required Hollywood star quality, to accept the award instead. The film also won the Special Prize at the Venice International Film Festival. The publicity gained from these awards was enough for Hollywood to bankroll Watkins' next project. The result was the feature film *Privilege* set in a near future police state and featuring Paul Jones as a pop star who is used to manipulate the general public. The crit-

> "Sequence after sequence inscribes itself in memory... stirred me to a level deeper than panic or grief."

ics savaged the film and it remains rarely seen.

Media reaction to *The War Game* was polarized at the time of it's making: "Sequence after sequence inscribes itself in memory... stirred me to a level deeper than panic or grief. It is more than a diagnosis; it is a work of art" — *The Observer*; "The film is the most sickening in the world today and one the public should never see" — *Manchester Evening News*; "Brilliant. But it must stay banned. It is a brilliant film, a brutal film. But I would never let any son of mine see it... I object to this film because it is propagandistic and negative in its approach, politically calculated in its effect. What producer Peter Watkins has made here is not a film about The Bomb, but a plea to ban it" — *Daily Sketch*; "This film must be shown. No wonder the Establishment wants to stop the film being widely shown. If several million people saw it, the campaign for the banning of nuclear weapons would receive an enormous impetus" — *The Daily Worker*.

With no TV transmission or wide scale release for his film Watkins instead took the matter into his own hands. He quit the BBC and without copyright clearance began to show the film wherever he could or was invited. In his introduction to the 1985 BBC screening Ludovic Kennedy estimated that an audience approaching six million, thanks to distribution in art house cinemas and the anti-nuclear movement, had already seen the film. Since the ban Watkins has never resided in England and at present lives in Canada after living in Sweden and many other countries.

The BBC still officially state that the film was banned because it was just too horrific for the medium of television, and viewed with nearly forty years historical perspective and put in the context of the Cold War, this was evidently true. But the conspiracy runs deeper than that, with recent research showing that the government and even the Prime Minister at the time, Harold Wilson, directly had a hand in banning the film.

In 1982 Watkins attempted to remake *The War Game* for Central TV, but it fell through. Over the following three years Watkins threw himself into the epic fourteen-hour-long film (understandably very rarely seen) *The Journey* that detailed the effects of nuclear power and possible war across the world.

The War Game was voted number twenty-seven in the BFI TV 100 poll in 2000 and received a DVD release in January 2003 from the BFI. The release contains a feature length commentary by Patrick Murphy and Watkins' short film *Diary of an Unknown Soldier* together with an overview of the banning of the film and a biography of Watkins. ⒼⒻ

Civil unrest and firing squads.
Scenes from *The War Game*.

Available on BFI DVD

GHOSTWATCH

by Andrew Screen

Screened only once on television, for years the BBC avoided any and all reference to the controversial drama, GHOSTWATCH, which many viewers believed was real. Here is the story of its production, its screening, and the fallout.

Over the centuries there have been countless reports of ghosts and ghouls, but the line between fact and fiction has always been unclear. Using the modern idiom of the outside broadcast Michael Parkinson, Sarah Green, Mike Smith and Craig Charles star in GHOSTWATCH.
Continuity announcement before transmission
followed by the Screen One ident

If we don't like a radio programme, we turn it off, but if we don't like a TV programme, the broadcaster shouldn't have made it! Somehow, people don't want to take responsibility for their own viewing.
Director Leslie Manning

NORMAL TRANSMISSION
WILL BE RESUMED
AS SOON AS POSSIBLE

Broadcast only once on Halloween, 1992, on BBC 1 at 9:25pm as part of it's Screen One strand, this controversial drama provoked a storm of complaints from viewers who believed the events unfolding before them were actually real. The writer Stephen Volk and the producer Ruth Baumgarten had been working together on *Ghostwatch* since 1990. Volk had written the scripts for the films *Gothic* (1986) and *The Guardian* (1990) and more recently continued his exploration of Reality TV with the Channel Four horror flavoured drama *Cyclops* for the series *Shockers*. Ruth Baumgarten began her career as a film critic in her native Germany before moving to England and continuing to review for publications such as *City Limits* and *The Listener*. She also produced *The Wyvern Mystery* for the BBC in 2000.

The ninety-one-minute play tells the story of a televised Reality TV investigation into the supernatural activities taking place in the house of a single mother, Pamela Early, and her two young daughters, Kim and Suzanne. Of course things go horribly wrong and in true Quatermass style — as the events escalate and the "viewing audience" becomes involved in a mass séance. The original script was actually a six part series set in a high-rise block in the 1960s with the live broadcast taking place in the sixth episode. It would tell the story of female journalist teaming up with a psychical researcher to investigate poltergeist activity in a council flat. Volk was encouraged to submit the idea to the BBC by his agent in October 1988 spurred on by the recent success of *Edge of Darkness*. However, the BBC were not keen to commit themselves to a six hour production, and Baumgarten felt that the story would work better as a one off drama for the Screen One strand. Volk drew upon many sources for the script. In part, he was inspired by the BBC's *A Ghost Story For Christmas*, and Nigel Kneale's *The Stone Tape*. He also had a keen interest in parapsychology and was intrigued by the idea of "need-based experiences" — the theory that under the correct conditions people will see what they want to see — which had been used to explain such phenomena as ghosts and UFO sightings. He also recalled the 1973 *Dimbley Talk-In* episode, which had made a star of Uri

Gellar and his spoon bending abilities. He also wanted to say something about the power of television itself. Volk recruited the services of Guy Lyon Playfair, an expert on poltergeist cases, to act as a consultant to the programme. Volk and Playfair had previously collaborated on the screenplay *Superstition* (the film was finally released in 2001 starring Mark Strong and Sienna Guillory).

Baumgarten had seen a news report on The Gulf War and how TV was being used to convince the public it was a "clean" war. She realised that the script could be a platform for making a statement about the unseen manipulative powers of televi-

Principal ghostwatchers. **Top, clockwise** Craig Charles, Sarah Greene, Michael Parkinson and Mike Smith.

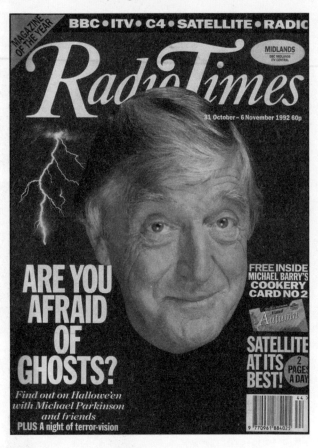

BBC • ITV • C4 • SATELLITE • RADIO

Radio Times

MIDLANDS
BBC MIDLANDS
ITV CENTRAL

31 October – 6 November 1992 60p

ARE YOU AFRAID OF GHOSTS?

Find out on Hallowe'en with Michael Parkinson and friends
PLUS A night of terror-vision

FREE INSIDE
MICHAEL BARRY'S
COOKERY
CARD NO 2

SATELLITE
AT ITS
BEST!
2 PAGES A DAY

Radio Times,
dated Oct 31
– Nov 6, 1992

Ghostwatch

sion and on suggestion that the whole story should be based around episode six to an agreeable Volk who set about rejigging the concept. Volk and Baumgarten watched every current example of the programme and incorporated many stylistic elements they encountered into the production as possible to give the finished production a realistic look. The updated script used the devices of a modern current affairs programme. It employed all the visual language, presentation and techniques of a live broadcast show in a convincing way (in fact too convincing for some) and utilized real-life TV presenters. Michael Parkinson, introduced the "live" broadcast from 42 Foxhill Drive with Mike Smith co-presenting, who was written in by Volk after Smith read the script when it was sent to his wife Sarah

Greene. Finally, playing on-the-spot reporters, were Craig (*Red Dwarf*) Charles and Sarah Greene (who had a previous telefantasy credit with an appearance in the Colin Baker era *Dr Who* adventure Attack Of The Cybermen). Also on hand were Dr Lin Pascoe (Gillian Bevan — most recently seen in the Channel Four drama *Teachers*), an expert in the paranormal and, via satellite, the sceptical Dr Emilio Sylvestri (Colin Stinton — most recently seen in the movies *Ali G Indahouse* and *Thunderpants*). As the programme proceeds the paranormal events at the house escalate, climaxing in Sarah Greene trapped in a cellar with a violent spirit, the studio erupting into chaos before ending with the sight of a possessed Michael Parkinson. The screen goes blank before the end credits role.

The spirit "Pipes" is seen briefly throughout the programme. His first appearance comes approximately twenty minutes in, when a tape is played back and at first a ghostly figure is seen standing against some curtains, though not when the tape is replayed for a second time. Pipes continues to make subtle appearances as the plot builds towards its climax. The phone number given on screen for the studio was real, but all the callers heard onscreen were actors. Viewers who did get through to the number were told that the programme was a work of fiction. Amongst the TV presenters originally considered for the programme were Anneke Rice and Nick Ross who the BBC bosses immediately said no to, preferring to use actors for these roles. Volk has commentated that he was very pleased with Michael Parkinson in the main presenter role as he quickly realised what the production was aiming for. Indeed, many viewers believed the show was real simply because Parkinson was presenting it. Volk recalls an incident which illustrates this point: A friend called him after the broadcast to say she had totally believed the events were really happening. Volk was puzzled by this as his friend was well aware that he had written it. When asked why, his friend replied: "As soon as I saw Michael Parkinson I thought you just have got it wrong."

The director entrusted with bringing a very technically complicated production to the screen was Lesley Manning who had previously handled the drama productions *Bloodrights* (1990) and *My Sisterwife* (1991). Volk, Baumgarten and Manning would later reunite to work on *Massage*, a stand-alone story in the BBC *Ghosts* TV series, starring Kevin McNally. Manning had to work hard to get away from the stylings of drama-making and concentrated on adopting the trappings of current affairs and news programming. One way in which she utilized these techniques was in the "vox pops" shown during the course of the programme. These were real people relating real-life incidents. The first block of recording took place in summer 1992 and completed all the location work three weeks before the studio work. Precise planning was needed, as most of this material would be featured "live", broadcast from Foxhill Drive, which would be viewed and reacted to in the studio by Parkinson and company. The editor, Chris Swanton, worked at breakneck speed to get all the footage ready for the studio-recording block. During the studio session Michael Parkinson was allowed to drift away from his scripted lines to help with his presentation and emphasise a more natural form of delivery. This clashed with Gillian Bevan's classical training and she had to work hard to react and deliver her lines on cue. Manning took a huge gamble as a transmission date for Halloween had not been granted when location filming commenced and she had insisted that the house be decorated suitably with pumpkins and apples on strings. If the Halloween slot had fallen through, the entire effectiveness of the production would have been destroyed. Executive Producer Richard Broke was given a preview screening of the finished production and voiced doubts whether the programme was scary enough. His solution was to hire Winston Ryder, sound designer on Stanley Kubrick's films, to fashion a soundtrack that would scare the living daylights. His main contribution was the tape played in the studio which took four weeks' work of layering sounds to achieve. Some of the sounds used apparently came from actual footage recorded by Guy Lyon Playfair during his researches. The interior of the outside broadcast van seen in the footage from Foxhill Drive was actually a set, as safety regulations denied the use of real vans. In total the production took six weeks to complete: three weeks on location and three weeks in the studio.

In the days following the broadcast the BBC came under severe attack from the press and a huge public reaction fuelled by the media frenzy. An estimated 20,000 viewers rang the BBC in the final five minutes of the show (just part of over 100,000 calls to the BBC about the show in total) from a viewing population of

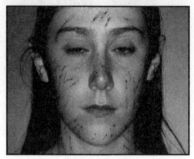

Top Mike Smith mans the *Ghostwatch* hotline.
Middle Dr Lin Pascoe (Gillian Bevan) and Michael Parkinson (as himself) in the studio (note cheesy picture hanging on the wall).
Above Ghostly scratches on the face of one of the Early children.

just over eleven million. Scotland Yard and Northholt police both received calls about the alleged events in Foxhill Drive, parents claimed their children where too scared to sleep after seeing the show, three women claimed in various newspapers that they went into labour as a direct result of watching the play and one woman demanded compensation from the BBC to buy new jeans — apparently her husband had been so terrified that he had soiled himself. There was even a much publicized newspaper story concerning the suicide of a teenage viewer. *Points of View* on November 4, was the first TV show to vent the anger that the public had felt with the production. The *Radio Times* dated 21–27 November, 1992, published a number of letters on both sides of the critical fence: "I describe myself as a pretty hard bitten sceptic, but by the time it had finished I was feeling very frightened indeed... All that was needed was to have a message flashed on screen every few minutes which would have informed people that this was a fictional account..." noted one viewer, whilst another stated "They pulled an Orson Welles off on the British public and it was really good. They should get a BAFTA award for it!"

Despite its late transmission time *Ghostwatch* was viewed by a sizeable child audience and the tabloids of November 1 had a field day: "My kids were terrified!" commented Mrs Valerie McVey in the *News of the World*, whilst Mary Jenkins was quoted in the *Mail On Sunday* as saying, "It's disgusting — thousands of children will be having nightmares." Other parents complained the programme had given their children sleepless nights and even worse, post-

> Scotland Yard and Northholt police both received calls about the alleged events in Foxhill Drive...

traumatic stress syndrome. Ruth Baumgarten personally responded to complaints from angry parents, taking time to write to the children detailing how the programme was made. Sarah Greene even made an appearance on *Blue Peter* to assure kids that she was still alive and unharmed.

The following weekend, on November 8, the *Mail On Sunday* and a number of other tabloids the following day continued their attack on the production. *This TV Programme Killed Our Dear Son* screamed the *Mail*'s headline. Teenager Martin Denham had watched the programme five days before hanging himself from a tree, near his home in Nottingham. A suicide note found on his body addressed to his parents read: "Please don't worry, if there are ghosts I will be a ghost and I will always be with you as a ghost." His parents blamed *Ghostwatch*, though the coroner made no mention of it at the inquest into the teenager's death. In June 1995 The broadcasting Standards Council did however uphold the complaints made about the programme by Martin's parents and many others:

> The degree of fear and distress shown in the programme was excessive...there was a deliberate attempt to cultivate a sense of menace (and) the BBC was mistaken in not taking additional steps to alert the audience to what they were about to see.

The BBC, as part of its remit to give its viewers a chance to ask questions and interview producers, programme makers and schedulers, broadcast a series called *Biteback*, introduced by Sue

Ghostwatch

Lawley. The November 15, 1992, edition featured *Ghostwatch* with a panel consisting of members of the public (in the main hostile to the programme and its content) and Ruth Baumgarten and Executive Producer Richard Broke. In truth, much of the anger and media attention was in frustration at having been duped by the production in the first place, and not in any potential nightmares that the programme may have created for viewers. However, the BBC effectively banned the production from ever getting a repeat showing, despite the high ratings, and the *Radio Times* was also forbidden from ever mentioning it again. Volk has stated that a BAFTA nomination for that year was also quashed. When Sarah Greene and Mike Smith later appeared on an edition of *Hearts Of Gold* and the studio lights failed, it was blamed on "Pipes", demonstrating that the programme had passed into popular culture.

The controversy around the drama has still not settled with Guy Lyon Playfair recently writing to the magazine *Fortean Times*. Playfair mentions his anger at the similarity between Volk's script and his book *This House Is Haunted*, which details the Enfield poltergeist case of 1977–78. He also felt that he was given a screen credit simply to keep him quiet about this and also to give the project some kind of stamp of authority. He contacted the Society of Authors with roughly twenty close similarities, who in turn approached the BBC. Shortly before the case was to go to court a healthy BBC cheque arrived through Guy Lyon Playfair's letterbox. Perhaps giving another reason why the play has never been repeated on TV?

Despite all the heavy pre-publicity stating that it was a drama production — it was introduced as one onscreen and billed as such in TV listing magazines — many people simply missed the point that Baumgarten and Volk were trying to make, and indeed the reaction to the programme demonstrated this totally. Television can be used to tell the version of events that whoever is in control of it wants you to see. Never believe readily and uncritically what you see on television. *Ghostwatch*, not unlike Orson Welles legendary 1930s *War of the Worlds* radio broadcast, demonstrated that audiences really would believe anything they see or hear if it has the stylings and trappings of a news report. This can only be a dangerous thing in a multi media rich society, which has seen the barriers between programme producers and programme viewers eroded with the advent of *Big Brother* and rise in popularity of Reality TV.

Ghostwatch was released on DVD by the BFI in November 2002 with an audio commentary by Stephen Volk, Lesley Manning and Ruth Baumgarten and DVD-Rom content including Volk's original treatment, screenplay and a ghost story by the writer, thus allowing a new generation of viewers to see just what all the fuss was all about. 𝕲𝕱

Available on BFI DVD

Ghostwatch | BBC | broadcast October 31, 1992

With: Michael Parkinson (himself), Craig Charles (himself), Sarah Greene (herself), Mike Smith (himself), Gillian Bevan (Dr Lin Pascoe), Brid Brennan (Pamela Early), Michelle Wesson (Suzanne Early), Cherise Wesson (Kim Early), Chris Miller (Cameraman), Mike Aiton (Sound Recordist), Mark Lewis (Alan Demescu), Linda Broughton (Yvonne Etherly), Katherine Stark (Wendy Stott), Derek Smee (Arthur Lacey), Roger Tebb (Local TV Presenter), Colin Stinton (Dr Emilio Sylvestri), Ruth Sheen (Emma Stableford), Diana Blackburn (Sandra Hughes), Brendan O Hea (Kevin Tripp), Keith Ferrari (Ghost)

Script Stephen Volk
Director Lesley Manning
Psychic Consultant Guy Lyon Playfair
Visual Effects Steve Bowman
Music Philip Appleby
Editor Chris Swanton
Executive Producer Richard Broke

For a detailed synopsis of *Ghostwatch*, see the article 'Hunting Ghostwatch' in *Headpress 22*. [w] www.headpress.com

A SHORT CONVERSATION WITH THE BFI

by David Kerekes

The British Film Institute (BFI) are responsible for releasing several key BBC productions under their Archive Television banner.

As the BFI's head of video publishing, ERICH SARGEANT took time out of his busy schedule to speak to CREEPING FLESH.

CREEPING FLESH *What is your official capacity at the BFI?*

ERICH SARGEANT I'm head of video publishing. This entails running a department which licences titles for home video and releasing them onto DVD and video.

How does the selection process work?

By looking at what's not out there, basically. Talking to people, that is a big proportion of what it is really about. What would people like to have and to see, what can we get the rights to. It's a process of negotiation, and also working to budget. There may be stuff we'd like to do but couldn't afford to do, being a non subsidised part of the BFI.

That kind of answers my next question, which is how do you go about choosing what to release given the wealth of material presently unavailable?

Well, that's what it comes down to. There's just so much not available. It's really just a case of talking to people to be honest, doing market research.

How does the physical condition of the source material in the BBC archive stand up?

It stands up okay actually. Film materials are good; video material is generally good, with some deterioration. The biggest problem is with what is available. For instance, *The Year of the Sex Olympics* had only been preserved by the BBC in b&w, whereas it was originally in colour.

Does the quality of material influence the selection process at all?

It hasn't as yet. We had to think about *The Year of the Sex Olympics* — in the end we decided to go with it because it still holds up in b&w. A lot of it also has to do with people's expectations — if you release older material, people expect a certain type of quality.

What kind of restoration is involved?

There are different kinds of programmes available, with more being developed all the time. What we try and do is remove scratches and blemishes. But you have to be careful with restoration in that it's always a trade off — in manipulating electronically, digitally, you can create little artefacts, so you have to balance what you're creating with the original.

You've released two of the eight A Ghost Story For Christmas. Is there any reason

why these two episodes in particular were chosen [A Warning to the Curious and The Signalman]?

Because they stood out really well. Simple as that!

Can we expect other episodes?

Not for a couple of years as we have other projects in the pipeline.

How did the BFI approach Ghostwatch? Were the BBC reticent to see it released given its bad press in the past?

No, no, the BBC were very keen that we did it. Very positive, very straightforward. "Do you want to do it? Great."

Because of course it has this baggage, doesn't it?

It does. Don't quote me on this [laughs] but maybe the BBC just thought "Hey, that's off our agenda, let someone else deal with it!"

Why do you think there has been this turnabout? And I'm not speaking specifically of Ghostwatch, but the Ghost Story For Christmas series as

well — because until recently you couldn't see any of this material for love nor money.

Well, the BBC has got its own agenda of what it releases; it's obviously got a huge mountain of material and can only release a certain amount of it. It does what it can do, and makes other titles available for other people to licence. And that's what we at the BFI do — as do other people as well.

What has been the response to your Archive Television series?

Very positive. Very positive. That's why we're doing more of it.

It is interesting that several of the Archive Television releases have been "difficult" films like The War Game and Ghostwatch. Does this aspect play any part in the selection process?

It does a bit.

Would you consider releasing material originally broadcast by ITV?

Oh yes, definitely. We've got plans to do some Dennis Potter. 𝔊𝔉

CREEPING FLESH readers will be thrilled to hear that the Archive Television releases include: *Whistle and I'll Come To You*, *The War Game*, *Ghostwatch*, *A Warning To The Curious*, *The Signalman*, *The Year of the Sex Olympics* and *The Stone Tape*.

"THAT WAS TRULY DIABOLICAL…"

by Phil Tonge

BBC misfire?
Not a chance.
An Appreciation of
DR TERRIBLE'S
HOUSE OF HORRIBLE...

Sometime in 2001, shoved away in the BBC2 schedules, there was an overlooked treat on the telly. The latest offering from Steve Coogan (aka Alan Partridge, Paul Calf, Gareth Cheeseman, Tony Ferrino etc), co-written with Henry Normal, fanzine editor-botherer (I still have the awful poems you sent me, Henry), and finally Graham Duff, actor, writer and British Horror Anorak. Blokes smart enough to remember that Hammer films were just as much about big tits as they were about "spine-tingling terror" (©1957 Any Hammer Copy writer).

What was it like, you ask? Well, you're watching BBC2… As the continuity announcer's bemused voice-over fades away we roll the titles. Barely animated cut-outs from penny-dreadfuls and gory old wood cuts flicker by as cartoon bats roll and weave their flappity way across a montage of red glow lighting and burnt twigs. Eventually we come to a paper cut-out of a "spooky" gothic schloss.

The titles appear and we leap into the drawing room of one "Dr Terrible" (Steve Coogan) a bald, big-toothed pervert with a white tuxedo jacket, big black bow-tie and several interesting skin diseases. After he introduces himself he launches into a very odd anecdote…

LESBIAN VAMPIRE LOVERS OF LUST

Opening Monologue (usually guaranteed to be the funniest part of the script — not to knock the rest of the episode, that is) *"So I put her in a sack..."*

A heady blend of Hammer's gory glory days of blood'n'big tits and endless "bummer gags" (as we called them at school). Concerning the Transylvanian honeymoon of one Captain Hans Broeken (Coogan) of the 23rd Light Rapier Dragoons and his virgin bride Carmina. We get a good idea of what we're in for courtesy of the scene where Broeken says "Ah, my pretty wife... can a man enjoy a finer sight?" followed by a point-of-view shot out the carriage window of two busty sorts snogging away like syrup-hoovers. Ending up at the castle of Castle Kronsteen, home of the eponymous vampire perv Countess Kronsteen (Ronnie Ancona — is that her real arse?) and her arch manservant Rehenor (Ben Miller — taking the camp ball and running with it all the way up Queer Street).

Ancona isn't too far behind though, getting her tongue around lines like "Can I take your cherry?" while Miller's having fun with "Like my seat?"

The production design is excellent, all the rich fabrics, stonework, matte paintings of outrageously impractical castles, an original excuse for the non-reflecting qualities of the undead ("It's not a very good mirror"), spy holes in paintings etc. There are even two buxom vampire twins (the Henderson sisters) and a vampire hunter — although it's not Van Helsing in tweed but Honor Blackman (always a guest star or two, natch) in black leather as Transit Van Hire... sorry, *Transeet Van Eyre*.

Coogan's performance is worthy of note too, pitching Broeken perfectly as one of those handsome, square jawed (but thick as pigshit during the acorn season) leading men we used to have in the British film industry. I'm thinking of Ian Ogilvy or Oliver Tobias, but more of him later. The episode ends with a suitably daft fight sequence, Broeken uses a bulb of garlic as a weapon by resting it on Kronsteen's cleavage and there's an impressive staking by occasional table (a sly reference to *Scars Of Dracula*, a film that looks like it was shot on half the money this episode cost).

Plus there's a twist ending that's the funniest in vampire fiction since *Fearless Vampire Hunters*, talk about starting how you mean to go on.

Closing Monologue *"But surely you say, there's no such thing as vampires... or lesbians?"*

Best Bit Far too many to sort out, but the line about *"Three barechested Cossacks were hungry for my end..."* takes some beating.

Note

This article reviews the episodes in the order in which they were originally aired. The actual running order as the makers intended ran as follows: *And Now The Fearing...*, *Frenzy of Tongs*, *Curse of the Blood of the Lizard of Doom*, *Lesbian Vampire Lovers of Lust*, *Voodoo Feet of Death*, *Scream Satan Scream!* This is the order in which the episodes appear on the BBC DVD.

That was truly diabolical...

CURSE OF THE BLOOD OF THE LIZARD OF DOOM

Opening Monologue *"The kitten however, lives on..."*

Edinburgh 1880. The Rabbie Burns' Burns Ward where our hero, Dr Donald Baxter, Burns Specialist (Coogan), works on scorched Scots for the benefit of a non-flammable future for mankind.

Essentially your standard tale of mad and misguided Victorian science based on the exploitation of an unusual range of lizard-based serums.

The sort of medical world where there really are big bottles labelled "Bad Acid" and a London School of Scorching. Plus a whole encyclopaedia of great off-colour Scottish references about thistles, haggis and things being "as plain as an Aberdeen oatcake".

With guest stars Graham Crowden (in full force) meeting a sticky end in Blind Alley and Simon Pegg discovering the drawbacks of "Overtongueularity".

Certainly the darkest episode, with the action slanted towards horror and *pastiche* rather than comedy and parody.

Closing Monologue *"...no animals were harmed during tonight's tale, still, you can't have everything".*

Best Bit The shed-skin scene (not funny I'll grant you but bloody effective).

VOODOO FEET OF DEATH

Opening Monologue *"That day I learnt an important lesson. Never eat your own chin."*

Lester Crown (Coogan) and his hot missus Beatrice (Sarah Alexander) are top dancers on the 1930s big band circuit. In fact Lester (The Man With the Liquid Feet) is deeply suspicious of his wife's relationship with tap-dance sensation Randolph Cleveland. "Why," he opines, "can't women be more like my size nine feet?"

This jealousy leads Lester to following his wife in the night to an unexpected appointment with a giant novelty shop sign in the shape of a giant pair of scissors. SNIP! Mr Crown is two feet shorter...

However, hope comes in the shape of a foot transplant from a Caribbean dock worker crushed by a crate of "Heavy Goods". Unfortunately for Lester the geezer was from a top voodoo family in the West Indies. Black magic murder ensues... as do a series of appalling foot gags.

This story is *Hands Of Orlac* done by a foot-obsessed Barry Cryer. See if you can catch the sly steal from Python's "Cheeseshop" sketch. Tom Bell and Johnathan Cake turn up to face "de feet" and it all ends with a suitably horrible denouement on the roof of a dance hall. I was thinking that this episode would have been better in b&w, but then you'd lose all that lovely Kensington Gore on display.

Closing Monologue *"Tread carefully!"* while being sucked off by a shaven headed woman. Nice work if you can get it.

Best Bit The bizarre amputation scene with the big scissors or failing that the sight of Sarah Alexander in her underwear (excuse me a minute...).

SCREAM SATAN SCREAM!

Opening Monologue *"...last Thursday."*

"Tygon, the potatoes!" With a swish of a cape and a landscape (well, soundstage) inhabited by people who are very slow on the uptake indeed rides our next offering... Taking it's main lifts from *Witchfinder General* and the rather odd *Captain Kronos, Vampire Hunter* we are catapulted into the witch-burning world of living, breathing *Viz* character Captain Tobias Slater, Witch Locater (Coogan) and his trusty sidekick, Tygon (Warwick Davies).

Slater's life revolves around burning women for such crimes as "yodelling with frogs" and the rest of the time "knobbing". Prevented from going to investigate the Glovely Girls' Finishing School for Young Virgins by a gang of thick peasants from the village of Devil's Hole, Slater sets up court at the Fist Inn. I never said it was subtle.

Nice to see the Henderson sisters return as two wide-eyed English Civil War innocents, as it is Slater during his investigations and "probings" (*"TWINS!"*). Like Matthew Hopkins in *Witchfinder*, Slater fucks with the wrong wenches in more ways than one. Firstly he picks on the local vicar's daughter and secondly burns the sister of two hardcore saucy lasses, sorry, *sorceresses*.

In no time at all there's brandings, burnings, magic potions, The Bend Sinister, curses (along the line of King Midas' other curse, yes, *other* curse, not the gold thing. Bloody hell, he must have pissed off a few minor deities in ancient Greece) and the flagrant planting of witchy evidence i.e. one badly-stuffed black cat.

Combine this with people who don't understand the most thinly veiled of threats — *"Your daughter has an appointment with some kindling... [blank looks all round...] and some flames... [still no response...] I'm going to burn your daughter to death!" [gasps of horror, finally]* — or know what "inundate" means.

This goes into the *"We've got this ducking stool"* routine which, had this series been seen by anyone, could have been *Dr Terrible's*

"This one goes up to eleven".

It all ends with a guest appearance by a rampant Satan who intends to have his revenge on Slater... with malice aforethought... in a most base area... The Devil is going to bum him to death.

Closing Monologue *"...You end up paying twice."*

Best Bit (and it's up against some stiff competition) Slater's jabberwocky-Latin prayer at the witch-burning. *"Maximum spurium... cunnilingus... Spirito Di Punto"* (after he's shouted *"Burn her, she's a slag!"* behind his hand).

FRENZY OF TONGS

Opening Monologue *"...because I can, and I don't like small dogs."*

Putting a kindly boot into those rather dodgy Fu Manchu movies of yesteryear. Set in Limehouse, 1910, under the grasp of Hang Man Chang (Mark Gatiss) — "The Sinister Boney-Fingered Menace From The East" — aided by his torture-fixated daughter Woo Woo and of course his long-reaching Tong.

Rallied against him Nathan Blaze (Coogan), Edwardian Inventor and gentleman adventurer (played as a mix of Adam Adamant and Jason King) and his trusty sidekick Sir Donald Tyburn (John Thompson) with his venerable neck.

I *adore* this story, I reckon there's a spin off series here, all that adventuring, intrigue and sewer-hopping. Outstanding. Certainly the first adventure show where a henchman is brained by a googly bowled with a ball of opium the size of a honeydew melon. Unless *The Avengers* tried it of course.

Mark Gatiss steals the show as Chang (*"The world has not seen my end!"*) and blatant conjugation of "thwart". Coogan's obviously having a whale of a time too (*"You Sir, are a large crab"*) handling all the cod-martial arts and utility canes with a deftness others couldn't have pulled off. Indeed, the story handles what could be seen as clod-hopping racism (which of course is the source material's fault) with such gusto that it actually gets away without offending anyone. Shame.

Nice references, re: Sergeant Rohmer. There are uncanny similarities to the *Doctor Who* story The Talons Of Weng-Chiang too, then again with noted *Who* fan Gatiss aboard, that's to be expected.

That was truly diabolical...

Closing Monologue *"Imagine a world with no torture, no pain, no misery... not very interesting is it?"*

Best Bit Chang having to explain who he is to Tyburn's daughter: *"Woo-Woo's Dad?"*

AND NOW THE FEARING...

Opening Monologue *"...while his wife peed into a Ming vase."*

A fantastic parody of all those mental *portmanteau** films that
Amicus produced in the early 1970s. In fact, the endless pointers to
the origins of this spoof are signposted by the makers so blatantly
that it becomes a gag in itself. Three obnoxious ciphers from the
seventies are trapped in a lift (*a la Vault Of Horror*), whereupon
they relate the tales of their troubling recurring dreams... First up
is evil capitalist Denham Denham (Coogan) and his dream of running over a tramp in his wife's car while pissed, ending up with him
on the streets, drinking meths and getting run over by his wife.

During journalist Stephanie Wise's (Julia Davis) tale of the
haunted coffee table (no more ridiculous than the haunted *killer*
piano in *Torture Garden*) who should turn up sporting an unconvincing Yank accent? Oliver Tobias. Small world, innit?

Then smug architect Michael Masters (Alexander Armstrong)
falls foul of some gypsies (led by Pete Walker's leading lady Shelia
Keith). He's evicted with a curse involving his own shadow. All the
time there's a recurring image of blank faced haunty types, last
seen in *Sapphire And Steel*.

Of course the stuck lift starts up again to dump our players on
the thirteenth floor, which leaves them stuck in faceless hell/loony
bin dimension in the established Amicus stylee.

Certainly my least favourite episode, mainly because at half an
hour it's not long enough to really get to grips with any one story,
which is a shame. An hour special perhaps?

* Portmanteau. It's the sister village to
Portmeirion where they filmed *The Prisoner*.
It isn't? Oh, fuck you then.

Best Bit Finding out Shelia Keith is still alive and working.

Why did *Dr Terrible* fail? Who can tell? Putting it on before the
awful ITV-quality sitcom *Mr Charity* couldn't have helped and it
wasn't promoted... at all. Then again neither were other Coogan
comedies that went ballistic viewer/fan-wise. Could it in fact be
down to the simple reason that it was just too affectionate in the
face of what Coogan's fan base were used to?

Perhaps the fans wanted big belly laughs and "I'm Count Von
Partridge, A-HA!" rather than mildly joshing spoofery, knowing
nudgey tomfoolery and rampant buggery gags. More fool them.

There's nothing so sad as a television programme that's been
carefully written, lovingly crafted and beautifully executed by a
team of artists and craftsmen only to be avoided by the viewing
public like a pint glass full of dogshit. *Dr Terrible's House Of Horrible* is merely the most recent. "Shame," I hear you cry. "That's
not my name," I reply as I playfully re-adjust your ball-gag.

"What have we learnt from tonight's story?... Bugger all. Good-
night." GF

Available on BBC DVD.

THIRTEEN REUNIONS: THE *HAMMER HOUSE OF HORROR* STORY

by Julian Upton

Late 1970s: Cinema was in decline and so it fell to television to rescue the movies. Given that their most recent big screen outing — To The Devil A Daughter — was a flop, HAMMER STUDIOS really had nothing to lose. Or so it seemed...

It was once famously said that, in the second half of the seventies, the British film industry was alive and well and thriving on television. Theatrically, of course, it was a different story. British film was seriously on the slide, and had been since the release of, say, NIGHT HAIR CHILD in 1971. It had since sank past the Cliff Richard vehicle TAKE ME HIGH (1973), scaled the depths of THE GHOUL (1975) and, by 1978, rested on the barrel bottom that was THE WILD GEESE, WARLORDS OF ATLANTIS and ADVENTURES OF A PLUMBER'S MATE. Pretty soon, things would go NORTH SEA HIJACK, and there was no turning back from that.

TV, by contrast, could boast the talent and the resources that British cinema lacked. TV could entertain the populous whilst stimulating the intelligentsia. It could satiate the morons whilst pleasing the subversives. It could follow a glorious half-hour of PORRIDGE with the new play by Dennis Potter; a challenging WORLD IN ACTION with the thick-ear hysterics of THE SWEENEY. Who would give up a night of that for two hours in a crummy provincial cinema — draughty, dank and in breach of at least eighty-five health and safety regulations — to sit through the ordeal of SILVER DREAM RACER? British cinema's darkest days were television's Golden Years; no wonder people stayed home in droves.

Hammer in Decline

Hammer Studios had been the most enterprising home-grown film outfit of the late fifties and sixties, but it could not weather these troublesome times. The seeds of the studio's demise were visibly sown in the early seventies. With *Dracula AD 1972* (1972), *The Satanic Rites of Dracula* (1973) and the offbeat *The Legend of the Seven Golden Vampires* (1974), the studio had desperately tried to woo the increasingly broad-minded audience that had deserted it for sex-oriented youth flicks and martial arts actioners. But this was to little avail.

The studio's final horror film, *To the Devil a Daughter* (1976) was a brave stab at distancing itself from its cheerfully anachronistic image and jumping on the lucrative post *Exorcist* bandwagon. But even international stars (Richard Widmark), a European production partner (Terra Filmkunst) and a more adult approach to the material (Natassja Kinski full frontal) failed to turn the company's fortunes around. *To the Devil a Daughter* was a dud; even its original author Dennis Wheatley agreed. (Actually, that is something of an understatement. Mr Wheatley was severely *pissed off* with the final product.) The future, then, looked very bleak for Hammer as a filmmaking outfit. So, in 1980, TV came to the rescue.

The show was marred from the outset by poor scripts and pedestrian execution. It was further hampered by a meagre budget.

Hammer on Television

Hammer had occasionally been linked to British television before, although none of the results were representative of its horror canon. In the 1950s, the studio had produced two *Quatermass* films (*The Quatermass Xperiment* [1954]; *Quatermass II* [1955]) based on the influential BBC TV

SF serials. The sixties saw its first series produced exclusively for television, *Journey to the Unknown* (1967, seventeen episodes), although here the focus was on mystery and fantasy thrillers. In the early seventies, the increasingly desperate studio followed just about every other British film company onto the sitcom spin-off bandwagon, producing *On the Buses* (1971) and *Man About the House* (1974). These were, of course, about as far away from *Dracula* and *Frankenstein* as it was possible to be. The challenge, then, of presenting, for the first time, a television series that was identifiably 'Hammer' was an exciting one.

Hammer struck a deal with Lew Grade's ITV franchise, Associated Television (ATV). ATV differed from other ITV companies in that its output consisted of a high volume of blatantly commercial programming, much of it made by Grade's company ITC, for sale on the international television market. *Danger Man*, *The Prisoner*, *The Persuaders* and *The Saint* were typical ATV products of their time: glossy, exotically-themed hokums with semi-faded international stars, shot in colour on 35mm film and highly suitable for US syndication. It was in this vein that *Hammer House of Horror* was commissioned.

Hammer House of Horror

Hammer's ethos had always been an undeniably populist one, so it is hard to imagine any other British TV company doing justice to the studio's name. But the overall style of *Hammer House of Horror* — first broadcast between September and December 1980 — was, sadly, as distant from its archetypal outings as anything else that the company had produced in its waning years. With a heavy focus on young couples in grotesque, modern-day, Guignolesque situations, *Hammer House of Horror* bore more resemblance to the dying days of the British horror film than it did to the Gothic camp of old.

The show was marred from the outset by poor scripts and pedestrian execution. It was further hampered by a meagre budget. But older ATV series such as *The Prisoner* and *The Avengers* had proved that TV could mimic the camp and colour of sixties cinema with style and flair even with modest means. Ultimately, *Hammer House of Horror* suffered more from a lack of energy and inventiveness than it did from its lack of resources.

But the flat direction made this lack of resources painfully obvious. Hampden House, a spacey Buckinghamshire mansion in generous grounds, was Hammer's production headquarters at the time. Shamelessly, the property and its surroundings are exploited *ad infinitum* in the series. This is understandable given the budgetary restraints, but the place is used so artlessly that it becomes quite hilarious. Gothic mansions may stand in well for retirement homes and exclusive clinics, and they provide opulent surroundings for black magic shenanigans and the like, but they aren't too successful in imitating modern hospitals and police incident rooms. Similarly, the same streets and stretches of road in the nearby town of Great Missenden continue to pop up undisguised with humorous frequency.

But, for all its failings, *Hammer House of Horror* did feature some watchable episodes, and even some of its worst instalments offered guilty pleasures. At the very least, fun could be had from seeing the horror turn to unintentional comedy, or by spotting the actors who weren't taking things too seriously. And the teasing title sequence — a Dracula-

like figure hovering portentously in the window of an eerie mansion (our first glimpse of Hampden House) — looked like a tremendous return to form. Sadly, this sequence was often the best thing about the entire show, its spooky iconography and thundering score providing a high point that the episodes themselves usually failed to live up to.

Episode Guide

Hammer House of Horror kicked off with "Witching Time," directed by Don Leaver from a script by Anthony Read. "Witching Time" begins, not uninterestingly, with a Gothic-period pre-title sequence that presents a woman disrobing in her chamber, framed by a sinister hand-held, point-of-view (POV) shot. At first glance, it looks here like Hammer are taking things up exactly where they left off in the early seventies — cardboard castle set, gratuitous nudity, portentous music and a strong whiff of careless misogyny. The woman turns to the unseen presence as the POV camera approaches, and screams. Cue titles. After the titles, we see that the sequence is in fact from a film that composer Jon Finch is writing the score for. So there's a nice little segue — from classic Hammer to 'something new'.

As the story unfolds — given some weight by Finch's reliably jumpy, aggressive, if characteristically humourless performance — the composer, conveniently housed in a 'remote farmhouse', encounters a crazy, flame-haired minx (Patricia Quinn), who turns up in his barn during a storm, claiming to be a witch from the fifteenth-century. She certainly talks like one — all "thous" and "thees" — and is quite clearly naked underneath her tabard. So far so good. Finch takes her inside and she appears suitably alarmed by the electrical appliances. Later, she

Thirteen Reunions

treats him to an eyeful of medieval flesh and bawdy session in the sack. But then his wife comes home...

"Witching Time" isn't that bad actually, but it seriously loses its way in the final third, and winds itself up with a lazy cliché — Quinn's effigy is burnt at the stake in a modern replay of the fate she'd escaped from in the first place. But as a series opener, it looked fairly promising, straddling as it did the quaint old Hammer films of the late sixties and the more graphic and salacious modern-day Guignol of Norman J Warren and José Larraz.

Episode two, "The Thirteenth Reunion", begins with a pre-credits sequence that has 'undertaker' Norman Bird (as petrifying as ever) proceeding to slice up a cadaver. Not much to go on there, but there is a satisfyingly squelchy sound as his meat cleaver hits the flesh. The story proper then starts, and we are into Brenda Starr territory. Wholesome-looking Julia Foster is a roving 'young' journalist (forty if she's a day) dispatched to investigate the controversial methods being practised by a successful slimming institute (housed in a Buckinghamshire mansion). Here she quickly makes a romantic acquaintance in the agreeable but unlucky-in-love Warren Clarke. One of the more successful slimmers, Clarke is, pay attention, being *fattened up*. Then, driving home one night, he drops one of his prescribed diet pills and goes doo-lally at the wheel. When he crashes and dies, one of the sinister undertakers from the pre-credit sequence is immediately at the scene.

Foster gets wind of this mystery and, being a hard-nosed journo, sniffs an exclusive (for the *Buckinghamshire Chronicle*, perhaps). She is then led into a web of intrigue that climaxes, not unpredictably, in cannibalism.

Directed by Hammer veteran Peter Sasdy, "The Thirteenth Reunion" is fairly entertaining hokum, although it misses most of its shock opportunities. The penultimate scene, with the disparate group of 'diners' is quite amusing, however, and looks like something from a panel of one of EC Comics' sillier stories. But, ultimately, the biggest mystery of the whole affair is why the bird-like Julia Foster would be allowed into a slimming clinic in the first place; she looks thin enough to warrant drip-feeding.

Top to bottom Episodes 1–3 *Witching Time, The Thirteenth Reunion* and *Rude Awakening.*

"Rude Awakening" (episode three) functions quite entertainingly in the contemporary psychological horror mould, and is one of the liveliest instalments of the series. Benefiting from a distinctly tongue-in-cheek performance of spiralling desperation by Denholm Elliott and some suitably surreal set pieces (the direction is again by Peter Sasdy), the episode follows an adulterous estate agent around in a circle of never-ending nightmares, many of which appear to revolve around a property in Buckinghamshire. Upon finally waking, Elliott fulfils a dark prophecy and seals his fate by murdering his wife.

"Rude Awakening" is perhaps the only episode of *Hammer House of Horror* where logic is 'logically' disbanded with. As Elliott himself says a third of the way through the proceedings: "What the hell is going on?" The episode plays like a dark, twisted *Groundhog Day*, although it falls far short of that later film's delicious contrivances. As entertaining as it is, "Rude Awakening" could have been much tighter and much more cleverly plotted.

Episode four, "Growing Pains" was perhaps the first real indication that *Hammer House of Horror* was destined for TV landfill. Full of petri dishes of evil sherbet and fluffy white bunnies smeared in uncooked casserole steak, this is a child's idea of a horror story, but without the finesse that the Children's Film Unit would have brought to it. (Any self-respecting thirteen-year-old director would have taken his name off it.)

Next page, top to Bottom
Episodes 4–8
Growing Pains, The House That Bled To Death, Charlie Boy, The Silent Scream and *Children Of The Full Moon.*

The pre-title sequence sees young William somewhat dysfunctionally neck a few grams of scientist daddy's coloured powder, throw an eppy and then crash to his death through the patio doors of his parents well-appointed Buckinghamshire mansion. Then the action, several months on, sees William's mother (rather mysteriously) picking up a replacement kid, James, from a nearby children's home (Hampden House, from the side). James is sinisterly polite and permanently clutches a stuffed rabbit; he also has an unerring ability to rub people up the wrong way. And when he joins the household, weird stuff starts happening, culminating in a ghostly appearance from little William.

There are a couple of good ideas and one or two memorable images in "Growing Pains" but they are all defeated by the numbing mediocrity of the project. The episode, ultimately, is a shambolic piece of television, and, like little William, is best left unearthed.

Director Tom Clegg leaves no cliché unturned in the onslaught of modern day, Amityville-style, haunted house shenanigans that make up episode five, "The House That Bled to Death." Dead cats, cracking plaster, bleeding walls, severed limbs, evil dentures, children's parties ending up in blood-soaked hysteria — it's all here, as a young family move into a dilapidated house where, years before, an old duffer carved up his wife with an ornamental machete (a scene we are treated to in the teaser sequence).

These rusty machetes are found in a drawer when the young family (Nicholas Ball, Rachel Davies, Emma Ridley) move in — somehow the weapons escaped the extensive police investigation that must have followed the discovery of the diced corpse — and appear to be the catalysts for the subsequent grisly goings-on.

"House" moves along fairly unremarkably, but offers a reasonable shock-per-minute value and at least has an ordinary suburban semi as the focus for the action, as opposed to the ubiquitous Hampden House. The plot takes an interesting turn in the final reel, as we find that it's all been one elaborate scam — Ball and his missus are in cahoots with a local hack who turns the 'true-life' haunted house story into a mass market best-seller and they all make a mint. (In retrospect, this is even more interesting, given that the Amityville

**Thirteen
Reunions**

saga turned out to be a money-spinning prank.) Ball *et al* retire to sunny California (or, rather, Hampden House's outdoor swimming pool) to live happy ever after. But someone has forgotten to tell the traumatised daughter that it was all a caper from the start, so a grisly comeuppance awaits the head of the household.

"Charlie Boy" (episode six) begins very badly, with a track-suited nomark falling unceremoniously to his death after trying, somewhat incongruously, to fit a cheap TV aerial to one of the gothic chimneys on the roof of Hampden House. A blunt cut to an ugly African carving leaves us in no doubt that there is spooky voodoo business at work here. The show itself picks up a little after the titles, however, and appears slightly more artfully made than most of the other episodes in the series. It also benefits from better performances by Leigh Lawson and Angela Bruce, who portray a mixed-race couple (which the show, thankfully, makes no reference to).

Would-be film financier Lawson acquires said African carving — Charlie Boy — and finds his life taking a dark turn forthwith. This is all heavily ploughed territory, but by this point in the series we are praying for the episode to offer some real hope, and for the first quarter of an hour or so, it looks like "Charlie Boy" might not let us down. But it does, of course — the plot goes decidedly awry, with some nonsense about everyone in a particular photograph having to die (even though only one of them has pissed Lawson off), culminating in a confusing burglary where Charlie Boy goes missing and… Oh, it's not worth it. Anyway, everyone dies in the end.

"The Silent Scream" (episode seven) is one of the most fondly remembered episodes, due in no small way to the presence of Peter Cushing in his final on-screen performance for Hammer. Indeed, Cushing's involvement here offers a nostalgic bond with the studio at its peak. But, as a Nazi pet shop owner (!), it is only his frailty that really disturbs us — the rest of "Silent Scream" is sub-*Avengers* nonsense. The Nazi traps an ex-convict (Brian Cox) in a suitably insane experiment in incarceration. This offers some scope for Cushing to revisit the evil Victor Frankenstein persona, with a nod to the jackboot exploitation of the mid seventies, but it is all far too humourless and pedestrian to evoke any excitement. And the downbeat ending seems quite unnecessary, coming as it does after a plot that could have been penned by Enid Blyton. Still, that's horror for you, and there are a few small pleasures to be had from "Silent Scream," although most of them come from Alan Gibson's ham-fisted ideas about direction.

"Children of the Full Moon" (episode eight) is hackneyed werewolf hokum, livened up a little by the fact that Diana Dors does not appear to be taking the events seriously at all. After a satisfactory teaser, in which an angelic young girl hovers over a slaughtered lamb, her mouth smeared with blood, we find the dependably decent Christopher Cazenove and his Grattan catalogue wife (Celia Gregory) losing control of their Beamer in the outer reaches of Great

Missenden, a convenient plot contrivance that had been used twice in the series already. Stranded, they head off to look for shelter and a phone and of course stumble upon Hampden House (this series really should have been called *Hampden House of Horror*).

Here they encounter a strange family of cherubic children decked out in turn-of-the-century togs, headed by a sinister matriarch, Mrs Arrr-doy (Diana Dors, bearing an uncanny similarity to Benny Hill doing his Somerset matron act — all "moi dears" and "these parrts" and "narsty turrns"). Mrs Arrr-doy is friendly enough, offering the couple a room for the night and even a few glasses of special red wine that "Misteraarr-doy" makes. (Christ, that's *not blood* is it??)

Later that night, Cazenove goes out to investigate a strange howling noise and a hairy face at the window, leaving Gregory to be attacked by an unseen growling beast. Attempting to rescue her, he falls from the drainpipe and wakes up in hospital.

Cazenove is haunted by the episode, but Gregory tries to convince him it was all a dream. After all, she is alive and well. Or is she? Soon, Cazenove notices a subtle change in her behaviour: brutal in bed, insatiable sexual appetite, taste for raw meat, etc. You know where it's going, of course. Anyway, she announces that she's pregnant, and another 'child of the full moon' is on its way.

"Children of the Full Moon" is well meaning enough, but for shock value it still falls way behind Hammer's own *Curse of the Werewolf*, made twenty years earlier. And in attempting to modernise the werewolf legend, the episode was already rendered obsolete by the punchy irony of *The Howling* (1980), and would soon be far, far eclipsed by the black comedy of *An American Werewolf in London* (1981).

Suzanne Danielle had the monopoly on attractive, promiscuous good-time girls in the late seventies and early eighties. At that time, no hour of British TV drama was complete without a shot of her stepping seductively out of a sports car in legwarmers and a sparkly headband. Sadly, she couldn't act to save her life, a trait she emphasises in the nauseatingly dull "Carpathian Eagle" (episode nine). Another instalment that tries to play up the sex (to no avail), "Carpathian Eagle" fails even as a routine TV *policier*, despite having a proto *Basic Instinct* plot. As a detective attempting to catch a seductress-killer, who rips out the heart of her horny victims with a distinctive dagger, Anthony Valentine tries his best to make at least a shred of this hooey convincing, but ultimately the odds, like Suzanne Danielle's breasts, are stacked against him.

Someone clearly forgot to tell co-writer/director Francis Megahy that "Carpathian Eagle" was supposed to be 'horror'. It is outrageously over-talky, and so concerned with academic explanations of the murderous goings-on that it forgets to be scary. In one mind-bendingly flat scene, Valentine and Danielle have to listen to Sian Phillips go on about some legend or other for what seems like half

Next page, top to Bottom
Episodes 9–12
Carpathian Eagle, Guardian Of The Abyss, Visitor From The Grave, The Two Faces Of Evil and *The Mark Of Satan*.

Thirteen

Reunions

the show's running length. Valentine is clearly struggling to stay awake; Danielle's eyes glaze over before Phillips takes her first breath. By the end of it, you couldn't give a fuck if the murderer gets caught or not.

"Guardian of the Abyss" (episode ten) is a cheap-looking black arts tale; to call this pedestrian would be to lavish praise where it is not merited. Nevertheless, the epsiode does seem to have gained some cult recognition for the supposed authenticity of the staging of its occult scenes.

"Visitor from the Grave" (episode eleven) competes strongly with "Children of the Full Moon" for the unintentionally hilarious honours. Alone in an isolated country cottage (just outside Great Missenden) "Visitor" sees emotionally fragile Kathryn Leigh Scott attacked by a brutal intruder (Howard from *Ever Decreasing Circles*), whom she impulsively blows away with her boyfriend's shotgun. Mortified by the episode (as I was, funnily enough), Kathryn descends immediately into mental instability, which, if comments like "we don't want them to put you away again" are anything to go by, has clearly affected her before.

Boyfriend Simon MacCorkindale (acting, with his usual one-note abruptness, like an annoying head boy who's secured the lead role in the school play) helps to sort out the mess by burying Howard, sinking his Land Rover in the lake and lying to a visiting curly-topped copper, who has very keenly mounted a full investigation into the disappearance of a powerful, fully-grown man six hours after he was last seen.

So far, so utterly worthless. Then, poor Kathryn starts to see the murdered man pop up in and around Great Missenden. She even sees his Land Rover. Mac has to dig the intruder up again just to show her he's really dead. But she continues to encounter this spectral presence, at drinks receptions and the like, and it drives her to despair. Eventually she agrees to bankroll the services of a peculiarly ruddy psychic Indian, straight out of *It Ain't 'Alf Hot, Mum*, to conjure up the dead man in an attempt to exorcise his obviously tortured soul. But, in the end, all this is too much for fragile Kathryn, and she blows her brains out.

In a shock epilogue that even Hanna-Barbera would have thrown out, we find that it's all been an evil wheeze — Mac was in on it from the start, and the Indian was in fact the copper as well. Even the dead guy isn't really dead. OK, he was shot at point blank through the head and then buried, but the nasty pranksters had obviously worked out a way of doing this without harming him, although the writer doesn't feel the need to explain it. Neither does he explain how they conjured up the 'dead' man's floating apparition at the end. They just did, *OK*? Oh dear. It is *very* hard to believe that this sort of lazy tripe could have passed for 'horror' as late as 1980. It is also very sad to find that it was scripted by Hammer veteran John Elder, also known as Anthony Hinds.

"The Two Faces of Evil" (episode twelve) is another corker from that delicate purveyor of subtlety, Alan Gibson. For sheer stops-out nonsense, it stands out from the rest of the shows. And, with its cheap thrills and juvenile attempts to cover budgetary restraints with Guignolesque surrealism, it is probably the most enjoyable segment in the series.

"Two Faces" begins with a family, straight from the cover of a knitting pattern, enjoying a day out in the Morris Marina. Foolishly, they stop to pick up a hooded hitchhiker, who looks from the word go like his only intention is to kill them all. This he proceeds to attempt immediately, attacking the husband, managing to turn the car over and landing them all in the quietest hospital in the world (that darned budget!). This pre-credits scene is nonetheless quite striking, perhaps the closest the entire series ever got to being genuinely frightening. And Gibson keeps this pace up for most of the show's duration, although when he strives for the macabre, he often achieves the comic — the father coming home half-dead from the hospital is hard not to laugh at, as is the psychotically obstructive ward sister.

Like a few of the other instalments "Two Faces" at least has at its centre a fairly believable central performance. Anna Calder-Marshall manages to retain our sympathy when everything else is descending into circus hysteria. The man she brings home from the hospital turns out not to be her husband, but his murderous Doppelganger — the mad hitcher they picked up in the first place. Some of this is surprisingly well handled, not least in the performance of Gary Raymond as the imposingly smiley, mute-monster husband. Raymond doesn't actually do much, but the fact that he looks like a cross between one of the white-gloved psychos in Michael Haneke's *Funny Games* and some sort

of freakozoid Derek Nimmo lends an unsubtle but occasionally unsettling power to the proceedings.

Finally, "The Mark of Satan" (episode thirteen) sees the series end with something of a bang, then a whimper. The episode was regarded as stronger stuff than most of the others, and consequently scheduled for a later showing on British television (it wasn't broadcast in the US at all). Peter McEnery is a mortuary assistant suffering from advanced paranoia about the significance of the number nine and its portentous occurrence in many aspects of everyday life (on telephone keypads, ice cream adverts, Europudding pop songs by Nena, etc). And just to underline the power of this demonic digit, the show's scorer strikes a couple of eerie musical chords every time it appears or is mentioned. McEnery's character (something of a minimum-wage David Icke) has a crazy theory about the spread of a evil cult, which is seizing control of all aspects of society. This being 'horror', his theory turns out to be true.

"Mark of Satan" has a lot of the usual failings, but it does stand up to a second viewing. At its best, there is a *Repulsion*-type power to the hysterical scenes of mental breakdown, and McEnery gives a convincing portrayal of paranoid delusion and social disaffection — he should be a better-known actor. And he is well supported by the reliably patronising Georgina Hale, here injecting a little intentional comedy into the proceedings (McEnery: "They're going to take over the world!" Hale: "Do you take sugar?") and Emrys James as the mortuary doctor, who, with his lively fascination for the morbid subject of his work, is the closest the series gets to presenting a three-dimensional supporting character. One climactic scene, three quarters of the way through, has been compared to the work of Ken Russell. Director Don Leaver might be Ken Russell on a bad day (and

Thirteen

Reunions

Russell had plenty of those), but he does a reasonable job of emulating the idiosyncratic director's brand of spiralling delirium — the gung-ho vicar, bursting into McEnery's madhouse with a plywood cross, is straight out of *The Devils*. Sadly, after this peak, "Mark of Satan" descends into the sluggish tediousness and contrived scripting that hampers many of the others instalments, and the "shock ending" is an impotent affair that sees the series finish on a banal note.

Aftermath

Regardless of its failings, *Hammer House of Horror* seems to have had a striking impact on the young audience to whom it really introduced the Hammer brand name. Its heady mix of horror and, occasionally, sex was a fairly unusual brew for television at the time, and one which preceded the permeation of similar, if more explicit, home video material by a year or two. Consequently, there was a strong element of titillation to be had, particularly from instalments such as "Witching Time," "Rude Awakening," "Carpathian Eagle" and "The House That Bled to Death." Similarly, the series' grisliness was quite apart from anything else on television at the time.

More shocking, however, for young audiences particularly, were the invariably downbeat endings. Formulaic television usually eschews such endings, opting instead for upbeat closure. But the remit of horror clearly allowed a subversion of this TV requirement. In the best episodes — "Rude Awakening," "The Two Face of Evil" — these nihilistic endings are quite effective. In the rest, they just add

> More shocking, however, for young audiences particularly, were the invariably downbeat endings.

a sour note of incongruity to the harmless mediocrity of the last fifty minutes.

Sex, gore and gloom, then, were *Hammer House of Horror*'s trump cards, and the show was a moderate ratings success. Plans for a second series went under way. A number of scripts were commissioned, but the second series failed to reach production after the commercial nosedive Lew Grade's ITC took in the wake of his catastrophic theatrical flop, *Raise the Titanic* (1981). (Grade: "It would have been cheaper to lower the Atlantic!") Further, in 1981, the UK Broadcasting Authority decided that ATV was not fulfilling its regional TV commitment and refused to renew its ITV franchise. ATV was forced to reconstitute itself as Central Television, and Grade was removed from outright control.

This manoeuvre effectively marked the end of British TV's colourful international period: Lew Grade had not just been responsible for the exotic travelogues that were *The Persuaders* and *Man in a Suitcase*, he had also been behind the formidable *Jesus of Nazareth* (1977), ground-breaking Gerry Anderson series such as *Stingray*, *Thunderbirds* (1965–66) and *Space:1999* (1975–76), and, in what was perhaps his most intelligent move, had provided a home for *The Muppet Show* (1976–81). Central nevertheless began to concentrate on more regionally relevant drama such as *Boon* and *Muck and Brass*. It was a good ten years before British TV again produced anything as shamelessly commercial as some of the shows in Grade's canon.

Hammer was knocked back by these developments but, after some delay, managed to cut a deal with Twentieth

Century Fox to produce a number of feature-length television films for broadcast in the US. The resulting series, *Hammer House of Mystery and Suspense* (*Fox Mystery Theater* in the US) was, however, an unqualified disaster. Fox had requested that the studio ditch the explicit horror approach and concentrate on intrigue and psychological drama. The series failed in the US when it was broadcast in 1984. In the UK, it was never even networked; occasional episodes turned up at the dead of night, but even if they had been shown at prime time, it's unlikely that they would have had any real impact.

After the failure of *Hammer House of Mystery and Suspense*, the company lay dormant, stirred only by the occasional rumour of a renewed production slate. Twenty years on, we have yet to see a new, recognisable Hammer production. When and if the studio eventually does produce a new film, or indeed a new television series, the management might want to look at the strengths and weaknesses of *Hammer House of Horror*, and approach the studio's re-invention either as an exercise in breaking new ground, or as something more in tune with classic Hammer sensibilities. ⒸⒻ

Hammer House of Horror: Credits

Witching Time
Director: Don Leaver; Script: Anthony Read
With: Jon Finch, Patricia Quinn

The Thirteenth Reunion
Director: Peter Sasdy; Script: Jeremy Burnham
With: Julia Foster, Warren Clarke

Rude Awakening
Director: Peter Sasdy; Script: Gerald Savory
With: Denholm Elliott, Pat Heywood

Growing Pains
Director: Francis Megahy; Script: Nicholas Palmer With: Barbara Kellerman, Gary Bond

The House that Bled to Death
Director: Tom Clegg; Script: David Lloyd
With: Nicholas Ball, Rachel Davies, Emma Ridley

Charlie Boy
Director: Robert Young; Script: Bernie Cooper and Francis Megahy
With: Leigh Lawson, Angela Bruce

The Silent Scream
Director: Alan Gibson; Script: Frances Essex
With: Peter Cushing, Brian Cox

Children of the Full Moon
Director: Tom Clegg; Script: Murray Smith
With Christopher Cazenove, Diana Dors

Carpathian Eagle
Director: Francis Megahy; Script: Bernie Cooper and Francis Megahy
With: Anthony Valentine, Suzanne Danielle

Guardian of the Abyss
Director: Don Sharp; Script: David Fisher
With: Ray Lonnen, Rosalyn Landor

Visitor from the Grave
Director: Peter Sasdy; Script: John Elder
With: Kathryn Leigh Scott, Simon MacCorkindale

The Two Faces of Evil
Director: Alan Gibson; Script: Ranald Graham
With: Anna Calder-Marshall, Gary Raymond

The Mark of Satan
Director: Don Leaver; Script: Don Shaw
With: Peter McEnery. Georgina Hale

Thirteen Reunions

HUNGRY IN A DREAM...
KILLER'S MOON

by David Kerekes

A coach comes trundling through the English countryside, a rather flat rendition of Greensleeves emanating from within. A lone jogger negotiates a trail through the woods, seemingly headed in the same direction as the coach. As the landscape peels away, England's oft quoted green and rich pasture presents a rather more sombre, muted picture — like the world just developed a cataract.

So begins Alan Birkinshaw's KILLER'S MOON.

Members of the Maidenhill School Choir are on their way to a concert in Edinburgh when the battered coach they are travelling on breaks down. Stuck in "the wilds of nowhere", the all-girl passengers, headed by two school mistresses — the fumbling Miss Lilac and the battleaxe Mrs Hargreaves, tired British caricatures dating back to the comedy films of Will Hay — manage to secure a night in the only accommodation around for miles: a big, empty, out-of-season hotel. The bus driver decides he would be better off staying in the coach.

Not too far away, in a tent in a field, Pete and a local girl by the name of Julie, encounter a freshly wounded dog, one leg having been hacked off. They also discover that their axe is missing.

Meanwhile, in Whitehall, London, a government minister discusses the matter of four criminal psychopaths having recently escaped from an isolated cottage hospital. The escapees were all undergoing experimental drug treatment, in which LSD was being used in conjunction with dream therapy. Of the radical treatment, a doctor explains, "We endeavour to tap the emotions freely available to the patient in his dreams. Of course, this should happen in a controlled environment."

A surreal blend of drugs, schoolgirls and murder, KILLER'S MOON is a rarely seen slice of British exploitation. Not well received on its release in 1978, and generally no better regarded now, CREEPING FLESH casts a fresh critical eye and (on p.87) interviews its director, ALAN BIRKINSHAW.

In essence, four psychopaths are roaming the countryside believing they're in a dream.

"My God!" exclaims the minister. "In my dreams I murder freely; pillage, loot and rape!"

"You do?" says the doctor accusingly.

And so the scene is set. Apart from this one brief sojourn to Whitehall, the film takes place entirely on the outskirts of an unidentified small village — in actuality, the Lake District and a couple of studio sets — where the small cast of characters try to evade, or fall victim to, the four lunatics on the prowl. The concept is formulaic, and the film directed without any particular flair. As a consequence, *Killer's Moon* is enjoyably idiosyncratic, with more than enough lame dialogue to keep Bad Film buffoons enraptured for a week. More than that, however, *much* more than that, it has the four lunatics living out their own fantasy worlds. And a dangerous obsession with schoolgirls.

Director Birkinshaw allows nothing to upset the film's unhealthy drive and interests. Despite their escape being discussed by the government, no one bothers to come looking for the lunatics and none of the victims tries *too* hard to leave the danger zone and seek outside help. Mid-way through the film, cornered by the lunatics, one suggestion of seeking any help is casually dismissed with the remark, "I don't think there are any cops around here."

The first we see of the lunatics they are jumping single file over a small stream. All wear white overalls which, curiously, fail to register stains or markings whatever the environment. We are informed that the four men share a history of child assault, mass murder, homosexuality, and religious delusion.

Darkness falls.

A local gamekeeper, sipping a cup of tea, tells his wife that he has a "feeling things aren't quite right out there".

Indeed they're not — the coach driver lies dead in the woods with an axe in his neck.

Another portent of doom, Mrs May, the only member of staff present at the hotel where the girls are spending the night, is worried that Julie, her help, hasn't yet arrived. Unbeknownst to Mrs May, Julie is having a bit of 'ow's yer father in a tent with Pete.

One of the Maidenhill schoolgirls — Sandra — volunteers to walk down to the phone box and report Julie missing to the police, but when she finds a bloodied body and an axe on the path, she panics and runs off, straight into Mike.

"That man! Lying there dead!" she blurts to the stranger.

Mike suggests the distraught girl ought to come back with him to the tent he shares with his buddy, Pete, and they can phone the police. His intentions are well-meaning, but needless to say, there is no phone in the tent.

In a continuity coherent world, it ought to be the coach driver who lies dead with the axe. It isn't, it's the gamekeeper — even though Mike later discovers the body of the coach driver, with the axe buried deep in his neck.

Back at the tent, the line of defence is pretty shambolic: Pete responds to the news of Sandra's discovery by stepping out into the night and yelling out loud that he's not scared.

Having set off for her stint at the hotel, Julie suddenly reappears back at the tent and tells Pete, Mike and Sandra that she's been raped by three men in white coats.

"Do you think they kill everything they come across?" Mike asks his buddy.

"They didn't kill Julie," Pete replies.

"As good as," Mike retorts, within clear earshot of the two girls.

Next page
"My dream is a land far away"...
Three of the acid-fuelled psychos of *Killer's Moon.*

Hungry in a Dream

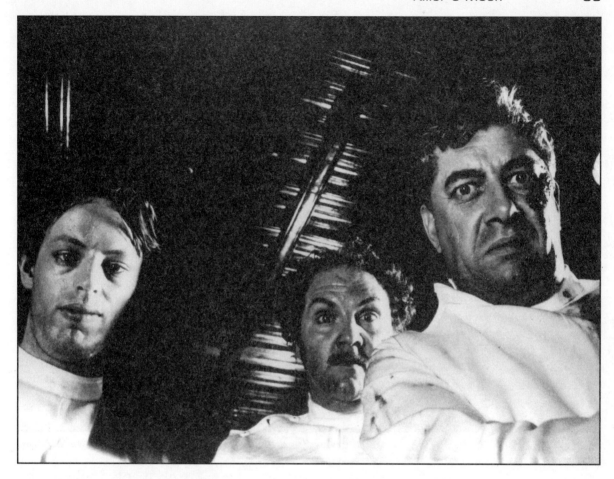

A shared dream is a rich dream

The lunatics — Messrs Smith, Trubshaw, Muldoon and Jones — who all address one another formally, are off on new pursuits. Mr Jones wanders into the gamekeeper's cottage and cuts off a cat's tale before turning his attention to the gamekeeper's wife. She manages to sink a kitchen knife into his neck (in gory close-up) before getting pinned to the back of a door with a knife through her own neck. There is a lot of neck trauma in *Killer's Moon*. Meanwhile, the other three lunatics have located the isolated hotel in which the girls are staying, and stand before it in a perfect line, singing.

There is an element of *A Clockwork Orange*'s droogs about the lunatics — no doubt intentional given their white outfits, and the fact that Mr Trubshaw conveniently locates a bowler hat which he dons and wears for most of the film. Their belief that they are ensconced within a dream world and not really doing anyone any harm is also a great excuse for some casual violence, and provides a handful of interesting platitudes, delivered with surprising confidence and engaging repartee.

With all the girls in bed, Trubshaw, Muldoon and Smith break down the door of the hotel. Miss Lilac faints at the sight of the intruders.

"Have you ever been hungry in a dream before?" queries one of the men.

Trubshaw rubs his leg nervously, reciting a bowdlerised version of Humpty Dumpty. He thinks the fainted woman is his mother.

"Never wake a sleeping lady, for we are gentlemen, even in our dreams."

"Are you sure you said 'mother'?" ponders Mul-

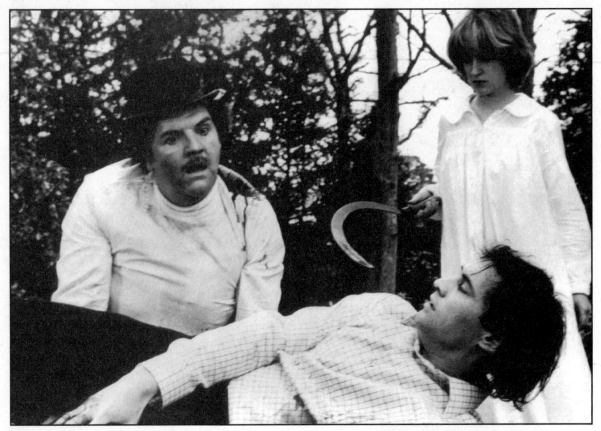

The end of Mr Trubshaw. *Killer's Moon.*

doon. "I often dream of mother — she doesn't look like that."

The rotund Trubshaw gawks at the hallway, licking his lips. One of the schoolgirls, in a night-dress and clutching a teddy bear, appears at the top of the stairs. The men claim they are friends of the family, on vacation. The girl enquires about Miss Lilac.

"You'd better come down and help," beckons one of the men, "sweet figment of my dreams."

"A shared dream is a rich dream," Muldoon empathises with his associates, grabbing the girl and dragging her down the stairs. Very slowly he tears open the girl's night-dress, slobbers over her, buries his head in her bosom, and rapes her. Perhaps more than any other, this scene shows just how much attitudes have changed since the film was made — it's a scene that certainly wouldn't be tolerated by the BBFC nowadays, as indeed one suspects the whole film would fall foul of the Board and be rejected.

Mr Jones arrives in time to strangle to death Mrs Hargreaves, who has been disturbed by the commotion. "She was a kind of accidental thought I had," Jones says of the lifeless school mistress before him. Convinced that their wanton actions are all part of a hospital controlled dream, a release mechanism encouraged by their doctors, Jones nonetheless deliberates on the strange consortium of characters his subconscious seems to be conjuring up. "I think I had her identified with the radiographer."

Hungry in a Dream

The group decide they need guns for when "they" come after them, as invariably "they" will. Jones returns to the gamekeeper's cottage, while the other three make their way upstairs, towards the rooms with the girls.

The girls panic. "They're coming! They're coming! Men! Horrible men!"

Jail bait

A short discourse on the adolescent porn fixations of *Killer's Moon*: Birkinshaw takes every opportunity to reinforce the fact that the principle victims in his film are supposed to be schoolgirls. Indeed, when all else fails, the viewer might care to try and spot all the references and innuendo. The girls are part of the Maidenhill School Choir — sounds a bit like maiden head. They clutch a lot of teddy bears. When not in uniform, they all wear identical, virginal white night dresses (and spend the latter part of the film running through the woods in them). The lunatics refer to the girls as "jail bait". Of the four rapes in the film, the three committed on schoolgirls are shown in lecherous detail, while the rape of Julie, the plump local girl, takes place off-screen (allowing more screen time for schoolgirls). In order to distract the lunatics, one of the girls starts to peel off her night dress, while elsewhere, a night dress, snagged on a splinter of wood, tears right open.

Greensleeves...

More singing...

Dark side of the mind

Mr Jones arrives at the gamekeeper's cottage to find Pete nosing around. Having discovered the woman's body stuck to the door, Pete nervously attempts to pacify the threatening lunatic with some dream-like dialogue of his own: "I was interested," he says. "It is very interesting, isn't it?" A strange blue pallor permeates several of the shots in this sequence, as it did when the lunatics first broke into the hotel. Pete escapes Jones' clutches.

Back at the hotel, the other lunatics manage to coax some of girls out of their rooms by yelling "Fire!"

"We want food fit for kings," the men tell the girls, leading them to the kitchen, "for kings we are."

"Supposing she's the nurse?" queries Muldoon of one of the girls. "We are in a hospital. This is the dream... Do you dream in colour, Mr Trubshaw?"

"Whenever possible," Trubshaw replies. "I like the flesh tints."

Mike, who has found the gamekeeper's shotgun in the woods, manages to sneak the remaining girls out of the hotel. Their paths

Psychos on the prowl...

Mrs Hargreaves is throttled...

Flesh tints.
Killer's Moon.

Hungry

in a Dream

cross with Pete, and the film becomes a cyclic cat and mouse chase as both men attempt to lead individual groups of girls to "safety", but somehow always managing to land them in the sights of another one of the lunatics.

Having just raped a girl by the edge of a lake — to a musical accompaniment that suggests "My dream is a land far away" — Mr Jones finds Sandra and Julie holed up in the tent. He prepares to spear them both with a pitchfork, but the three-legged dog from earlier makes a sudden reappearance and tears his throat out.

In order to lure the remaining lunatics away from the girls in the kitchen, Pete dons a night dress. Out in the hallway he clobbers Trubshaw and quickly discards his disguise. "First it's a girl," the bewildered Trubshaw informs his associates, "and then it changes into a boy — oh well, that's dreams for you."

Mike and the girls hide in the cellar. One of the girls, distraught after being raped in the kitchen by Muldoon (who also dropped food stuffs onto her), is

told not-so-compassionately by a friend, "Look, you were only raped. So long as you don't tell anyone about it, you'll be all right."

Mike decides he must leave the girls so that he can look for a lamp, and sure enough, the lunatics find the girls while he's gone. By now, however, Mr Smith is having serious reservations about all of this being a dream.

"It's the dark side of the mind down there!" Smith determines of the cellar.

Something suddenly bursts into flames, and Smith throws himself into the fire.

Back in the woods (every door that opens seems to provide direct access to the heart of the woods), Trubshaw has acquired the shotgun and is chasing Pete. "There's no escape!" Trubshaw hollers. "In my mind I shoot your bloody head off — and that's what I'll do!"

"Go to hell, you bastard," Pete responds. "You're mad!"

Cornered and wounded, Pete is advised by Trubshaw that he is going to die slowly. Unbeknownst to either of the

"WE HAD THIS MASSIVE CASTING SESSION FOR A THREE-LEGGED DOG..."

men, a schoolgirl in a night dress appears on the horizon. Trubshaw shoots Pete in the leg and is about to drive a knife into his skull when a machete swings into shot and buries itself in his neck. "I couldn't stop myself," the girl from nowhere sobs.

Like falling dominoes, deaths come quick and fast in the last moments of the film. Even the three-legged dog finds its happy hunting grounds, collapsed at the foot of a tree. Completely exhausted of fatalistic scenarios in which to place the players, the film falls back to Mr Muldoon for some last minute close-up eating of raw egg. The squishing of yoke between the teeth must surely stand as one of cinema's most cost-effective invocations of madness. With that, *Killer's Moon* limps to its impetuous climax — a painful 'homage' to the granddaddy of psycho movies: Miss Lilac recovers from her fainting spell to the sound of crying, and follows it the cellar where Mr Muldoon lies slumped and forlorn at the feet of, what appears to be, one of the schoolgirls. On closer inspection, it's actually the skeletal form of the burnt Mr Smith, dressed in a night dress and a wig.

And should you be wondering whatever happened to the hotelier Mrs May — she simply disappears from the story. Those people fortunate enough to have caught *Killer's Moon* on its initial theatrical release will know that Mrs May's *mysteriously dead form* appears briefly as a kind of post-end titles after-thought. Those watching Inter-Ocean Video's pre-certificated tape of the film will be denied such a pleasure. **CF**

AN INTERVIEW WITH ALAN BIRKINSHAW

by David Kerekes

CREEPING FLESH *Am I right in saying that* **Confessions of a Sex Maniac** *in 1974 was your first feature film?*

ALAN BIRKINSHAW That is correct.

That was a film about a sex-obsessed architect, who has the idea of designing a building in the shape of the perfect breast?

He wasn't sex-obsessed to start with, but he became obsessed when he had a dream... His boss had gone away on a lecture tour leaving him in charge and he had to come up with this shape for a building. He had a dream and all these buildings turned into breasts and he realised that the perfect shape was a breast, but then he had to find the perfect breast.

How did you land the job of director?

I found the money and put the deal together, in fact.

Scene from
*Confessions of
a Sex Maniac.*

speak. We decided that the sex comedy was probably the easiest sort of film to get distributed and... we had learned the ropes... it wasn't just a case of making the film, it was also a case of the subsequent distribution of it and everything else. The financier and myself, we decided this was the best sort of film to make, commercially.

And your next step was* Killer's Moon *in 1978, a horror film.

We decided that the horror film was more up-market than sex comedy and it would sort of lead us onto bigger and better things. That was the idea. We decided that horror film was a natural progression.

***It's fitting and ironic that* Killer's Moon *was released at the same time as* Carry On Emmanuelle, *which was essentially the death knell of the sex comedy... Can you recall how you came up with the idea and the story for* Killer's Moon?**

Yes, the idea was to try and find a group of vulnerable people who, when isolated, would make an interesting story and we sort of put a couple of heroes in and then found some vulnerable... psychopaths basically. So I think that all the people involved were vulnerable one way or another and that was the mix: You would take an isolated location, nobody was going to turn up to help them and there was twenty-four hours to see what happens.

***I do like the central idea of the film, the idea of thinking you're in a dream when you're not. Of course this has been used since in films like* A Nightmare on Elm Street. *Were you at all influenced by* A Clockwork Orange?**

Had you had any film experience before this?

I had directed commercials, TV shows and documentaries. I've done commercials for the Milk Marketing Board, Barclay Card, British Steel, Shell... all sorts of things.

Could you understand the popularity of the sex comedy films, because they drew considerable box office at that time?

It was probably the only way one could get to see naked people legally, I guess.

And of course you had Norman J Warren, Derek Ford and so on... who started their careers in a similar way.

**Alan
Birkinshaw
Interview**

Well the thing is, we were just looking at a progression and we decided that we hadn't a clue what was going to happen when we made a film, so we wanted to make a film to test the water, so to

I've been asked this before, but no I wasn't. Is this because of the way the maniacs look?

Well, you're got the way they dress, in white outfits, and there's a bowler hat in there. And at the core of the film is this radical idea for treating criminals.

Well the idea was that, in a strange sort of way, they were innocent too. Maybe that was too subtle. And the girls racing round in their nighties were also innocent and that was just sort of a thing in the background really. I mean one tries to put a bit of depth in these things although sometimes it doesn't really come through.

And of course you've got the LSD. Was that aspect of the film based on anything going on at the time, in the news, say?

I don't think so. I can't remember anything. It just sort of seemed to be the way to go.

The Monthly Film Bulletin *actually cited* Texas Chain Saw Massacre *as an influence, though I can't actually see that myself. Do you have any idea why they might have said that?*

No, I don't know.

Can you tell us a little bit about the shooting of the film? For instance, the great location. I presume that Killer's Moon *had a bigger budget than* Sex Maniac?

Yes, it was about three or four times as much, maybe more. We had a money crises on the first day of shooting because we realised that we were probably already into most of our budget at that stage. We had to find some more money, which we did. The consequences of that were that by the time we got to finishing the film, we only filmed in the Lake District for four weeks and there were some scenes that were shot in a London studio and in barns. Some of the sequences with the jogger at the start, although they look as if they all match in the Lake Dis-

trict, were in fact shot in London. Otherwise, the location I knew about because I went to school up the Lake District and it was a fabulous backdrop for a film; you can isolate people quite easily there.

You are credited with co-writing the musical number, My Dream, a tune which I quite like. Did you have any involvement in the music beyond this?

No, I didn't actually write the music, I wrote the words. But also, some of the dialogue was written by [novelist] Fay Weldon.

The dialogue in the movie?

Yeah. She happens to be my sister.

So how would you go about the writing process; was it backwards and forwards?

Yes, and since then we have written two or three projects together. She didn't want a credit on the film, she just did it for fun. She just added certain bits and pieces to it. Some of the fun lines actually came from Fay.

Did you have any problems with the BBFC?

I think we did originally. I know we had to make some cuts, but I can't remember what they were.

Did you liase at all with the Board during the making of the film?

No, because the situation was that in those days… I remember giving a script to, I think, John Trevellyn, the director of the BBFC. Basically, if he said the script was alright then everything was fine. But he picked up on absolutely everything and wrote a four page letter saying that this film would be nothing but trouble. I realised that to show a script was quite a dangerous thing, unless it was doctored. 'They make love,' what does that mean? It can be rude or crude or unattractive or fantastic, so it's a very dangerous thing to do as I discovered. So, did I liase with the Board? No.

How was the film originally received by the general public, do you recall?

Actually, if you are interested in the distribution and things like that, I can take you back one step. When we had distributed *Confessions of a Sex Maniac* we had all sorts of problems with the distributors, ending up with legal action and God knows what! So we decided that we would distribute *Killer's Moon* in the UK ourselves. (We had someone dealing with overseas sales.) So what happens is, you show it to the circuits, and all the bookers — the bookers have different regions, for which they are each responsible. You have one guy who is responsible for the North West of England, one for the NorthEast and so on and so forth. And they all sit and watch the film and make notes and they hand the notes to the chief booker who decides whether they are going to release the film or not. The exhibitors were so-so, they were not particularly wild about the film, so they gave us three trial dates — one of which was Gravesend, I remember. The other two were not much better. Gravesend really is the pits as far as cinema…

Its so happens that we had in the film the Doberman — you know, the three-legged dog? The casting of the dog was quite interesting because the dog had to have his leg cut off for the film and I realised that a four-legged dog that had to pretend it only had three legs would find it very difficult walking. I then had the bright idea of getting an actual three-legged dog and sticking a bit of blood on it, so that everybody thinks, "Oh God it's had its leg cut off!" We had this massive casting session for our three-legged dog; a whole stack of

Alan Birkinshaw Interview

dogs turned up to my offices in Greek Street and we eventually chose this one called Hannah. Hannah was a dog that lived in a pub. The pub was held up one day by a man with a gun; the dog leapt across the bar at the gunman, the gun went off and Hannah got shot in her leg and had to have her leg amputated. The dog won the doggy VC for bravery, so when it came to promoting the film I took the dog and we had a press call/ photo call in a place called Peppermint Park, which was right next door to Stringfellows in those days — it doesn't exist anymore; it was one of these fabulous cocktail lounges. So we had a press call/photo call in the morning with the dog and two of the girls from the film. There obviously wasn't a lot of news that day because all the newspapers turned up, the consequence being that we got a fabulous photograph of Hannah sat up at the bar with a straw in its mouth and a girl sitting on either side. We just hit all the national press with this story, the doggy and the girls, and when the film opened in Gravesend and the other two awful cinemas, it did incredible well. On the back of which we then got a full release, and all the other cinemas on the ABC circuit were opened up to us.

The Last Hard Men went out as *Killer's Moon*'s support; it was a good double bill… And that's how we got into the distribution business.

In the theatrical print, the actress Hilda Braid who plays Mrs May, is shown dead after the end credits have rolled. On the original Inter-Ocean Video release in the 1980s, however, this scene is omitted. Do you have any idea why?

It must have been a mistake.

I guess so, because you're simply

*left wondering what on earth has hap-
pened to Mrs May!*

I think that during the course of the filming,
what happened was we realised that we hadn't
actually made any arrangements for Mrs May,
so we put her in the end scene. The camera
pulls back and there she is lying dead.

*Any significance in the names of the four
killers?*

No, they were just fun names that I came up with.

*Nowadays, the idea of a British film in-
volving schoolgirls being menaced by
murderers and rapists wouldn't get past
the starting post. Was there any problem or
hesitation back in 1978?*

I don't think so, no. I don't think they are
meant to be all that young necessarily, they are
all over the age of... whatever. I can tell you a
funny story about the filming of one of the rape
scenes if you are interested: The location was
Armouthwade Hall, which is now a five class
hotel where they fly you in from Newcastle in
a helicopter. It's a very expensive hotel, but it

was the quiet season just before Easter and the
agreement was we would stay there with the
crew, but could also use it for location. So they
did quite well out of it, considering it was out
of season. But the deal was that if any of the
guests wanted to walk where we were filming,
then they had right-of-way. So we had set up in
the afternoon to shoot the rape scene in what
was in fact the big main hall, which sort of
doubled up as an afternoon tea area. We were
set up on a couch and I seem to remember that
there was a line of couches with tables in front.
So we set up to shoot the rape scene where the
maniacs had carried the girl off down to the
chair, rips her dress and then starts raping her
with the others all watching.

We had set up on one of these couches and then
an American couple aged about sixty-five or seventy came along and sat on the next door couch
and ordered tea. So the assistant director said
to me, "Well, we'll have to ask them to move"
and I said, "Well, if the management get to hear
that we've moved any of the guests, we really
will be thrown out". Because I think there had
been one or two other problems. They were a
bit upset about our presence, I don't think they
had quite realised what they had taken on. So I
said, "We can't ask them to go. We're just going
to have to see what happens."

Anyway, they sat there and ordered tea and
they obviously weren't going to take it quickly.
We also had a horrendous schedule problem, so
we got a couple of sheets of polystyrene which
are used for reflecting light and stuffed them
between the two couches. And I said, "Right,
this has to be the quietest rape scene ever shot
without any noise whatsoever and we'll put
the noise on after." So we shot this rape scene
in absolute silence. It's the most extraordinary
situation because if you stood back from behind
the camera, you could see this very dramatic
rape going on next door to a couch where this
American couple were having afternoon tea and
scones and strawberry jam.

*So the hotel was in full use during the
filming?*

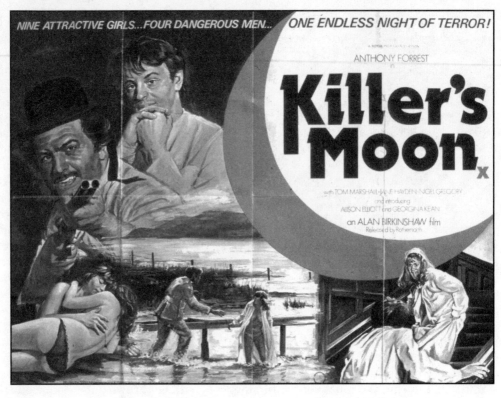

NINE ATTRACTIVE GIRLS...FOUR DANGEROUS MEN... ONE ENDLESS NIGHT OF TERROR!

ANTHONY FORREST in

Killer's Moon x

with TOM MARSHALL · JANE HAYDEN · NIGEL GREGORY
and introducing
ALISON ELLIOTT and GEORGINA KEAN

an ALAN BIRKINSHAW film
Released by Rothernorth

Killer's Moon received only a very limited release on video in the UK in the days of pre certification. FAB Press brought the film to a new audience when they resurrected it (along with director Alan Birkinshaw) for their Horror Show film festival in June 2001 — the only time the film has been publically screened since its initial release.
British quad poster courtesy FAB/Harvey Fenton

Top left Sleeve for *Killer's Moon* scarce British video release on Inter-Ocean, pre certification. *Courtesy David Slater*

It wasn't very full but there were guests floating around. That was quite funny.

What was it like seeing** Killer's Moon **again after all these years? [This interview was conducted shortly after the film was screened at the Horror Show — see sidebar.]

It was very strange because I've learnt a lot about tension and timing and rhythm and things which I didn't really know in those days. The editor had edited some other film before but not feature films. So the both of us together were a little bit in the dark about that sort of thing. Seeing it now, you can see how inexperienced

we all were. As I said to the audience the other day: Look, just don't take it too seriously, because we set out to make a film, but it was a lot of fun and we were not taking ourselves too seriously, and I never have in my life either but hopefully you enjoy the film and don't expect too much from it. I think there are some good parts in it.

If you could make** Killer's Moon **again, today, what would you do differently?

I could do it now and I could make everyone jump every ten minutes, or whatever. I would have people jumping out of their seats and I could do that quite easily now. In those days, I hadn't quite twigged how to do it. And it's incredibly simple, its just a technique. Look at any of the *Friday the 13th* things or *Halloween*, which I think came out just after my film or around about the same time. John Carpenter had got his act together in terms of making people jump, and I learnt a lot from those other films… from the Americans. That's what I would do, I would be far more successful in making it much more dramatic, and in making people jump out of their seats.

Moving on to 1982 and your next film, Invaders of the Lost Gold… *I presume that this is a* Raiders of the Lost Ark *cash-in?*

Vaguely, yeah.

You made this in Italy. How did that come about?

We actually made it in the Philippines. It was an Italian production with Italian money. I knew the producer, I'd met the producer and he asked me to direct it and he got together some of the actors. The problem with it was that the script was absolutely dreadful, so we re-wrote it as we went along — which is not the best way to make a film, but that's the way it was done. So every night, I would go off and re-write the next day's script and present it to the actors at breakfast and we would have a fight about what was going to be said and what not. And then off we went and shot it.

And that starred Laura Gemser, Stuart Whitman and Edmund Purdom.

It also had Woody Strode and Harold Sekata.

Who played the Indiana Jones character? I guess it had one?

Yeah, Stuart Whitman was the main man.

What was it like to work with Purdom.

Edmund Purdom is an eccentric actor who

is great fun… in his time when he was working in Hollywood, he had starred in the most expensive film ever which was *The Egyptian*. He would have been one of the biggest names around, except he was having a good time with various females and had to flee Hollywood. He's very eccentric and he went off and ended up marrying Tyrone Powers' wife after he died, Lynda Christian. Well he certainly lived with her, I think he married her. Because he lived in Rome for so long, he became a bit of an eccentric and was probably quite a difficult character to work with. Great fun. But if he'd stayed in Hollywood… He was incredibly good looking and he had the most beautiful James Mason-type voice and he could have been as big as anyone. But I think he was having an affair with a head of the studio's wife or daughter or something like that and had to flee Hollywood.

Laura Gemser had already starred in numerous films in Italy, notably the Black Emanuelle *series.*

Yes, I didn't actually cast her, she was part of the deal sorted by the producer. Originally they had Britt Ekland, but she dropped out because they couldn't afford to pay her as much as she wanted, so they got Gwyneth Barber who had just appeared on the scene in England and was up-and-coming.
One of the other characters was Harold Sekata, who played Odd Job in the Bond movie *Goldfinger*, you know the guy with the bowler hat? Woody Strode had starred as Sergeant Ruttledge in a John Ford picture. Stuart Whitman had been nominated for an Oscar for *The Mark*. It was a very good cast actually.

In 1983 I think you did the Best of Gilbert and Sullivan?

That was not actually a film, that was a big television thing, which I wrote. We did that in the Albert Hall.

Towards the end of the eighties you were involved in three films: The House of Ush-

er, Ten Little Indians *and* Masque of the Red Death. *All were filmed in South Africa and produced by Harry-Allen Towers. How did that come about?*

I'm just trying to think which film came first. I think it was *Ten Little Indians*. I had just been to India, making a film of the life of Nero, for the government of India, which was a sort of semi-dramatised documentary. I'd been there a year and a half and I went to South Africa and made another film — which you haven't got on your list there — called *Sweeter than Wine*, which was a love story. That was supposedly set in the south of France but we shot it in South Africa, in the wine growing area, Pall, just outside Capetown. So then suddenly the possibility came up of directing a Cannon film, *Ten Little Indians*. I was put up for it, got it and went off to do that.

When was Sweeter than Wine?

It was made the same year as *Ten Little Indians*. We made that at the beginning of the year, about 1989.

Harry-Allen Towers has quite a reputation. How did you find working with him?

What was his reputation?

Well, let's say "crafty"...

The thing with Harry-Allen Towers is, in spite of what people may say about him, he does make movies. He's made probably 150 movies — some of which have been made several times under the same name — over the years. But he does make movies and I think he's probably made four or six in the last year or two. He's quite extraordinary,

he's certainly given a lot of people a lot of chances and opportunities and he gets the deals done — although occasionally the scripts may be wanting a little bit for various reasons, normally because it's all part of the package. Those who have accepted the package at the beginning or the end, wouldn't have any changes made and so we were a little bit stuck to a degree, with what was there. But anyway, he does enable people to make movies. So, much maligned Harry-Allen Towers... I think the *Variety*'s of this world, like to run him down. Sometimes their comments are fair and sometimes they're not.

He seems to have a particular fondness for Ten Little Indians *doesn't he? He's made it a few times.*

Yes, well he owns the rights to it you see. I think it's an Agathe Christie stage-play that he owns the rights to. Anyway, whatever, he can roll it out every so many years and make it again.

I believe he once said he could get off a plane anywhere in the world and within twenty-four hours he would have a film rolling.

I don't quite know how that would work, but yes, he does tend to... I don't think he does it so much now, but he used to write the script on the aeroplane and there it would be, ready; "Roll in the actors and let's get shooting." He's sort of like a dealmaker: he brings various parties together and sets the project up. He supplies reasonably big names and the people who are putting up the money are quite happy with the deals. They can pre-sell them. Some movies are better than other movies, but he does make movies. I think that there are two sides to movie-making; one, the end result — and one can be critical or snobbish or whatever else, turn your nose up — and the other side is, it's bloody difficult getting films together. I've got some fabulous scripts now and it's very, very difficult, whereas Harry is churning them out.

Do you think it's actually more difficult now to make movies than it was when you were starting out in filmmaking?

I think so, yes. Films are quite expensive to make nowadays and I think people are always looking for what's going to happen next or trying to jump on the bandwagon or find out what the new bandwagon might be… They're very snobbish about it and a lot of people are making movies because of television, Channel Four for example. Which is absolutely fine, but quite often the films that are made are called films but in actual fact are really *television films*. By the nature of the deal, the films have to be shown at a cinema somewhere, but they don't work very well at the cinema for all sorts of strange reasons and the city or the financiers say, "Well, if this is movie-making, we don't want to know." So, although it's quite good in one way, in that it gives people the opportunity to make movies, quite often they're not very commercial and it doesn't do filmmaking much good. It's a funny old business.

The films you made in South Africa again boasted quite an impressive cast. We're talking about Oliver Reed, Donald Pleasance, Herbert Lom…

Frank Stallone, Brenda Mcara, Moira Lister…

I presume that Mr Towers brought these people together, or did you cast them?

I think they were part of the deal.

Given some of those actors involved, you must have had some pretty volatile situations on your hands!

Yes, well Mr Oliver Reed was very entertaining to work with. Not an easy person… he used to drink a lot. Although having said that he was never really drunk on the set and he always knew his lines. But I think the amount of drink that he drank sort of dampened his performance shall we say, by about forty percent. I should think he could have been totally brilliant if he didn't drink. He had a most extraordinary screen presence and I think he could have been really something fantastic, as maybe his last film shows, *Gladiator*. Certainly if he had not been drinking the last six years of his life, he would have been something totally awesome.

Donald Pleasance?

He was wonderful to work with. One of my favourite films ever is *Cul-de-Sac* by Roman Polanski.

Going back to Mr Towers, I read an interview in which he said of Ten Little Indians — not your film particularly, but the story in general — "You always kill off the most expensive stars first." Who was it to go first in your version?

In fact that probably wasn't true in my instance. That was just a sort of colloquialism that came about from somewhere or another. I remember being asked to direct this film which I thought was odd, where the American producer had all these star names lined up — the story had this nuclear bomb being dropped, and so the idea was that after the first week of

> I remember being asked to direct this film, where the American producer had all these star names lined up — the story had this nuclear bomb being dropped, and so the idea was that after the first week of shooting, all the names had to wear these helmets…

Killer's Moon (1978)

Dir/Script Alan Birkinshaw
Prod Alan Birkinshaw and Gordon Keymer
Ph Arthur Lavis
Ed David White
Asst dir Cormack Clark
Music John Shakespeare

With Anthony Forrest (Pete), Tom Marshall
(Mike), Georgina Kean (Agatha), Alison Elliot
(Sandy), Jane Hayden (Julia), Nigel Gregory
(Mr Smith), David Jackson (Mr Trubshaw),
Paul Rattee (Mr Muldoon), Peter Spraggon
(Mr Jones), Jo-Anne Good (Mary), Jayne Lester
(Elizabeth), Lisa Vanderpump (Anne), Debbie
Martin (Deirdre), Christina Jones (Carol), Lynne
Morgan (Sue), Jean Reeve (Mrs Hargreaves),
Elizabeth Counsell (Miss Lilac), Charles
Stewart (Bert), Edwina Wray (Enid), Hugh Ross
(government minister), Graham Rowe (prison
governor), James Kerry (psychiatrist), Carol
Binstead (telephone operator), Hannah (three-
legged dog)

Alan
Birkinshaw
Interview

shooting, all the names had to wear these helmets. The idea was that you wouldn't be able to see who the hell was in the helmets. As long as the dialogue for the rest of the movie had been recorded, you could then have extras walking around in big helmets for the next five weeks and still be able to use the names. But I said that the people who are paying a lot of money to see these actors in the film, would actually like to see their faces and quite frankly I don't think it would work.

I think from that idea grew these stories about killing your expensive actors off first. But in fact the version of *Ten Little Indians* I made had Frank Stallone — he was as expensive as any of the other stars and he was in it all the way through.

Into the 1990s. You did **Space Precinct.** *Now, I've also got something here called* **Punch...**

Punch was a Swiss/German/French co-production and the producer was a guy called Walter Saxer who had worked with Werner Herzog. The person who was originally set to direct it also wrote the script, but it didn't work out with him directing, so I was asked to come on board. I added quite a lot to the dialogue, for which I didn't get credited. So we made this picture, and there was a bit of a hue and a cry because the co-production treaty were a bit amused that this French/German/Swiss co-production

should have an English director. They eventually decided that it was alright, though. I worked with Donald Sutherland on another picture which I took over, called *Ordeal by Innocence*. Again an Agathe Christie story. For that I wasn't credited either — although I was the additional director and had directed about twenty-five minutes of the film.

You did something for German TV...

Yes, *Umberstechlicker*. That was actually three ninety-minute films that I made as part of a series, directing in German, which was quite interesting.

Is there anything I've missed?

Yeah, there's a German TV series called *Zorc*, which was an action series I did a few episodes of, starring Klaus Loevisch. Loevich was in *Cross of Iron*, I think. Anyway he was a very charismatic, but very wild actor. If Klaus Kinski was the madman of German films, then Klaus Loevich was the madman of German television and German directors were terrified of him. I wasn't because I seem to enjoy working with these lunatics. But anyway, that was an action TV series and that was shot in Italy. He was sort of like a private-eye type character, pulled in to solve unsolvable crimes if you like. Ⓕ

HEATHEN CHEMISTRY

by Gary Ramsay

Published by Hutchinson in 1967, RITUAL is a short novel revolving around pagan lifestyles, the occult murder of a young girl and its subsequent investigation by a puritanical policeman who befalls a sticky end. Ring any bells? This little book carries a reputation that twenty-seven year old author David Pinner would never have guessed at nor believed at the time of writing, as RITUAL is now inextricably linked to the iconic 1973 British horror film and cult phenomenon <u>par excellence</u> — THE WICKER MAN.

The Wicker Man has loomed over British horror cinema for the last thirty years, particularly over the last decade, where it has been examined in microscopic detail. Devotees now regularly traipse around Scotland in search of a souvenir, or stray fragment to remind them of the film. It's an important and memorable film, but for all its oppressive atmosphere and dalliance with twisted religion, *The Wicker Man* has triumphed as a survivor of the fickle world of film distribution, and as a supreme example of reputation over quality.

For readers steeped in Wicker Man lore the story of David Pinner is familiar territory. For those unaware of Pinner and his book, the story is very simply this: Robin Hardy (director of *The Wicker Man*) and Anthony Shaffer (writer of the original screenplay) used Pinner's book as a template for their exploration of religion and alternative belief systems, then jazzed it all up with hefty doses of sex and sacrifice. Hardy and Shaffer have often squirmed when questioned about the relationship between the book and the film. It has been suggested they 'borrowed' many aspects of the book for the movie, and have explained countless times their film merely drew its inspiration from the novel and was not a straightforward regurgitation.

Which is right. *The Wicker Man* is not a carbon copy of *Ritual*

A glimpse of RITUAL, the book that inspired THE WICKER MAN. While on p. 101 we appraise THE FANTASIST, Robin Hardy's follow-up to THE WICKER MAN.

Front cover of the scarce book, *Ritual*.

A Pagan Party

The story is set in the isolated Cornish village of Thorn. It begins with the discovery of a young girl's body at the foot of an oak tree. Fastened to the trunk by a hat pin are a shriveled monkey's head and three garlic flowers. Little Dian Spark is victim of an obvious ritualistic killing.

The village finds out about the murder via a group of menacing lawless children who are straight out of John Wyndham's *The Midwich Cuckoos*. Cue discontented mumbles from the village hoi polloi. The hub of Thorn is the local pub — The Green Fingers in My Hair — full of macabre locals in mid séance, gibbering in tongues and acting suspiciously. There is an unspoken mystery to the village.

Enter Detective Inspector David Hanlin. Huffing and puffing, and clutching a photo of the young murdered girl, here is a man uncomfortable with religion, sex and any kind of grotesque hedonistic behavior. Sent from Scotland Yard to investigate the killing, meet a man destined for trouble as his reality is peeled away before his eyes.

Along with Hanlin, the main characters we meet are: Lawrence Cready, retired actor and all round sinister dandy; Reverend White, aware of the occult high jinx of the village, but unable to change anything; Squire Fenn, the flute playing gardener; Gypo, the mysterious forest dwelling arrowsmith; and teenage rumpot Anna Spark, the voluptuous daughter of the sweet shop owner and sister of the murdered girl.

At every stage of his investigation Hanlin is stonewalled by the locals and slowly becomes a hapless pawn lost amongst the riddles of the villagers. Cready in particular is constantly probing at Hanlin's chaste demeanor and tries to tempt him to become fully involved with village life: *"It's true the village children often come to play in my*

by any stretch of the imagination. But the film and book share similar characters and a flavour of pagan festival, warped mind games, occult weirdness, and explicit sexual abandon. The characters and plot of *The Wicker Man* are well known and copiously documented elsewhere, but what is the novel like? *Ritual* is difficult to find and has long been out of print with original copies now fetching tidy sums amongst collectors. One copy recently available on the internet was selling for £150. My copy was tracked down via the good old British Library with a wait of seven months!

garden in the butterfly season. Should you care to join us in some of the more advanced games, you are welcome. We always appreciate innocence."

It seems everything in Thorn is brewing up for the Midsummer Celebration. Hanlin is eventually led by a procession of transvestites and villagers dressed as wolves, hares and goats to a throbbing beach orgy, where in the polite vernacular, there is much *"fornication and rutting"*. Crowds gather in sweaty heaps drinking and screwing. Here a vivid scene takes place where a galloping horse is beheaded for the 'invocation of the moon'. Amongst the sand, spurting blood and viscera, the drunken rabble eat the animal in a fury while children stuff dandelions and dog roses into the horse's ears before the head is floated out to sea on a raft.

Unfortunately, David Pinner spoils some effective scenes when he tries to inject a little ribald humour into proceedings. As the climax to the book starts to pan out and Hanlin begins to lose his mind, he phones his superiors in London. Here we meet Chief Inspector Peter Thornton, who comes out with many priceless lines. He bellows at Hanlin: *"Who the bloody hell is that at this time of night? If that's you Hanlin, I'll have you out on your diarrhoea ear!"* and *"Why, in the name of Leicester Square urinal, didn't you ring me before?"* or *"Stop bleeding well patting yourself on your sanguinary back! Give me the crudding facts!"*

It is sometimes difficult to separate this 'serious' book from comedy. Throughout there are some excruciating pieces of dialogue that are unintentionally hilarious. For example, as Hanlin is berating Cready about the villager's morals, he comes out with the fantastic line:

"Incest. I understand it's as common as fish and chips in back-water villages. Though, I must admit I haven't seen a fish and chip shop yet! But I can smell incest!"

Or his insane rant on the moonlit beach.

"You've made a mistake, animals," David began quietly. "You've returned to the grunt of the pig-sty, revealed yourselves for what you are!

Maggots rutting in slimy cheese. You've dragged down witchcraft into the sexual abyss! Don't pretend even to yourselves, that this is an act of worship! No this is anarchy! Licence! Glutting yourselves on your bodies to avoid the present! You've given up life. You've thrust your pubic hands into your own excrement! And now you're really enjoying yourselves! You're eating it."

Superbly terrible.

The police eventually come crashing into the village. Along with barking dogs straining at leashes they turn the place upside down to flush out the killer. The denouement in the nearby woods, involving another dead child and Gypo is confusing but suitably hysterical before the unlikely murderer is revealed. Hanlin himself. The closing image has the schizophrenic policeman sitting in a brilliant white room with a doctor handing him his sunglasses. A mildly loopy finish.

The Temptation of Hanlin

There is one scene that has travelled from the book to the movie. In *The Wicker Man* we have the infamous scene where Britt Ekland (and body double) prances around her bedroom, while in the room next door Edward Woodward works himself into a lather. In *Ritual* the same scene centres around the hellcat Anna Spark — owner of *"rhythmical hips, perky nipples and moist lips"*. Hanlin is lodging at Anna's parents. During the night, Anna tries to wind up Hanlin's libido to bursting point and lure him to her room. With a *"shine on her bottom lip"* Anna begins to rub herself against her bedroom wall. The gasping Hanlin is glued to the other side of the wall.

She leant against the thin plaster wall, adjoining David's bedroom. David listened with his groin… he felt himself drawn towards the wall. He knew her hot body demanded through the stale mortar. He knew. Still with hips hard against the wall, she removed the first layer of her skin. Her sweater. She loosed her breasts.

After doffing her clothes completely.

Author
David Pinner.

She amused herself, knowing David was stroking the wall. She savoured erotics for their own sake. Anna believed in everything for its own sake. David slid his hands over his side of the wall, lingering where the subtle incline of her navel would be… she mapped her body, from mountain to citadel, on the blank page of the wall.

Hanlin is left, literally, licking his wallpaper while Anna gambols off to bed giggling.

Some of *Ritual* will make your toes curl — really. But the basic concept of paganism, sex and murder has a universal appeal, and it certainly struck a chord in the imaginations of Hardy and Shaffer. Originally published by Hutchinson under it's New Authors Limited imprint, the plan was to publish new young writers with 'something to say'. It is a bold little story. Albeit faintly ludicrous, it has the surreal aftertaste of 1967 about it. Why it has not been reprinted (if only to cash in on *The Wicker Man*) is a bit of a mystery. *Ritual* has definite charm and curiosity value and if you are a fan of *The Wicker Man*, it really is essential reading.

Pinner — Past and Present

What of David Pinner? *Ritual* was his first novel and in the years that have passed since 1967, he has become a respected playwright and theatre director with several plays and radio productions in circulation. A long list of plays include *Hereward the Wake* (1973), *An Evening With The G.L.C.* (1979), *The Last Englishman* (1990) and *Lenin In Love* (2000). The likes of Philip Madoc, Kate O'Mara and Marayam d'Abo have all popped up in his productions.

During the 1960s and early 1970s, he had dozens of supporting parts on TV including appearances with John Hurt, Colin Blakely, Kenneth More, David Hemmings, Susanna York and a young Tim Piggot-Smith. His *The Potsdam Quartet* was screened by the BBC in 1980, and *The Sea Horse* was produced by Thames TV in 1985. Indeed, *Ritual* was written whilst Pinner was playing the lead in *The Mouse Trap* at the Ambassador's Theatre in the West End of London.

As of writing Pinner is involved with directing his own play *All Hallows' Eve*, that will take him to Hong Kong, Singapore, Shanghai and the USA. It seems he has lost none of his touch for the slightly crazed and hyperactive. The synopsis of the play reads:

a library in an old English mansion is haunted by the sound of Chopin's Nocturne Op 55 no. 1. The temptations of the supernatural. A disjointed family brought together by loss. Then when a limping stranger with a sinister presence unlocks all secrets on *All Hallows' Eve*, the full impact of the past is horrifically brought to light. *All Hallows' Eve* is permeated by blossoming sexuality, sublimated violence and predatory spectres from the past.

I'll leave it up to you to draw your own comparisons between the novel and the film. Without a doubt *The Wicker Man* will continue to excite and be talked over for years to come, whilst *Ritual* remains a lost book. In some respects it deserves to be lost. The narrative is incomprehensible, the dialogue often puerile and clunky and some of the settings badly drawn. But, the atmosphere it conjures up is unsettling and in the context of 1967 Britain it takes a healthy swipe at the establishment taboos of sex and religious faith. If nothing else, *Ritual* remains the inspiration for one of the most obsessive British horror movies of all time — *The Wicker Man*. ⒼⒻ

KILLING JOKE

by Gary Ramsay

THE FANTASIST (1986) is the second foray into motion pictures by Robin Hardy, the director responsible for the seminal British horror classic THE WICKER MAN (1973). Set in Dublin, the tale is based on the novel GOOSEFOOT by Patrick McGinley, the respected Irish author whose novels are noted for their dry wit, sinister characters and dark plot.

On first viewing, there is a definite tingle of excitement. THE FANTASIST has echoes of Michael Powell's startling PEEPING TOM (1960) and FRENZY (1972) — the film that Anthony Shaffer scripted from the Arthur Le Bern novel and which Alfred Hitchcock moulded into the last classic film of his career. In the absence of a wordsmith such as Schaffer to inject some style (Shaffer wrote the screenplay for THE WICKER MAN), Hardy penned the screenplay himself and this is where the problems with THE FANTASIST begin. Sadly, Robin Hardy cannot sustain the literary subtleties that Shaffer could and only succeeds here in revealing a clumsy and faintly misogynistic heart beating beneath the guise of a classy chiller. Hardy has excised the bizarre characters of McGinley's original novel and replaced them with farce, caricature, laughable dialogue, hysteria and a confused and muddled narrative. On top of this, there are some catastrophic acting performances that will make your blood curdle.

Considering that it's director is Robin (THE WICKER MAN) Hardy, is THE FANTASIST one of the most disappointing films ever made?

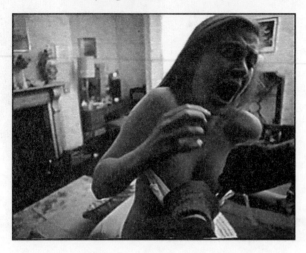

Country Girl v Urban Woman

Above
Sex-murder in
the opening
scenes of *The
Fantasist*.

Next page
Patricia gets
an obscene
phone call.

The film follows Patricia Teeling (Moira Harris) a wholesome rosy-cheeked country lass with a brand new Degree in Agriculture, who flees the rural nest to sample the delights of the big city — or as her Auntie describes Dublin, "that cesspit" — and also find some love and saucy thrills along the way. In doing so, she becomes embroiled amongst the murders of a serial killer, the eponymous Fantasist, who contacts his intended victims over the telephone. He waxes lyrical in mellifluous tones, entrancing them with pseudo-romantic psychobabble such as:

"I'm the bounce in your instep when you stride out flaunting a brand new dress, I am the melting feeling in your tummy when you hear music so sublimely beautiful you want to cry… the universe is your box of toys, you dabble your fingers in the day fall, you are gold dusty with tumbling, a good word amidst the stars."

As the women listen to this guff and become misty eyed, he breaks in and despatches them with the standard issue butcher's knife. He then arranges the corpse in the pose of Francois Boucher's rococo erotic tableaux *La Morphise* (a painting of the nude Mary Louise O'Murphy, an Irish actress who became the darling of the French Court and teenage mistress of Louis XV).

We first meet Patricia Teeling having a farewell meal in the bosom of her family on the family farm. This is intercut with the death of the Fantasist's first victim. With theatrical carving of the Sunday roast, Teeling is given a royal send off by Uncle Lar, recovering alcoholic and patriarch of a sad stereotypical bumpkin family. Patricia tootles to Dublin in her yellow Citroen 2CV, winding through some idyllic Irish countryside to take up her new post as a schoolteacher. Some fine cinematography and a lilting folk soundtrack capture the scenic beauty of Ireland perfectly and are about the only two aspects of the film that are effective. There are a couple of sumptuous landscape scenes that are reminiscent of *The Wicker Man* — for Patricia in her car, substitute the aerial shots of Sergeant Howie flying to Summerisle; Robin Hardy offers up two individuals imbued with innocence who are travelling to meet their destiny in unknown and possibly dangerous territory.

Once in Dublin, her first task is to check out somewhere to live. After ten seconds of entering her chosen digs Patricia has an excruciating conversation with her gawky roommate about losing their virginity and what constitutes their ideal man. Patricia reveals her Mr Right is "… *hard, always hard… strong, reliable, inscrutable, an imaginative rock… a beautiful rock.*" It has to be said that Moira Harris' Irish accent is as close to a comedy impression as you can get. Possibly hamstrung by the fact she's from Pontiac, Illinois, it wobbles throughout the entire movie, but it's truly fascinating waiting for the next clichéd twang to pop out.

The killer could be one of three men

that Patricia meets in Dublin and forms some kind of relationship with. Our paramours are Inspector McMyler, a limping policeman investigating the killings, played by TV stalwart Christopher Cazenove, who seems strangely to have been dipped in brilliantine; Timothy Bottoms as Danny Sullivan, writer, chirpy philanderer and all-round Yankee clot; and John Kavanagh as Robert Foxley, the weirdo bearded English schoolmaster with a particular fondness for having his tummy rubbed and an unexplored, and sadly unresolved, fetish for rubber and party balloons.

Patricia, now living in the big city, and swilling back the Guinness like a good 'un becomes a pleasure seeker and checks out the local nightspot — *The Coconut Grove*. The film has dated pretty badly, and the sight of Level 42 churning out their hit Love Games in a dreadful cheesy disco set piece is particularly hair-raising. Fashions change, haircuts change, but Level 42 were always shite. In the disco, she meets Danny Sullivan (Timothy Bottoms) the painfully jokey writer and possible camp killer who attempts to sweep Patricia off her feet and asks her out for a date.

It transpires that Sullivan and his wife Fionnuala actually live in the flat above Patricia. During the night arguments and disturbing sounds filter down through the ceiling, all hinting at a violent marriage. Inexplicably, and knowing it to be wrong, Patricia accepts a date with Sullivan and they meet at a house on the coast he is looking after for a friend. Here we see the character of Patricia transform from coy innocent frump to compliant husky voiced adventurer.

During the short stay in the house, Sullivan attempts to seduce Patricia. He asks her to slip a coin down her knickers while he attempts to find it via a divining rod attached to his head. As she hides the coin, he nips off to the kitchen to make a few dirty phone calls. (Yes, just like that.) Pretending to be an Albanian osteopath, he hams down the phone:

"I love the erotic wrinklings of your crotchless panties, why crotchless panties you may ask in your innocence, if they weren't crotchless how could I have you while you are waiting for the traffic lights to change. Look when I cum, the

flow of cream coloured light moulding the glowing crimson of your ass...!"

Patricia steams into him mid-flow and berates him about his disgusting ravings. Sullivan makes his excuses and palms off the conversation as part of a fantasy that he and his wife regularly play out: *"When a man can't make an obscene phone call to his own wife, what the hell is the world coming to?"* Patricia brands him a panty fetishist and heads home to take a bath. This scene is pretty funny for all the wrong reasons.

Fantasy v Reality

Sullivan's wife is soon murdered by the killer. But who cares? He sure doesn't, and strides out of her funeral without an ounce of remorse, announcing to the congregation and priest that the sermon is all: *"Lies, lies, lies, lies, dead, dead, she's as dead as a trussed up turkey."* As the movie now enters a crucial phase, the limping Inspector McMyler is firmly on the case and decides to follow Sullivan whom he suspects as being the likely culprit for the murders. He tails Patricia and Sullivan to a horserace and then to a nearby pub, where the Inspector wins a war of words with a drunken Sullivan. Here we learn a little of the oblique reference to Goosefoot. Does it pertain to the hobbling policeman? Or is it a reference to an evil smelling herb? Spinach perhaps? This is not expanded on at all, and for my money the relevance of Goosefoot

strikes me as pointless and unconnected to the structure of the film completely. Nevertheless, Patricia is now beginning to have some kind of fatal attraction to the Inspector as well as Sullivan.

Patricia goes home to see Uncle Lar who has fallen under the drunken spell of her cousin, Hugh Teeling. Sullivan follows her to the country and winds up having a meal amongst her hillbilly blarney-filled caricature family. Sullivan throws an inexplicable wobbly at the dinner table and brands her family lunatics and Patricia a prick tease, before fleeing back to Dublin. Ultimately, Patricia's country ties are finally broken with the drunken death of good old Uncle Lar who leaves his estate to her pissed-up cousin Hugh.

As the film moves towards its climax, Patricia returns home to find she has the fruity tones of the Fantasist on her answering machine. After listening to his usual romantic claptrap, she is disturbed by a mysterious intruder. She climbs out of her window and scarpers as the visitor enters her room. It is the weirdo bearded schoolteacher. Has he returned to the flat to see how she is? Practice some balloon blowing? Or is he the killer?

After staggering down some scruffy Dublin streets, Patricia manages to find the Inspector's house where he is casually putting his bin out. Here the film shifts up a gear. The Inspector has a suitably foreboding front room with a copy of the Tibetan Book of the Dead, statuettes of Kali and acres of imposing dark furniture. After enquiring whether she wants to see a little hobby of his, the Inspector shows her into his photo studio where he has numerous photos of her pinned up that he's snapped whilst tailing her and Sullivan. Here Inspector McMyler reveals himself to be the Fantasist, the obsessive killer and purveyor of eloquent telephone calls.

As it becomes clear that the Inspector is circling his next victim, he casually asks Patricia *"Do knives interest you at all?"* before lecturing her on the blue tinge of tempered steel. Patricia once again changes from a strange giggly schoolgirl to knowing sexpot. The Inspector asks her to undress and with a steely resignation Patricia

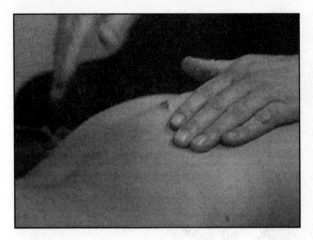

peels off her matronly kit to reveal herself as a fleshy bombshell. Through many enticing shouts of *"that's grand!"* the Inspector frantically takes more photos of her in the pose of *La Morphise*. He then straddles her and begins to use her buttocks as a pair of tom-tom drums, patting her rump to the beat of some atonal sub-metal sludge from his ghetto blaster. Honestly, this scene has to be seen to be believed. In a surprising spin of submission to dominance, Patricia flips the Inspector over and screws him leaving him in a sweaty heap in his dingy house.

The final barmy endgame is played out on a ferry. Patricia is presumably leaving for another new life across the Irish Sea when Inspector McMyler suddenly appears from nowhere. They have a brief struggle before he falls into the sea leaving Patricia aghast and clutching his artificial leg! The final unforgettable scene sees Patricia pushing her way to the ferry bar brandishing the Inspector's limb, and with a final farcical flourish announces *"… man overboard!"* The frame freezes as the dumbo Sullivan enters screen left. *The Fantasist* comes to the end of its *long* ninety-four minutes.

Average v Awful

There are many flaws to *The Fantasist* and it would take an age to deconstruct it fully. But there are a few prime aspects of the film that grate. Firstly: the voice of the killer over the telephone. This is totally ludicrous. He has the theatrical tones of the Speaking Clock, even within the film itself he is described by one character as sounding like a *"superior newsreader"*. A killer with artistic flair is to be celebrated but instead of a potent killer, we are served up with some namby pamby Hampstead antique dealer reciting bad poetry.

The performances of the main characters range from adequate to downright pathetic. Moira Harris is pretty solid throughout, except for her risible accent, but she battles through it all well. She swings from foolhardy to tough cookie too easily but still manages to exude strength of character. And there is a definite sensuality lurking beneath the brown tweedy ankle length skirts. Last seen in Jonathan Mostow's *Breakdown* (1997) with Kurt Russell, Harris is perhaps best known for being married to Gary Sinise (*Forrest Gump, Apollo 13, The Green Mile* etc) for the last twenty years. An accomplished actor like Christopher Cazenove must cringe when viewing this again. His po-faced limping policeman is pure *Carry On Screaming*. Timothy Bottoms turns in an enormously irritating, and in my opinion, possibly one of the most inept professional acting performances in film history. He is desperately bad every second he's on screen. Having started his career in major films such as Peter Bogdanovich's *The Last Picture Show* (1971) and Dalton Trumbo's *Johnny Got His Gun (1971)*, it really is a tragedy to see him flounder so hopelessly in the confines of *The Fantasist*.

A singularly unappetising feature of the film is the silly hard loving, hard drinking, Irish bog snorkelling stereotypes. They are weary, uneasy and badly drawn. Why didn't Hardy have the killer beat his victims to death with a shillelagh to complete all the clichés in the book?

This could so easily have been a triumph. There are several compelling polar opposites at work in the film but not much time is devoted to exploring them fully, or even at all. Patricia's transmogrification from country girl to city slicker is glossed over. The concept of innocence and experience (explored so expertly in *The Wicker Man*) is cast aside and the theme that underpins

the entire movie — fantasy versus reality — is explored in an amateurish and frankly slapdash manner. We learn nothing about Inspector McMyler at all and what could have triggered his fantasies, or who Patricia really has feelings for. Her coquettish behaviour is pointless. The worlds of fantasy and reality only seem to mesh together in one scene — the bravura nonsense that takes place in McMyler's photo studio towards the end of the movie. Attempts at injecting some deadpan humour are not funny, but just faintly embarrassing. Try as you might, it is impossible to watch *The Fantasist* without comparing it to *The Wicker Man*. As Hardy has only been involved in these two motion pictures, it's tough not to try and draw some parallels. They both incorporate the central tenet of the doomed innocent — genteel victims thrown into the chaos of sacrifice and murder. But, unlike *The Wicker Man*, where Sergeant Howie is led to his fate in such a subtle way that you hardly notice it, the figure of Patricia Teeling is a donkey lead by the nose.

Unfortunately, *The Fantasist* is so weak, that it throws some cautionary light on Hardy's talent as a filmmaker. Was *The Wicker Man* a 'happy accident'? A strange victim of circumstance, several talents — Anthony Shaffer (Writer), Seamus Flannery (Art Director), Harry Waxman (Director of Photography), and Paul Giovanni (Composer) — combining together to paper over the cracks of Hardy's shaky directorial abilities? In *The Fantasist* his 'helping hands' are stripped away and we are left with Robin Hardy alone at the helm and it's clear that he's lacking in filmic muscle to carry on. If there were more projects in Hardy's career to compare and contrast, we may view this as a blip on a stellar career path (what would we make of David Lynch if he had stopped making films after *Dune* [1984]?), perhaps he should have persevered and made a few more films, practiced a bit more. Instead, all we do is look at *The Fantasist* and worry.

Essentially a psycho-slasher movie with dollops of fetishism, *The Fantasist* is a curio and is worth watching... once. It cannot be viewed as a lost classic and considering the pedigree of Robin Hardy, this is certainly one of the most disappointing moments in European fantasy cinema over the last twenty years. With his third big screen movie allegedly in pre-production and scheduled for release in 2004, Hardy has apparently lined up Christopher Lee and Vanessa Redgrave to star in *May Day* (previously titled *The Riding of the Laddie*, but changed for obvious negative sexual connotations). We can only hope it has far more to offer than his beleaguered Irish murder mystery, *The Fantasist*. **CF**

THE CURSE OF THE PISSING CHIHAUHAUS: PETE, DUD AND PAUL'S *HOUND OF THE BASKERVILLES*

by Martin Jones

THE HOUND OF THE BASKERVILLES

...Yet Another Adventure Of Sherlock Holmes And Dr. Watson By A. Conan Doyle

"A hound it was, an enormous coal-black hound, but not such a hound as mortal eyes have ever seen. Fire burst from its open mouth, its eyes glowed with a smouldering glare, its muzzle and hackles and dewlap were outlined in flickering flame. Never in the delirious dream of a disordered brain could anything more savage, more appalling, more hellish, be conceived than that dark form and savage face which broke upon us out of the wall of fog."

THE HOUND OF THE BASKERVILLES, Sir Arthur Conan Doyle

Here's Sherlock Holmes as Conan Doyle never quite envisaged him: playing the violin, but badly. Wearing a hairnet, a grubby-looking corset under his dressing gown and sporting a broad (to say the least) Jewish accent. He takes a sip of tea and spits it out in disgust. And Doctor Watson? He's Welsh and wearing an apron,

Warhol Factory worker PAUL MORRISSEY decided to make THE HOUND OF THE BASKERVILLES with PETER COOK, DUDLEY MOORE and a host of aging British comedy stars. The result was panned by its stars and critics alike.

Starring

PETER COOK
as Sherlock Holmes

DUDLEY MOORE
as Dr Watson

The Curse
of the
Pissing
Chihauhaus

more housekeeper than doctor. From beyond a doorway within 221b Baker Street he asks, "Holmes, are you there?"

"No, Watson," the sleuth answers. "I'm in Budapest!"

There's much more where that came from. Waiting for Holmes are three nuns, anxious for him to recover a relic stolen from their church (it turns out some members of the congregation — flocking cripples — nabbed it). Holmes proposes to use the newly discovered 'picture-fit' method. "Oh, yes," says one of the sisters. "That's when you piece together the face of the criminal?"

"Alas, no," the grave-looking Holmes replies. "I can only piece together the *appearance* of the face of the criminal. I cannot piece together the *actual* face. I wish I could, 'cos of course once you've captured the criminal face, the other criminal parts are not hard to find. The criminal body being situated directly beneath the criminal face, joined, of course, by the criminal *neck*."

This is Holmes and Watson as played by Peter Cook and Dudley Moore respectively, directed by Paul Morrissey in the eighth celluloid version of *The Hound of the Baskervilles*. As the opening credits roll out, the pair go about their domestic day accompanied by a silent movie/cliff-hanger piano score; a hysterical, moustache-twiddling pastiche with shouts and whistles aplenty. Somehow, it runs perfectly with the scenes on show: Watson serves food to Holmes, Watson mugs about with a huge magnifying glass whilst Holmes reads *Guilt Without Sex* by 'S Freud'; Watson removes the top of a human skull and shouts into the void...

When belatedly released in Britain in 1978, *The Hound of the Baskervilles* was — to quote an older Peter Cook — grabbed by the throat, wrestled to the ground and kicked to death by critics and cast alike. This is a situation that has for the most part remained the same over the years in film guides, biographies and articles. A recent book, *Pete & Dud: An Illustrated Biography*, speeds past the film with a snappy "irredeemably dire" comment. But *Hound* was a three-legged dog, the last appendage being Andy Warhol acolyte Paul Morrissey. By the mid seventies the once-harmonious comedy partnership of Cook and Moore had diluted, and bringing in the cult presence of an auteur like Morrissey to their project certainly made things odder. It's a situation mirrored in one of the opening scenes of the film, when Watson journeys down to Dartmoor with Dr Mortimer (Terry-Thomas) and the new heir, Sir Henry Baskerville (Kenneth Williams). In their train carriage, Mortimer reels off a list of the folk living on and around the family estate, ending each description with the words, "a *strange* couple" (words Spike Milligan, playing a policeman straight out of *Q5*, also uses to describe a brief moors encounter with Watson and Sir Henry). *Hound* is a film created by a strange couple, or an estranged couple, with the director coming in as the intruding element. Or is it the other way round? Whose film is *The Hound of the Baskervilles*?

A brief narrative interlude...

Doctor Mortimer descends on Baker Street to tell Holmes and Watson of the Baskerville curse, and of the fate that befell poor Sir Charles: his death before the dreaded hound. "Oh," Watson exclaims. "Does it have huge, dripping jaws and great oozing eyes and enormous private parts?"

"*Enormous*. But how do you know?"

"Well, I used to have a little Pekinese like that, y'know. It used to leap up on the bed and bear its fangs and then, when I was least expecting it—"

"Calm yourself, Watson!" Holmes interjects.

After they are introduced to the young Sir Henry, Holmes puts Watson in charge of the case and inexplicably disappears from the scene. "Holmes," Watson pleads, "I've never done anything on my own before!"

"I think you have, Watson!"

Down at Baskerville Hall, the dusty, randy old housekeepers, Mr and Mrs Barrymore (Irene Handl and Max Wall) offer them a supper of cheese and cold tea, shove them into a water-logged bedroom, and tell them when they are *not* available, but that, "from four o'clock to four fifteen, all yours."

Watson sleeps with a photograph of Holmes next to him.

Back in London, the Great Detective pays a visit to the Piccadilly Health and Relaxation Spa de Paris, then visits his mother (Moore again) who is holding a séance aided by her meek friend, Iris (Lucy Griffiths). When Iris inappropriately laughs, Mrs Holmes slaps her and announces, "I like to strike a happy medium."

Sir Henry and Watson discover strange goings-on at the Hall, what with Mr Barrymore signalling someone out on the moors at night with a lamp ("It's moors code"), and Mrs Barrymore entertaining a group of ne'er-do-wells with luxurious food and drink downstairs; one of whom happens to be her sister, Ethel (Roy Kinnear), even though she looks suspiciously like an escaped convict.

After being pelted with fresh meat by a madman on a horse and cart, Watson goes to the village Post Office-cum-horse stable to send a telegram to Holmes summarising his progress so far. Then he walks over to Grimpen Mire and finds more fresh meat, only to be hooked and reeled in on a fishing rod by the madman, Frankland (Hugh Griffiths), who is also after the hound. Frankland despised Sir Charles — "THAT GUTLESS BASTARD!!" — and only buxom Mary (Dana Gillespie), storming in with a dead deer on her shoulders, can calm him down. But as Watson makes his escape, Frankland loses it completely and attempts to strangle the girl.

Back on the moor, Watson is mistaken for Sir Henry by Stapleton (Denholm Elliot), owner of two incontinent Chihuahuas. He invites the sopping wet doctor back for tea. There, Watson is served by Stapleton's myopic sister, Beryl (Joan Greenwood), who reveals that she was molested by the hound.

"'Ow 'orrible!" Watson exclaims.

"Mmmm," says Beryl, shrugging. Then she tries to seduce him. But on discovery that he is not in fact Sir Henry, Beryl uses some archaic force to throw him out of her bedroom window.

Sir Henry becomes hysterical when the Barrymores begin auctioning off the family heirlooms in order make up their unpaid wages. Holmes turns up in disguise and makes a successful bid for a strange, colourful portrait which, when turned upside down, reveals itself to be of the hound. Watson gets excited: "That means Sir Charles actually saw the 'ound *and* painted it before his death!"

"Yes, I think he *did* paint it before his death, Watson," Holmes replies. "I don't think he painted it afterwards."

Watson and Sir Henry are invited to dinner at the Stapletons. Crossing the moor, accompanied by Holmes, they witness Ethel being attacked by the hound. He was wearing one of Sir Henry's jackets. At the house Watson pulls out a revolver (but not before knocking over a bottle of wine), eats some leftovers that one of the Chihuahua's has pissed in, and is forcibly ejected by Mary. Holmes's mother turns up with Iris, and predictions of an erupting volcano.

It turns out that everyone was after Sir Henry, and that the hound was the true heir to the Baskerville fortune. During a climatic chase, Holmes

**The Curse
of the
Pissing
Chihauhaus**

changes around the path signs, and the scheming group all get caught in Grimpen Mire. "Don't look, Iris," Mrs Holmes exclaims. "Hermaphrodites!"

Back at the Hall, a volcano does indeed explode, killing everyone except the dog, who runs off with the painting between his teeth (that is to say, the dog ran off with the picture…).

Our two heroes meet an American gent…

Holmes: This is a job for an imbecile!
Watson: Quite right, Holmes. Let me deal with this!

By 1977, Peter Cook and Dudley Moore had nowhere left to go as an act. Between 1971 and 75 they had worked intermittently together on *Behind The Fridge*, a stage show of old favourites and new material that played in Australia, England and North America. But Moore's desire to relocate himself to California and Cook's rampant drinking eventually brought it to an end. The partnership that had grown from the groundbreaking 1960 *Beyond The Fringe* review (which also featured Jonathan Miller and Alan Bennett) to four series' worth of successful TV shows *Not Only… But Also* (1965, 1966 and 1970; BBC2) and *Goodbye Again*, (1968; ATV) had become fractured through broken marriages, alcohol, jealousy, and each man's unwillingness to acknowledge that they needed the other to spar against. Also, Cook and Moore's onscreen roles were now cast in stone: Peter was the literate antagonist, more often than not belittling Dudley and reducing him to a mess of laughter (as in their classic Pete and Dud conversations); Moore was the put upon fool, the innocent loser who literally looked up to Cook's superiority. Occasionally the tables would turn in their sketches, and later in real life, but after seventeen years together, that was how audiences of television, stage and screen saw them.

Notable success on the big screen had so far eluded the pair. Cook had made no secret of the fact that he wanted to be the new Cary Grant, or, failing that, a pop star. But where Cook was tone deaf, Moore was an accomplished jazz pianist and fledgling film composer, certainly a more plausible route to worldwide adoration. The pair made a cinematic debut together at the height of their popularity in *The Wrong Box* (1966), a star-strewn Victorian black comedy of corpse disposal based on Robert Louis Stevenson and Lloyd Osbourne's nineteenth-century novel. They then went on to co-write (and Moore score) 1967's *Bedazzled*, a Mephistophelian Carnaby Street clash in which — fittingly — Cook played the Devil and Moore a suicidal soul up for grabs. But after the big screen adaptation of Spike Milligan and John Antrobus's post-apocalyptic play *The Bedsitting Room*, and the American formula chase movie *Monte Carlo Or Bust* (both 1969), two things became apparent:

Dudley Moore was quite the natural in front of the camera; Peter Cook was not. In fact, he was somewhat *unnatural*. The masterful presence caught on the small screen was lost somewhere in the transfer, making him appear not so much Cary Grant as Scary Grant. Their cinematic characters were in fact chipped out in two solo projects: Moore in *Thirty is a Dangerous Age, Cynthia* (1968), and Cook in *The Rise and Rise of Michael Rimmer* (1970). In the former, Moore played a jazz musician unlucky in love, but not without a girlfriend; in the latter, Cook modelled the ascent of a cold bureaucrat on his comedy nemesis, David Frost. They were parts that stuck: the sympathetic fool and the emotionless manipulator.

Apart from *Bedazzled*, perhaps the pair's most successful attack on cinema in their heyday was a sketch in the third series of *Not Only... But Also* entitled 'The Making of a Movie'. In it, Cook is a cardigan-wearing, pipe-smoking author, poet and playwright called Robert Neasden — author of *A Man For All Neasdens*, *A Lion in Neasden* and *Anne of a Thousand Neasdens* — who lives a quiet life in the country with just his wife, children, dogs and the occasional television crew. One day, he gets the idea for a film:

> I was in the cinema at the time. Just me, my wife and children and dogs. I was watching this film…and suddenly I thought, "a film — that's it, a film". It was so simple I almost wept.

He goes to famed producer-director Bryan Neasden (Moore), who is just about to start shooting *When Diana Dors Ruled the Earth*. "I see it as a film about people," he tells the director. "People… who need people."

'The Making of a Movie' was the result of Cook's experiences in the film world. It wasn't a place appreciative of his on-set wit, so he ridiculed it in the medium he knew best: television. Obviously the lesson was forgotten by the time *The Hound of the Baskervilles* reared its shaggy head. This is a film in which Dudley Moore acts, and Peter Cook *lurks*, like a public school Clint Eastwood ("…my philosophy was, it's Clint Eastwood time, the less you do the better," Cook told *The South Bank Show* during filming, "and Paul kept saying 'Come on Peter, a slightly bigger reaction'; so I'd go 'RUARRGH!' and he'd say 'That's good!'"). Right from the beginning, when Dr Mortimer visits Baker Street, Holmes appears to do nothing more than sit around and watch the others act as the story unfolds before his wild eyes and tight-lipped mouth. No wonder he disappears soon after, almost as if he realises that Moore will be the better focus of the film as Watson. Even though by this point *his* character seems to be heading in the same mad direction as Harry H Corbett in *Carry On Screaming* (or maybe not: on the train journey down to Dartmoor, Watson, curiously cutting up a jacket, seems to be deep in thought; or is it Moore, wondering what favours this film isn't going to do him?)

A dumping ground for the cream of British comedy… how could *Hound* possibly fail?

Previous page Terry-Thomas, Spike Milligan and Kenneth Williams.
This page Max Wall and Irene Handl, Roy Kinnear and Joan Greenwood.

At home with Holmes
and Watson.

On that fateful journey, young Sir Henry relates the story of his turbulent sea voyage from Canada, in which he was swept overboard and almost drowned. "Did you manage to drag yourself up on deck?" Doctor Mortimer asks.

"Oh no," Sir Henry replies. "I just dressed casual."

A line ripped from the corpse of a *Carry On* film and fitting for a director such as Paul Morrissey, for whom *Hound* became a platform for his own particular interests...

Morrissey came to Warhol's New York Factory in the mid-1960s. Still in his early twenties, he worked in the multi-media set-up as a production assistant and cameraman before directing *The Chelsea Girls* (1966) for his employer. He then went on to add some much-needed stability (and editing) to art-house successes such as *Flesh* (1968), *Trash* (1970) and *Heat* (1971), all of which starred Warhol beef-rack Joe Dallesandro. Morrissey's horror connection began with two Italian films, the gory *Flesh For Frankenstein* and the sombre *Blood For Dracula* (both 1973). Uninterested in the genre, he was however tempted by the chance to work in Europe, making a 'Frankenstein' film in 3-D. Offered more money, he agreed to make two films back-to-back, which he did in two months, aided and/or abetted by the Italian director Antonio Margheriti. The movie's backers brought him on board because of Warhol's name and Dallesandro, who appeared in both films; and both projects were sufficiently removed from the Factory constraints, but with some droll, black humour uncommon in Italian horror flicks. Like Antony Balch, another director who came from an art-house background, Morrissey managed to make a name for himself away from his ethereal master. Pity that when the films were released, Warhol's name took precedence over his own, and that for years after, some would contest that Margheriti directed both movies. Understandably, Morrissey passed on the chance to direct *Andy Warhol's Bad* (1976) and went looking for something further removed from his origins. Perhaps something that would allow him to indulge in his one true obsession, a passion for British film comedies, particularly the *Carry On* series.

Despite touching the hem of ghastly art, Cook and Moore had so far stayed clear from straightforward horror projects. Sure, there's *Bedazzled* and *The Wrong Box* (written, after all, by the creator of Jekyll and Hyde), each drawing on aspects of the genre; but before tackling Conan Doyle, Cook and Moore's most revealing glimpse of their darker sides was a sketch entitled 'Mini Drama', written especially for the *Behind The Fridge* tour. In it, Cook plays a sinister Scottish cabbie whose fare is inpatient Lord Nesbitt (Moore), late for his speech at the House of Lords. Nesbitt steadily looses his authority and becomes increasing nervous as the calm driver gradually lets it slip that he may well be a maniac, complete with a handgun in the dashboard compartment. Cook completes the image by wearing his *Bedazzled* devil glasses and — in a homage

**The Curse
of the
Pissing
Chihauhaus**

to *Dr Strangelove* — a black leather glove on his left hand. It's a postcard from a comic pairing at the end of their respective tethers — Cook in charge, Moore cowering — owing more to Beckett and Pinter than The Goons.

The 1970s may have been the pair's wilderness years, but they still managed to find a new audience, by pure accident. In '73 they went into a studio to improvise a sketch about "the worst job I ever had" (for Peter it was pulling lobsters out of Jayne Mansfield's arse), and from there, Derek and Clive — smut-obsessed, obscene, taboo-breaking, evil, sick, sad and sometimes very funny alter egos of Pete and Dud — were born. Over the next few years, bootleg tapes of their drunken recoding sessions began to appear, becoming favourites with Bacchanalian rock bands such as The Who and Led Zeppelin. In the summer of 1976, Island Records released some of the sessions as *Derek and Clive (Live)*, and it became a best seller. Suddenly, Cook and Moore as a comic partnership were hot property again. Producer Michael White offered to finance a film featuring Derek and Clive's more restrained creators. Moore, who had been trying to start a movie career in Los Angeles, returned to Britain in the autumn of '76 to begin writing again with Cook. They took as their starting point a sketch from the second episode of *Goodbye Again*, 'Sherlock Holmes Investigates...The Case of the One-Legged Dog', in which Cook essayed his future role as Holmes and Moore was an unimpressed Watson. Splitting the time between London and Los Angeles, they set to working eight-hour days on the script, informing the press that it would tell the familiar story from the hound's point of view...

Early in 1977 Michael White presented Cook and Moore with the idea of Paul Morrissey as director for *Hound*. They liked it. A hip director of the same generation as them, with a number of cult films under his belt, seemed a renegade choice in the world of British comedy. As Cook's biographer Harry Thompson later wrote, 'Morrissey's involvement promised to contribute both kitsch intelligence and an awareness of mainstream tastes; at least, that was the idea on paper.'

The awareness of mainstream tastes was what Cook and Moore were aiming for, hoping that the financial backing (and trust) they had been given would secure a box office hit; also, from the improvised nature of his Warhol work, they assumed Morrissey would be easy to get along with. What they didn't count on was Morrissey's lust for auteur status after the outside interference — intentional or otherwise — on his previous films. Firstly, he took the completed script and began rewriting it to the specifications of his own *Carry On* obsessed mind: innuendo and wordplay suddenly made a rude appearance in scenes. Morrissey also wanted one quarter of the script to be made up of *Not Only... But Also* sketches, an idea that must have made Cook and Moore groan after five years of touring with the stuff. The fact that they had to be thrown in regardless of plot structure meant nothing to the director. By this point Cook and Moore were no doubt wary of Morrissey's intentions and knew that their script was being taken away from them. The final straw must have been the director's idea of filling the film with a host of British character/comedy actors and 'novelty' faces, a move akin to getting the keys to the sweetshop for Morrissey; but, as Cook and Moore already knew, it was more a way of pasting over the cracks. By the end of May, Morrissey had a final draft and copies were sent off the actors' agents, one eventually ending up in the hands of *Carry On* stalwart Kenneth Williams (after Charles Hawtry had passed on it, natch).

Williams' famous diaries — which he kept all his life — show in occasional detail how the initial enthusiasm for filming dissipated. On June 2 he received the script and wrote, 'It made me laugh out loud: some of it is v. funny.' But by August 5, when he and the cast watched the sixty-three minutes in the can so far, he commented: 'it was all rather depressing.' This was the insider's view of the battle between Pete and Dud and Paul (Williams makes no mention of it in his 1985 autobiography, *Just Williams*, which ends as the *Carry Ons* are dying a natural death).

The Hemdale/Michael White Ltd production of *Hound* began filming at Bray Studios — once home for Hammer productions (their last film to be shot there was *The Mummy's Shroud* in 1966) — in July 1977 and continued for four months, the main delay being that Morrissey contracted

Dud and Pete in happier times.

The Curse of the Pissing Chihauhaus

hepatitis at the beginning of August. Promotion was started early with a screen test stunt to cast the hound, but it soon became clear that the film's nominal stars and its director had vastly different views on how *Hound* should evolve. Dudley Moore summed it up to his biographer Barbra Paskin much later: 'It could have been the funniest thing, but it didn't work because he [Morrissey] was somewhere else. I had no *idea* what he wanted.'

Is *The Hound of the Baskervilles* really that much of an abortion that no one wants to acknowledge it? Cook and Moore were up for a retelling of the famous story. So was Morrissey: according to him, executive producer Andrew Braunsberg proposed the project, then hands-on producer John Goldstone approached with the idea of casting Cook and Moore in the leads. Morrissey, the comedy student, thought this was a good idea. He wanted to make it a companion piece to his previous retellings of horror legends,

to use the improvisation skills learnt at the Factory. But, even from the director's angle, things weren't right. 'I wasn't confident in it,' he later told Maurice Yacowar. 'I lost control over it at the very beginning when it was suggested that the two main actors each write a section of the film.' Regardless of where the two main actors were heading, Morrissey wanted a different feel to the movie, a pre-*Carry On* homage featuring a host of characters actors (Moore: 'Basically he wanted something comedic to happen whenever we did anything'). Michael White's company had already given audiences an intoxicating dose of TV-turned-cinema with 1975's *Monty Python and the Holy Grail* (John Goldstone would go on to produce 1979's *Life of Brian*), but Morrissey wanted to move away from the possibility of *Monty Python's Hound of the Baskervilles*, further back to the age of Music Hall, a setting fitting for his supporting cast.

The main feature...

On 21 June 1977, Kenneth Williams wrote in his diary, regarding *Hound*:

> Peter E. [Eade — agent] phoned and said: "I've fixed your contract for the film. I've got you 7½ and a car!" and I admitted it was better than anything I'd got before. The first bit of good news for a long time.

The *Carry Ons* were drying up (Williams would go on to do *Carry On Emmanuelle* straight after this film, the last and worst of the lot), and, like many other typecast actors, he found his main source of income was in advertisement voice-overs. No matter that he was prone to depression, hypochondria and terrible doubts about his sexuality. Apart from Cook and Moore, whose careers were at a standstill, *Hound* became a dumping ground for many comedy stalwarts as dusty as the Bray studio set: Terry-Thomas, Joan Greenwood, Max Wall, Irene Handl, Hugh Griffith and Williams himself. Morrissey's allusions towards a music hall homage extended to surrounding himself with these dying specimens, a vindication of his comedy theories, as all would soon find out.

The South Bank Show, LWT's well-respected arts programme, descended on the set in order to chart Paul Morrissey's new film. They were far more interested in the cult New York filmmaker than yet another vehicle for Cook and Moore's machinations (the programme was aired in April 1978). Morrissey was a walking encyclopaedia of British comedy and approached the trisected script with the reverence of a student. This delighted Williams, but made Cook more wary, as he told *TSBS*: "Paul Morrissey has made me as grotesque as I've ever been, apart from in private life, which is almost continuously." That private life was coming apart again, with his second marriage to the actress Judy Huxtable (one of disco-vampire Michael Gothard's victims in 1969's *Scream and Scream Again*) already under strain. Cook had returned to his old ways: a car would collect him at 6.30 am and by the time it reached the set he'd polished off a bottle of wine, chasing it with amphetamines for the rest of the day. As ever when his life was disintegrating, Cook took to ridiculing Moore. "Dudley is still not quite sure how to play Dr Watson," he informed a *Daily Mail* reporter just before filming began. "I tell him that Dr Watson is basically a small, bumbling, ineffective fool, but Dudley has some objection to playing himself."

But Kenneth Williams was flattered at Morrissey's knowledge from the beginning, when the director asked him to contribute lines, if he wanted. He was happy to go along with Morrissey's plan, that of installing aging character actors in familiar roles so that the process would appear to be to wheel them out, let them do a turn, and put them away again. This inevitably became a game of scene stealing, and stalling: 'We started off with the scene where Mrs Barrymore shows us into the attic room. Irene was rather halting & her work didn't have great flow (as I'd expected) & Paul went again & again.' (July 19.) The filming of *Hound*, it seemed, would be a kind of race against death, getting the most out of the actors before they copped it. Williams himself was buffed by Morrissey's attention, but while publicly lauding the film (whilst denying to the *Evening Standard* that it was another *Carry On*, he declared the script to be 'screamingly funny') he wrote up his doubts in the diary (at a script meeting):

> Peter Cook reiterated: "Sir Henry must be very mild and vulnerable... be careful you don't get that *edge* into your voice..." It's ludicrous the way he and Dudley talk about *truth in characterisation* the whole time, 'cos the script contains a mass of inconsistencies...The seriousness with which everyone sits around discussing the merit of this word or that word for inclusion in this hotch-potch of rubbish is the sort of thing Cook would have ridiculed in his undergraduate days. [4 July]

Those undergraduate days also reappeared when Morrissey recreated a number of *Not Only... But Also* sketches for the film, dressed in period trappings. "We were very worried about that," Cook told *TSBS*, "because we said, 'it will just look like we're rehashing old material,' but he said 'No, it's stuff which works. If you look back to the Marx Brothers, they did stuff on film which they'd done on stage for years and years, and they did it on film because it worked.' I hope he's right." The pair were correct to be nervous, as such a move appeared to be more crack-filling, most notably with the scene when Holmes interviews a Mr Spiggott (Moore) for the job of a message runner across Dartmoor, circumnavigating around the fact that the applicant only has one leg. This was 'One Leg Too Few', a sketch that Cook wrote seventeen years previous and personally held to be the best thing he ever created. It was the only classic to survive the final cut, although the climax of *Hound*, where Holmes changes around footpath signs on the moor to confuse the villains, mirrors an old *Beyond The Fringe* dig at Britain's WWII civil defences.

By the end of July, Cook, Moore and John Goldstone were aware that Morrissey was seeing the film in a clearly different, over-the-top light. The evidence was coming out in the rushes. 'The character looks *other* than me,' Williams wrote on July 22. 'It's a good wig and the alopecia is convincing. The moments when I stay in character are good... the odd bits (snorting etc.) when I don't, are bogus. The whole film looks lavish & expensive.' But when Morrissey contracted hepatitis and the filming was put on hold for a month, Williams and anyone else who cared had the chance to see what *Hound* was becoming:

To Audley Square, where everyone gathered to watch 63 minutes of what has been shot so far on *Hound of the Baskervilles*. It was all rather depressing. Again & again in the script, I've thought "That is hilarious" yet the fact remains, there is nothing hilarious in any of the stuff I saw in the cinema

Next page
Dana Gillespie with a happy Hugh Griffith.

The Curse of the Pissing Chihauhaus

today. It looked as if cues weren't being taken up with enough expertise & there are certain bits (the sex-talk between Holmes & Watson, and the one-legged man) which don't really belong to the story at all. [August 5]

Although he was spared the onscreen fate of the rest of the cast (involving a studio-bound swamp), Williams' last day on *Hound* was as confused and slapstick as the filming itself, as his entry for September 23 notes:

P.C. said stay for lunch at the Crown in Bray. I had far too much to drink & we drove back to the Old House and suddenly P.C. started this "you're wanted on the set for another shot of you & the dog" stuff, and he and Charles Knode [costume designer] pushed me into some stables & pulled my clothes off. It was like some daft sort of public schoolboy cruelty and had a curiously sinister undertone. I was shoved in front of the camera and Paul kept giving me directions about kissing the dog, but it was all rather perfunctory & I could see a lot of people giggling expectantly & I suddenly realised they were hoping I would make a drunken exhibition of myself.

Williams was driven back to London drunk, asleep and snoring, woken at the end of the journey as if from a nightmare, as no doubt many of the cast were.

In this all-hands version of Conan Doyle's story, the hound itself only gets about two minutes of screen time, as it's got a bit of a fight on with the other actors. Everyone's willing to fill up space, get the camera's attention. In populating his film with comedy grotesques, faces unwilling to play it straight, Morrissey papered the cracks in the largest way possible. These were characters let loose to wander around Bray Studios, its 'ram-

A FEW WORDS WITH DANA GILLESPIE (MARY FRANKLAND)

by Martin Jones

bling & derelict house with dirt, decay & cobwebs everywhere' (Williams, July 18) and sound stage moors, accompanied by dry ice and a slightly surreal air, like Vivian Stanshall's Rawlinson End if it had ever opened to the public. Nevermind the waterlogged bedroom in the attic: "even the mice have webbed feet!" cries Sir Henry. This version of *Hound* contains the "strange couple" mentioned by Terry-Thomas and Spike Milligan, and more. It begins with Perkins (Geoffrey Moon), the mole-like driver who takes Sir Henry, Watson and Dr Mortimer across the moors, towards a house full of the creatures.

Morrissey was used to working with oddballs. They tended to provide distractions. Kenneth Williams' Henry is a fay, staring creature, dressed in an ill-fitting hairpiece, accessorised by alopecia and dandruff. Morrissey's appreciation comes through in his performance, the apex of the huge gestures the director wanted: Williams spends half his screen time flaring his nostrils and winking conspiratorially. But his route down Camp Alley is blocked by Denholm Elliot as Stapleton, with his pissing chihauhaus, soaking Watson in a never-ending stream of urine whilst their owner chastises Sir Henry for upsetting them. The dusty living elements of Baskerville Hall are supplied by the Barrymores, music hall relicts of Morrissey's

A veteran blues singer with more than thirty-seven albums under her belt, before Dana Gillespie appeared in *The Hound of the Baskervilles* she had released a couple of folk records in the 1960s, appeared in the original stage productions of *Jesus Christ Superstar* and *Tommy*, and recorded 1973's *Weren't Born A Man* with the production/writing help of David Bowie. Gillespie's acting career includes work for Hammer (*The Lost Continent*, 1968), Ken Russell (*Mahler*, 1974) and Nicholas Roeg (*Bad Timing*, 1980) — not forgetting a part in the 1983 British exploitation flick *Scrubbers*!

CREEPING FLESH *Can you tell us about your role in* **The Hound of the Baskervilles?** *It's quite feisty: throwing deer and men around!*

DANA GILLESPIE I played Hugh Griffith's lover but Dudley Moore fell for the cleavage!

What did you know about Paul Morrissey? Was he easy to work with?

Cont on p.119

Left On the set of *Flesh for Frankenstein*, Paul Morrissey (with Dalila di Lazzaro). **Right** Denholm Elliott and *Hound*'s pissing chihauhua.

The Curse of the Pissing Chihauhaus

mind. Irene Handl looks like Alfred Hitchcock in a regency wig, sticking to the P's & Q's pronunciation that served her career. Max Wall appears as the Dickensian ghost of himself, all furrowed face and bared teeth (used again in another John Goldstone production, *Jabberwockey*, the same year), a comedian basted in flour. But both remain effective: at the close of *Hound*, the Barrymores — under the clairvoyant guidance of Mrs Holmes — decide to up roots and move to America. Kentucky, to be precise. "She saw chickens in my lifeline," Mrs B tells our heroes. "And frrriieeed potatoes in mine," Mr B grimaces, with all the weight his marriage can lay on his creaking bones (Wall looks even dustier at the auction earlier, with Handl sometimes missing from his side).

Elsewhere, there's not so much trace of the dust of age. Each section of the film has a silent movie title card, in the style of a book chapter; but when 'Chapter IV: Sherlock Holmes Seeks Consolation' is reached, a sepia photograph of three naked Victorian girls is swiftly brushed off by a hand possibly belonging to Holmes. The madam of the Spa de Paris is a surprisingly dirty/posh Penelope Keith, moonlighting from her dirty/posh role in BBC sitcom *The Good Life*. No matter that her girls are actually rancid old fishwives (one of which is a man — Mohammed Shamsi) who pinch and pull Holmes into frustration. The *real* lookers are hard to find: tabloid 'Page Three' model Vivien Neve appears briefly as one of the nuns at the beginning; and Dana Gillespie lays waste to all male eyes, but that's about it. In the local

Post Office (where Watson, surreally, is served by Henry Woolf, as a slightly shorter version of the doctor, even down to identical clothes) lurks *Fawlty Towers'* Prunella Scales, as Glynis the postmistress who knows a code of opposites, and Daphne (Anna Wing from *Eastenders*) with a "sausage and mash" code. "I'm getting a bit confused," Watson remarks. "Don't you worry, sir," replies the shopkeeper. "I'll combine all three codes and send it in Latin!"

In the totally bizarre scene where Watson follows a trail of fresh meat cuts across the moor, he is eventually captured by mad Frankland, acted to the brandy-soaked hilt by Hugh Griffiths, all wild eyebrows and alcohol-glazed eyeballs fit to burst. Frankland is a screaming loon only calmed by Mary, a gypsy girl (played by twenty-seven-year old folk/blues singer Dana Gillespie) with straining corset and a frightening dose of lusty aggression.

But perhaps the strangest actors to be dragged up by Morrissey are Joan Greenwood and Terry-Thomas. As Stapleton's sister Beryl, Greenwood is a frail but eerie presence, a spectre on heat; and no man, or animal, is safe. At their cottage she pours tea for Watson, but in fact it's just water. Then she temps Watson into her bedroom, where something quiet extraordinary happens. It's hard to figure whose idea it was, but for some reason twisted beyond all help, someone saw fit to hammer in a pastiche of *The Exorcist*, just four years after its release. Thinking Watson is Sir Henry, Beryl becomes possessed. The bed crashes up and down, her eyes flash red and green, a lizard-like tongue protrudes from her mouth, and then she pulls open her dress to reveal a chest bearing the flashing red words 'LOVE ME' (a reference to a scene in *Bedazzled*, where Moore played a Tom Jones-style crooner singing a song of the same name). Later, as most of the cast converge on the Stapleton's cottage, Greenwood caps the effect by spinning her head 360 degrees and spraying puke over Watson and Sir Henry. Demonic Beryl looks like a hairdresser's model head, but with real hands.

As for Terry-Thomas, Kenneth Williams rightly deduced that he was in the grip of Parkinson's Disease, although it barely shows on screen, ex-

Dana Gillespie continued from p.117

I knew that Paul Morrissey had worked with Andy Warhol, and had no problems with him.

As they were supposedly at loggerheads with Morrissey, what was it like working with Peter Cook and Dudley Moore?

They were not really compatible.

Kenneth Williams, in his diary, describes the climatic scene in the Mire thus: Hugh Griffith drunk, atrocious heat, everyone struggling to stay above water (Terry-Thomas appears to be unconscious). It all looks pretty chaotic...

It was chaotic — everyone had to wear all-over rubber suits! To keep out the cold the water was heated — very steamy! Hugh Griffith had been refuelling on Brandy! It was like a sauna, Hugh kept slipping over, off the ledge we were sitting on, and I had to keep leaning on his feet to keep them below water level! After several hours he virtually expired and had to be hauled out to be revived with yet more brandy!

Given that no one — cast or critics — seemed to have a good word for the film after its release, did you ever see it once completed?

I did see the completed film, and have an affectionate memory of the making of it.

What was your one happy memory of the experience?

Lots of good memories — warm sunny days, the hilarious in-between gags cracked mainly by Dudley Moore, that reduced me to helpless laughter all the time, mainly off camera! GF

Thanks to Greg Upchurch at the Dana Gillespie website
[w] www.dana-gillespie.com

More pissing...

The Curse of the Pissing Chihauhaus

cept for a scene near the close, when he — along with Gillespie, Griffith, Greenwood and Elliott — is trapped in Grimpin Mire. Williams looked on at the chaos:

> At the studios we did the falling in the Marsh Pool. I was relieved to find I was excluded! Joan Greenwood, Denholm Elliott & Lucy Griffiths & Hugh Griffith & Dana (& eventually Terry-Thomas) were all put in. H.G. so pissed that he kept reeling over & floating & crying out "Oh! For fuck's sake shoot the bloody thing!" The heat was atrocious. [September 16]

There is a blink-and-you'll-miss-it glimpse of Terry-Thomas, to the right of the screen, propped up against the side of the Mire whilst Holmes explains his theories. Head lolling, he's definitely unconscious. It's a perfect example of Morrissey's wheel-them-on-and-hope-for-the-best attitude. Comedy and despair. Sometimes it worked, sometimes it didn't.

The restorative benefits of rising damp and alopecia...

So whose film is *The Hound of the Baskervilles*? Who was innocent? Who was to blame? Everyone and no one. It was one of those brilliant accidents where chaos took up the challenge. If Paul Morrissey had been left alone with a low budget and no names to carry, he may well have turned out a third film to match the literary reinventions that were *Flesh For Frankenstein* and *Blood For Dracula*. If Peter Cook and Dudley Moore had been accompanied by a less individualistic director, someone who had no intention of writing his thoughts onto the screen, then they may have ended up with a movie to stand in the company of *Bedazzled*, their best film together.

Morrissey said that *Hound* was the only film he wasn't in total control of, but obviously the others felt the same way, with Cook acknowledging that the script was a "very bad compromise" between the three of them. He later described it as "a mess with some funny moments. Asking Paul Morrissey to direct English comedy is like asking me to direct an improvised movie about junkies in LA. Not compatible at all." Whilst Moore tied together a musical score, Morrissey edited his version of the film straight after leaving Bray. Cook, Moore and John Goldstone rejected it, thinking it too horrible. Cook and Moore edited their own version, removing all the old TV sketches Morrissey had filmed, with the exception of 'One Leg Too Few'. This was the version that would eventually be released, sometime. Officially, it was due out in April 1978, but distributors kept shying away from the job, postponing and postponing it, thinking of any excuse not to let it out: a summer release was out of the question, for instance, because of the football World Cup. *Hound* eventually crept out in November 1978 for a few weeks, by which point everyone involved had forgotten, or had pretended to forget, about it. Kenneth Williams' dairy entry for November 2 found him at Alan Bennett's house: 'Peter Cook came "I'll just have a tonic water" & sat smoking fags & gleefully relating the worst notices he'd read for *Baskervilles*.'

Two years later, the film was re-edited again for its USA release, with several scenes appearing in the wrong order.

Evidentially, no one knew what to do with the film: it was a mess, an accident, a woeful example of good ideas gone bad. But there *are* great things about *Hound*, simple things that pepper the movie. Such as after the announcement, 'Chapter IX: Watson Crosses His First Hurdle', cutting to a scene on the moor with Watson, crossing over a hurdle. Or when Watson and Sir Henry observe Mr Barrymore signalling to someone on the moor: Ethel the escaped convict busts into the hall, and there is a silent movie moment as he and Barrymore flash their coats open and shut, revealing lamps tied to their belts. Or at the auction where Stapleton — mistakenly believing that the bearded Holmes is Sir Henry — tries to point his sister in the right direction. "He's the one picking his nose," Stapleton tells her. Cut to about ten men all with a finger up their hooter. There's even unintentional stuff, like when Watson phones Holmes (geddit?) from the Post Office, unaware that his friend is actually standing behind him, disguised in moustache, glasses and hat.

And there's always the rather psychedelic Hound portrait.

Morrissey may have returned to the independent film scene, and Cook to a vagabond life of drink, drugs, laziness and the occasional small/big screen appearance, but the winner of *Hound* was Dudley Moore, and his prize was Hollywood stardom: a part in Blake Edward's hyped *10* was but a few years away. At the séance run by "Shirl"'s mother — something that would have appealed to Conan Doyle — Holmes stands outside, looking in, watching what is going on. This is Cook's role in the film: he always appears to be observing something, on the periphery of the action, eyes darting between actors as they talk out the plot. Moore has more things of significance to do. As Holmes' mother (a suggestion made by Morrissey), sporting a voice he used for Derek and Clive, he is brilliantly domineering: grey hair, glasses and a collapsed tea chest of a bosom. Mrs H carelessly hits Sir Henry with her handbag at one point, chastising him: "Saw you looking at my breasts!" As the musical composer, he's perfectly equipped with nothing but a loud voice and a piano: the title sequence is almost matched at the climax when, as our heroes and villains prance through the studio fog, Moore hammers out a shouting "THE HOUND! THE HOUND IS LOOSE!" Even redoing for the millionth time Mr Spiggot in 'One Leg Too Few', Moore manages to hold his own (well, he almost tumbles at one point) as a throaty, grumbling uniped with numerous facial ticks. The film ends as it began, with Moore at the piano. After the credits Dud rises to take a bow, only to be pelted with rotten veg by an unseen audience. As usual, he got the blame for everything, even a collaborative, chaotic curiosity such as *The Hound of the Baskervilles*. ⒼⒻ

The author would like to extend his gratitude to the Very Reverend David Kerekes and Lord Oliver Tomlinson of Moseley for their assistance with this article.

Note

At the time of writing this article (February/March 2003) the obligatory DVD of *Hound* appeared, released by CDA Entertainment. The original theatrical version of the film — nicely turned out in widescreen — is tucked away in the 'special features' section, whilst the main version, for some curious reason, is panned and scanned and at least ten minutes shorter, with the scene in Frankland's hut missing; also, Moore's score has been completely rerecorded (his top-and-tail appearances at the piano are also mostly missing) and there's a new inferior title sequence replacing the old 'Holmes and Watson at home' one. Despite an advert in the February 2003 issue of *Viz* promising "never before seen footage" there appear to be no additional scenes, unless the theatrical version is supposed to fulfil that role when compared to the other. The only other features are a five-minute contemporary interview with Paul Morrissey and biographies for nine of the cast members, now all dead.

Bibliography

Davies, Russell (Editor), *The Kenneth Williams Diaries*, Harper Collins, 1993

Games, Alexander, *Pete & Dud: An Illustrated Biography*, Chameleon Books, 1999

Paskin, Barbra, *Dudley Moore: The Authorised Biography*, Sidgwick & Jackson, 1997

Thompson, Harry, *Peter Cook: A Biography*, Sceptre, 1998

Yacowar, Maurice, *The Films of Paul Morrissey*, Cambridge University Press, 1993

LOOKING FOR A MOMENT: THE UNKNOWN CINEMA OF MICHAEL J MURPHY

by Darrell Buxton

MICHAEL J MURPHY — who is he? Where is he? Director of INVITATION TO HELL, THE LAST NIGHT, TORMENT and SECOND SIGHT, is he still making movies? CREEPING FLESH can claim the following to be the most in-depth analysis of Murphy's films published to date...

Rumour has it that the British horror film died a couple of decades ago. Stuart Mitchell's seemingly defunct and somewhat Hammer-centric Ghoul Britannia website carried a chronological filmography which dried up at around 1985, and although the publication of TEN YEARS OF TERROR (FAB Press 2001) proposed the work of Pete Walker, Peter Collinson, Peter Sykes and Jose Larraz as a movement which ripped through the British industry, the book's concluding chapter suggests that they may have also torn it apart.

So what really happened? Once the Eady levy and tax dodges had been snatched away by a Conservative government, keen to promote 'family values' and therefore none too happy to find themselves indirectly funding the likes of *Emmanuelle in Soho* and *Inseminoid*, Britsploitation divided down the middle. Those who had been simply in it for the money moved on to greener pastures, and we realised in retrospect just how lucky we had been — most of our filmmakers at the commercial end of the market had clearly entered the business to make a quick buck, so the fact that a high proportion of them actually showed skill behind the camera was a combination of our good fortune and their necessity to beat the competition in securing that all-important slot at the Odeon or ABC triplex. Once the financial acumen of these accidentally-talented plunderers had lured them towards non-filmic opportunities for profit, the three major areas of popular home-produced cinema fare lapsed into temporary obscurity; the comedy/sitcom spin-off disappeared almost completely (there's a huge gulf between *Rising Damp* in 1980 and *Kevin and Perry Go Large* in 2000), the sex movie vanished for a while, to eventually mutate into the video gloss of *The Lovers Guide*, and the horror film got an upgrade. At least, that's how it *appeared* to be. As Chris Wood states on his British Horror Films website [**w**] britishhorrorfilms.co.uk, the 1980s were a time of "ra-ra skirts, batwing sleeves, Rick Astley, and some right poncey arthouse rubbish masquerading as horror", and indeed, while Pete Waterman svengalied his way into the public consciousness, British shock cinema seemed to take a turn down the Merchant-Ivory path. It was titles such as Palace's insufferable *The Company of Wolves*, the Dylan Thomas-linked *The Doctor and the Devils*, the confused *Dream Demon* and the symbolism-loaded children's fable *Paperhouse* which attained theatrical release, as I well know from the occasions I found myself stranded viewing them in echoing, near-empty halls.

In the absence of Pete Walker and Norman J Warren, then, who could save us from Stephen Rea and films without a perceptible beginning, middle or end? Like bare-knuckle boxing, the real horror movie went underground. Old lags like Lindsay Shonteff turned to cranking out video-only productions (*Lipstick and Blood*, *The Killing Edge*, both 1984); regional types such as Manchester's David Kent-Watson got ambitious (securing the services of Donald Pleasence and Ronald Lacey for *Into The Darkness* (1986), casting a black panther and a Northern action hero in *The Eye Of Satan* (1988), and directing a gory space opus called *Firestar: First Contact* in 1991, starring Oliver Tobias and dear old Charles Gray). And in 1982, at the height of video rental fever in the UK, a double-bill of semi-professional featurettes crept out on the Scorpio Video label. "*INVITATION TO HELL*", screamed the packaging; "your nightmares will never be the same again."

Courtesy of Scorpio, the unwary viewer would discover *The Last Night* — described on the box as a 'supporting feature' — and *Invitation To Hell* itself. Both were X-rated, and are often the subject of animated discussion today whenever children of the video age congregate. They were the early outpourings of perhaps our most obscure, elusive exploitation director — Michael J Murphy. As David Flint wrote in *Ten Years Of Terror*, "all attempts to find further information on Mr Murphy and his work have come to naught." Until now.

I'm sorry to report that I haven't traced Michael J Murphy, don't know where he hails from, whether he is alive or dead, or even if he is still making movies. However, the quest for additional enlightenment bore fruit one night in the mid 1990s, when, at a meeting of London's Gothique Film Society, my good friend Ian Bellerby

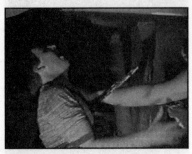

Scenes from *The Last Night*. The film title (**top**) is ambiguously displayed only as a banner pasted over a poster for 'Murder in the Dark', the play-within-the-film.

Looking for a Moment

turned up clutching a tape containing two items recorded from the late, lamented HVC channel. The Holy Grail or what? A pair of *new* Murphy features! Namely, *Torment* (1990) and *Second Sight* (1992). So, assuming that his local newspaper or parish magazine hasn't been reviewing his work for years, and guessing that his output fails to extend beyond this aforementioned quartet, *Creeping Flesh* can surely claim the following to be the most in-depth analysis of Murphy's films published thus far...

It's been difficult for researchers to accurately date *Invitation To Hell* and *The Last Night* — opinion among those who have written about this pairing in the past seems to be that they were both shot in the late 1970s, largely based on the hairstyles and dress sense of the cast. One reviewer even picked out the number plate of a motor vehicle as a determining factor! However, a brief reference to President Reagan on a radio broadcast at the start of *The Last Night* would appear to confirm that the films could have been produced no earlier than 1981. I'm not entirely certain where Murphy and his actors hailed from, but there are more than a few performers here whose dialogue is tinged with a West Country burr, and it's safe to say that whatever might have been fashionable in the West End in 1979 probably didn't filter through to Somerset & Avon for some time after!

Jonathan Rigby's description of *The Last Night* (in his book *English Gothic*) as "threadbare", and his comment that its companion piece is "even less appetising", is fairly typical of the critical reception Murphy's films have encountered. Writing in *Flesh & Blood* some years ago, Nigel Burrell said of *The Last Night* that it "leaves a putrid taste in one's mouth" and called it "one of the all time lowest points in British Horror". Extremely unfair — Murphy's direction is competent, mixing use of low and high-angle shots with close-ups effectively, employing enough zooms to satisfy even the most rabid Jess Franco nut, and eliciting decent performances from what I assume to be a mainly amateur cast comprising his friends and neighbours. The plot sees a bunch of local theatricals, the Prestidge Players, staging a sub-Agatha Christie production, *Murder In The Dark*, to ever-diminishing audience interest ("nineteen so far" says one weary thespian, having peeked through the curtain, "that's three more than Tuesday"). As they prepare for the final evening show, and a surprise party for one of their number who is celebrating a birthday, two violent criminals on the run from Broadmoor decide to use the theatre as a handy hiding-place. Gary (Colin Efford) and Mike (Steven Longhurst, a Chris Tarrant/Peter Cleall look-alike and Dave Prowse sound-alike) proceed to bump off various members of the troupe, events taking a somewhat surprising turn when their activities are discovered — Mike decides that 'the show must go on', as a means of concealing their presence from the audience, and takes it upon himself to assume the role of director, intending to dispose of the players at a more convenient moment. ("I'm your new producer, and if I don't like your acting, Gary is gonna slit her throat"). The killers acknowledge their dilemma, being unable to rid themselves of those cast members expected on stage, since their failure to appear would be a sign that something was awry — however, in a scene which brilliantly anticipates the chilling 'rehearsal murder' in Michele Soavi's masterpiece *Stagefright*, one actress adapts her dialogue in order to give the game away, only to be shot from the wings by Mike, with her traumatised friends having to disguise the shocking death as fake, showbiz, all part of the act. Murphy has up until this

> She staggers off stage, drenched in gore, startling the revellers who have gathered to wish her a happy birthday. It's my party...

point frequently juxtaposed backstage stabbings and knifings with shots of the applauding theatregoers, in a rather obvious and ham-fisted way, but this particular comment on the art/reality divide is exceptional, and offers an early indication of the territory into which the director would later delve in the complex and intricate *Second Sight*. *The Last Night* wraps up briskly in a maelstrom of havoc, with Mike inadvertently wounding Gary while murdering a male victim; Gary, the brutish half of their *Of Mice and Men*-style partnership, hangs Mike using a scenery cable, only to himself be bloodily knifed by Helen (Catherine Rowlands, a Murphy regular). She staggers off stage, drenched in gore, startling the revellers who have gathered to wish her a happy birthday. It's my party...

Scenes from *Invitation to Hell*.

Val Lewton always claimed that the formula for success in the classic B-movies he produced at RKO was to ensure that what-ever else happened, the film should contain three moments or events which would keep the cinema crowds talking on their way home — the famous *Cat People* 'bus' being a prime example. It's a tenet followed by Michael J Murphy in his own way — clearly aware of limitations in both budget and ability, Murphy plays to his strengths. Amid the cups of tea, home-made cakes, and Abbey Crunch biscuits which represent genteel 'normality' during *The Last Night*, for instance, the director is not averse to hurling in a vicious multiple stabbing followed by a bout of necrophilia! And while *Invitation To Hell* may be inferior overall, it too contains one particular twist on an old cliché which arrives with genuine impact. This one features Jacky, a young student who is lured to 'Manor-farm' (sic) on the pretext that some old friends are staging a fancy dress party, only to find that she has been earmarked for sacrifice to an ancient demon; cleverly, she decides to seduce her boyfriend, safe in the knowledge that the devil only wants her for her purity,

Scenes from *Torment*.

Looking
for a
Moment

but in a spectacular display of coitus interruptus her partner has a huge carving knife rammed through his neck, emerging from his throat, and leaving Jacky intact and still vulnerable. Efford and Longhurst pop up again with another variant on the 'George and Lenny' duo, the former playing a silent, musclebound farmhand acting as a vessel through which the demonic entity causes rural carnage, while his cocky pal occasionally finds himself possessed, growling out instructions to his hulking mate. There's a rather odd and understated homo-erotic tone to their teaming this time, as Longhurst takes considerable interest in watching Efford pump iron in front of a wall covered in girlie pictures (against which he is crucified towards the end of the movie), and delivers loaded lines such as "you ought to come down with the pub with me — I know you ain't gonna talk, but you'd be something to look at" and, bafflingly, "take your boots off before you get into bed"! *Invitation To Hell* is otherwise a pretty routine satanic chiller, but rings the changes on the usual template by having the participants fully aware from the start that they are endangered by dark forces, yet leaving them powerless to do anything about their predicament.

Murphy's two early 1990s films tend to reject the traditional trappings of British horror, while developing themes from *The Last Night* to interesting and somewhat daring effect. *Torment* and *Second Sight*, like *The Last Night*, centre around the world of entertainment, and offer a scathing view of celebrity status and the demands of the media. Anna Bell (Debbi Stevens), the Bonnie Tyler-like pop singer who acts as the focal point of *Torment*, and novelist Ray (Patrick Olliver) of *Second Sight*, both appear to despise their success — Anna is never happier than when out of the public spotlight, retiring to a country cottage to relax, pen a few new songs, and enjoy an affair with a handsome handyman, while Ray, struggling with a new horror story, has shut himself away in a remote mansion with his young American wife and a vow to never sell out, not permitting the sale of film and TV rights to his work until after his death. In Anna's case, however, her ideal lover is revealed to also be the psychotic stalker chopping his way through her entourage; while for Ray, his self-enforced isolation causes paranoia and the belief that his spouse, who stands to benefit financially, is in league with his gardener and odd-job man Nick in developing a *Les Diaboliques*-like plot against him.

As pointed out by Kim Newman in *British Horror Cinema* "there are almost no British slasher movies", in the sense that our filmmakers have rarely copied the American model epitomised by Sean Cunningham's *Friday The 13th* and its horde of imitators. *Torment* may be as close an approach as the British horror movie has made to this brand of cinema, although it spirals off into far more disturbing territory during its final third, and predates Ray Brady's *Boy Meets Girl* (1994) in certain aspects. One curious trait of Murphy's films sees suspicion heaped upon blue-collar workers, with Colin Efford's country simpleton from *Invitation To Hell* doing the devil's dirty deeds, James Reynard's self-styled "jack of all trades" from *Second Sight* becoming embroiled in his lover's schemes and burying bodies in the nearby orchard, and Rob Bartlett as Mat in *Torment* seemingly sympathising with Anna's desire for an easy, carefree existence but wiping out her friends and colleagues in order to help her achieve her dream. Anna may be "looking for a moment, looking for some romance" as the lyrics of her hit song Torment have it, but the reality is so unexpected that it drives her to take torturous revenge. Once again, Murphy adapts a basic horror/thriller plotline, here the mad stalker/obsessive fan, and flips the concept over — Anna's response to the death and destruction around her is to kidnap Mat, depriving him of food and water for an unspecified but lengthy period, playing psychological mind games with her helpless victim, eventually murdering her own manager when he arrives at the cottage, and in an extraordinary finale which recalls Buñuel's *Un Chien Andalou*, driving the dying Mat down to the beach, where the killer couple, entwined by insanity, lie waiting for the engulfing tide to end their mutual misery.

Scenes from *Second Sight*.

Murphy's cleverest and most sinisterly playful film, 1992's *Second Sight*, demands extremely careful attention from the viewer, as it could easily be mistaken for one of those 'fiction-come-to-life' stories *a la Screamplay* (1984) or the 'Method For Murder' episode of *The House That Dripped Blood* (1970). Ray (Patrick Olliver, memorable as the camp choreographer in *Torment*) is an embittered writer working on a new horror novel featuring a deranged surgeon, Dr Purcell. Ray has a need to visualize his characters, and bases his mind's-eye view of Purcell on a neighbour (seen just once by us) whom he spies from his study window. Thereafter, Murphy intercuts the domestic drama played out between the writer, his sexy young wife, her secret American husband, and estate manager Nick, with scenes of 'Purcell', envisioned by Ray, cackling dementedly as he gruesomely scalps his victims. As the film progresses, Ray's visions of Purcell become increasingly personalised, with the doctor's bon mots seemingly passing comment on his creator's own predicament, and Purcell appearing to manifest himself in the real world on more than one occasion, indicating the author's own cracking mental state. This truly original plot thread is interwoven into a more recognisable 'bump off the old man for his money' scenario, yet even that hoary old idea is given a twist of its own with the injection of a second husband arriving unexpectedly, albeit soon to be despatched with a handy pair of scissors and buried in a tea chest. Ray is temporarily blinded following an 'accident' in the pool house — though he suspects his wife of attempting to bash his brains in with an empty wine bottle — and he continues to feign sightlessness even when his vision returns. Purcell continues to plague his thoughts, and Ray appears to concoct a fiendish scheme of his own in which Nick will unwittingly inter the writer's claustrophobic spouse alive. *Second Sight* at this point bears comparison with George Sluizer's chilling *Spoorloos/The Vanishing* (1988), and if it weren't for a neat but rather unnecessary final revelation or two, culminating in Ray becoming impaled on his own white walking-cane, Murphy's film could have rivalled the Dutch movie in intensity and sheer nerve-shredding ghastliness at its climax.

And that, as far as I'm aware, is that. The HVC channel, which aired *Torment*, *Second Sight*, and a handful of other British obscurities during its brief heyday, has disappeared into the ether, and Michael J Murphy remains as unheralded and phantom-like a figure as ever. I'm not trying to state any sort of case that Murphy is an undiscovered genius, but the four films of his that I've been fortunate enough to see all have their merits, and would certainly appeal to anyone wishing to claim Britain as the true home of transgressive, taboo-breaking terror. If you're anywhere out there, Michael... 𝖢𝖥

Filmography

THE LAST NIGHT (1982)
Directed by Michael J Murphy
Produced by Caroline Aylward
Cast Mike/Steven Longhurst; Helen/Catherine Rowlands; Trevor/David Bruhl; Gary/Colin Efford; Arthur/Antony Peyton; Sue/Lindsey Greer; Eileen/Yvette Gunter; Marilyn/Patricia Dolby; Jill/Marina Bolton; Dave/Clifford Gardiner; Bert/Al Greer; Stan/Peter Neal; Clive/Tim Morris; Rita/Nanda Arkin
50mins | Released by Scorpio Video

Notes The title *The Last Night* appears simply as a secondary flyer being pasted on to a poster for 'Murder In The Dark', the play-within-the-film. | Michael J Murphy is not credited officially as 'director'. His credit reads: 'A Film By Michael J Murphy.'

INVITATION TO HELL (1982)
Directed by Michael J Murphy
Produced by Caroline Aylward
Cast Jacky/Becky Simpsom ('Simpson' on video box); Ed/Joseph Sheahan; Maurice/Colin Efford; Alan/Steven Longhurst; Rick/Russell Hall; Laura/Catherine Rolands (spelling on credits); Liz/Tina Barnett
Production Screenplay/Carl Humphrey; Photography/Stephen Childs; Editor/Mike John; Sound/Tony Ward; Music/Terence Mills; Production Design/Joyce Bernard, assisted by/Elizabeth Morris

42mins | Released by Scorpio Video

Notes Catherine Rowlands' name is misspelled in the credits. | Again, Murphy is not officially credited as 'director'. The film's titles state: 'Michael J Murphy Presents *Invitation To Hell*.' | The Scorpio Video release gives a running time of 'Approx. 98 mins.' on the back of the videocassette box, but this is obviously intended to include *The Last Night* also. The actual combined running time is 92mins (at 25 f.p.s.). | *Invitation To Hell* was later re-released in a slightly edited version.

TORMENT (1990)
Directed by Michael J Murphy
Produced by Michael J Murphy
Cast Anna/Debbi Stevens; Mathew/Rob Bartlett; Mike/Philip Lyndon; Fiona/Catherine Rowlands; Craig/Alan Jansen; Village Girl/Sarah Payne; also with: Jessica Day, Denise Burden, Elise Meldrum
Production Screenplay/Leo Golding; Songs written and produced by/Mark Thomas; Sung by/Debbi Stevens; Production Assistants/Steve Sexton, Carole Shipp, Bill Stote, Steve Butt; Photography/Michael Melsack; Sound/Tony Pitcher; Editor/Arthur Childs; Special Effects/Bernard Baker; Production Manager/Caroline Aylward; Transportation/Steve Moore; Research/Dave Lyndon; Props/Rob Brown; Catering/Brian Hill; Costumes/Joyce Bernard;

Design/Nino Farnochia; Continuity/Judy Salmon; Makeup/Gaye Sizer; Exec Producer/Jeanne Griffin
86mins | Merlin Films

SECOND SIGHT (1992)
Directed by Michael J Murphy
Produced by Rick Arthur & Jeanne Griffin
Cast Ray/Patrick Olliver; Vicky/Amy Raasch; Nick/James Reynard
Tanith/Judith Holding; Sean/David Charles; Madeline/Caroline MacDowell; Doctor Purcell/Neil Goulbourn; Doctor/John Flanagan
Alice/Odette Forse; Young Man/Robert Richards; Nick's Friend/Sarah Payne
Production Screenplay/Michael J Murphy; Associate Producer/Carole Shipp; Assistant Director/Ian Owens; Production Assistants/Andy Dunn; Leigh Wood; Location Advisors/Bob & Cheryl Bryant; Video Facilities/Viv Gregson; Script Consultant/Carl Lajeunesse; Music/Philip Love; Photography/Michael Melsack; Sound/Tony Pitcher; Editor/Arthur Childs; Special Effects/Bernard Baker; Production Manager/Caroline Aylward; Transportation/Steve Moore; Research/Dave Lyndon; Props/Rob Brown; Catering/Brian Hill; Costumes/Joyce Bernard; Design/Nino Farnochia; Continuity/Judy Salmon; Makeup/Gaye Sizer
85mins | Merlin Films (mis-spelled on opening credits as 'Murlin Films')

NO SLEEP 'TIL MANCHESTER!
THE CURIOUS HISTORY OF *SLEEPWALKER*

by Darrell Buxton

Full supporting programme. Three words which struck terror into the hearts of provincial cinemagoers throughout the 1970s and early 1980s, promising as they did the icy threat of a dread-filled hour comprising tacky ads (King Cone, anyone?), trailers which all seemed to feature the same growling voiceover (you know the one), and most painful of all, the short.

Ah, the short. A holdover from the days of the 'quota' system, designed to ensure that British fleapits played a fair proportion of home-grown product, and a means for any Tom, Dick, or Harry with access to a camera, a few thousand quid, and a mate in the business who could secure Warren Clarke or Gabrielle Drake for two days work, to get their twenty-five-minute epics up on screen — to the vast annoyance of a horde of paying punters eagerly awaiting the new Bond instalment or Irwin Allen catastrophe. The news was not all bad, however, and the occasional gem surfaced from the morass. Sture Rydman's exquisite and elegantly-crafted Bierce-based frighteners *The Return* and *The Man and the Snake*, Stanley Long's delirious *Killer Punch*, and the fang-in-cheek par-

Ramsgate-based filmmaker SAXON LOGAN's 'lost' horror classic SLEEPWALKER, has rarely been seen since it was completed in 1984. Following its recent rediscovery, the movie is now being given a new lease of life...

Above
Sleepwalker's
excrutiating
restaurant
sequence,
courtesy the
Paradises and
the Britains.
Next page
More
restaurant
business.

No Sleep 'til Manchester!

ody *Vampyr* all gave audiences an unexpected bonus half-hour of entertainment prior to the main feature attraction.

And suddenly it was over. The withdrawal of government funding in the early days of Mrs Thatcher's tenure killed off the short format, along with much of our beloved 'film industry', without remorse. Meanwhile, however, in a small corner of Hampshire, a young associate of Lindsay Anderson, one Saxon Logan, toiled away on a forty-nine-minute featurette whose promise was to remain unfulfilled for almost two decades...

I first encountered the title *Sleepwalker* in No 10 of Harvey Fenton's esteemed fringe-dweller's bible, *Flesh & Blood*. Harvey and contributors were busy compiling a completist's guide to the modern British horror movie (eventually to develop into the essential tome *Ten Years Of Terror*), and Kim Newman had hauled up distant memories of Saxon's movie from the recesses of his trivia-cluttered mind. Kim claimed to have attended a press screening of *Sleepwalker* in early 1985, in his capacity as film critic for the now-defunct *City Limits* magazine, and offered a tantalising description of what he referred to as "the most obscure horror movie ever made in Britain". At the time, I was hard at work collating information for my own UK horror filmography, an ever-expanding beast presently

harnessed on the web under the banner Pass The Marmalade [**w**] www.british-horror.fsnet.co.uk, and duly listed *Sleepwalker* — albeit as an example of a title I never expected to actually *see*.

Before too long, however, my suspicions got the better of me. Kim is noted for his affectionate refashioning of genre concepts and clichés, not to mention his meticulous attention to detail, and I began to ponder whether the unknown *Sleepwalker* might be a concoction of his own devising, created to confuse and bewilder fellow researchers. Had he made the whole thing up? After all, 'Saxon Logan' sounded a most unlikely, possibly anagrammatical or otherwise significant signature; the *Flesh & Blood* review also claimed the film to be a battleground upon which the social dramas epitomised by Play For Today collided roughly with the red-raw nu-horror represented by *Friday The 13th* and its ilk; and surely the likes of Fulton Mackay and Michael Medwin would have had better things to do with their time than involve themselves in a project of this nature? The clincher for me was Kim's bizarre claim that the award-winning Scottish director Bill Douglas, best-known for his grimly nostalgic trilogy *My Childhood/My Ain Folk/My Way Home*, should appear in one of the lead roles! I was convinced — surely this was no more than a playful fancy, a clever hoax on Kim's part? Deciding to retain the film's entry on my website, I nonetheless added a codicil indicating my doubts about *Sleepwalker*'s authenticity, as well as putting out a rather hopeful request for any further information/confirmation. And for the next two years, that was that...

Until, upon accessing my e-mails one evening in January 2002, I was staggered to receive a message from Saxon Logan himself! Apparently a friend had spotted Saxon's name on my website while browsing, and contacted him to inform him that some herbert was claiming that neither he nor his movie actually existed! Fortunately, Saxon seemed to see the funny side of all this and was most amiable about the entire matter. For my part, once I'd recovered from the initial surprise, my natural response was that if *Sleepwalker* was genuine, could there be the slightest possibility that we might get to view it one day? To my delight, Saxon revealed that he had a 35mm print of the film stashed away at home, but that following an acclaimed performance at the Berlin Film Festival and a few scattered screenings in the mid eighties, he had virtually expunged the entire project from memory. Before long, and with my encouragement and assistance, the print was dredged up out of storage and we arranged a private showing of *Sleepwalker* in February 2002, staged at Paul Cotgrove's preview theatre at the British Council offices just off London's Oxford Circus. This event, attended by various associates of Saxon, plus a handful of Gothique Film Society members rounded up by yours truly, proved a minor triumph, especially when the film's executive producer Robert Breare turned up just after the start of the movie, having flown in from Paris for the show.

Saxon had already sent me a VHS copy of *Sleepwalker*, so I knew exactly what I was in for — the film's main quartet comprise a ruthless, high-flying Thatcherite, his troubled wife, and a socialist brother-and-sister couple who have inherited a crumbling mansion estate significantly named 'Albion' (and hence representing 'Britain in microcosm', for the more allegorically-minded viewer). Opposing viewpoints are established in the powerful first half of the story, with a heated political debate leaving everyone mistrusting everybody else once each individuals' dogma has been presented, analysed, and dismissed; meanwhile, comments about sleep traumas and an unconscious murder attempt offer the first stirrings of the strong genre content which is to follow. The atmosphere gets progressively stranger overnight at the old dark house, ultimately leading to the gruesome deaths of three of the party — but have the horrific murders taken place in reality, or in some nightmare world? The film's climactic shot is reminiscent of Siegel's great political SF classic *Invasion of the Body Snatchers*, with definite echoes of Kevin McCarthy's desperation contained within Bill Douglas' terrified admonition "Wake up! Wake up!" (aimed at the on-screen somnambulist/killer — but on an entirely different level, a screaming protest against 1980s apathy, targeted directly toward the audience). It was with some trepidation that Saxon unspooled the film in February, but *Sleepwalker*'s social message — and, for that matter, its ghastly violence — proved extremely contemporary and resonant, and the event was judged a great success by all who attended. Excited by this, Saxon and myself put out feelers in an attempt to drum up further interest in bringing *Sleepwalker* to a wider audience. All credit to the late Harry Nadler, whose lifelong enthusiasm for fantastic cinema ensured that our offer to take

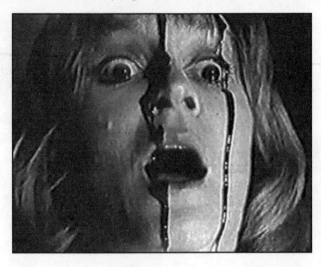

One of the murder victims in *Sleepwalker...* or perhaps not.

Sleepwalker to the Festival Of Fantastic Films in Manchester was warmly and whole-heartedly accepted, and to Tony Edwards who helped co-ordinate the presentation of the film at the Festival following Harry's passing.

Sleepwalker was shown at the Festival Of Fantastic Films at 6pm on Saturday August 31, 2002, in the early-evening slot following the Festival's annual (and hugely entertaining!) auction, presided over by Ramsey Campbell. Ramsey's ebullience and *joie de vivre* always attracts a sizeable throng, a fact from which we certainly benefited, since many of those present for the auction appear to have stayed seated afterwards, curious to witness this 'lost' gem of British horror, being presented to a paying audience for the first time since 1986. Once again, the film seemed to excite and capture the interest of those present, with nostalgia buffs enjoying the on-screen appearance of Raymond Huntley, Michael Medwin and Fulton Mackay, gorehounds salivating at the final reel's parade of bloody mayhem, and the socially-aware appreciating the finer points of the literate screenplay and the political underpinnings. Saxon's mentor throughout his early film/television career was the

No Sleep 'til Manchester!

legendary, humanist, British director Lindsay Anderson (best man at Saxon's wedding and helmer of the magnificent *O Lucky Man* on which the teenage Saxon worked as an assistant), and clearly the master's influence had rubbed off on his pupil, as *Sleepwalker* shares with Anderson's *Britannia Hospital* an acute awareness of genre and its importance in the history of British film culture, deftly managing to interlace elements of classic English terror into a 'state of the nation' satire. Indeed, might *Sleepwalker* have even been somewhat ahead of its time? Audience member Mark Renshaw (whose own *I am Peter Cushing*, winner of the 'best amateur short' award at that year's Festival, similarly toys with viewer expectations and the conventions of Hammer horror to fine comic effect) stood up to praise *Sleepwalker* and to comment in particular on the movie's splendid 'restaurant' sequence, comparing its snappy dialogue and character interaction to the hip nineties-defining work of Quentin Tarantino, no less!

As for the future, Saxon and myself are continuing to present *Sleepwalker* at venues around the UK, and perhaps beyond. The film formed part of a highly successful Halloween double-bill at the Metro Cinema in Derby; the Cobden Club, an exclusive gathering of media folk centred around the Notting Hill area, booked the film for their Christmas get-together; and the re-appearance of this long-dormant movie is also gaining attention from cult film websites such as The Spinning Image [**w**] www.thespinningimage.co.uk and The Zone [**w**] www.zone-sf.com — with tentative discussions also underway concerning the possibility of a release on video or DVD. From Saxon's basement to the shelves of your local Woolworth's — who knows? It's been a long, strange journey. ⒼⒻ

BOY MEETS GIRL
AN INTERVIEW WITH
RAY BRADY

by Stephen Portlock

A man goes to the home of a woman he has just met at a bar, only to wake up a captive of hers, strapped to a dentist chair in a dark basement. He is systematically tortured and abused by the woman. This, essentially, is Ray Brady's BOY MEETS GIRL, passed uncut for cinema release in Britain in February 1995 but rejected outright for video in September that year.
This decision was reversed in September 2001.

CREEPING FLESH *How did the idea for Boy Meets Girl come about?*

RAY BRADY *Boy Meets Girl* was a complete construct. I had issues with the way that films were being censored in this country. James Ferman who was the head of the BBFC at the time was trying to shelter a nation, but I think he was in fact desensitizing them to violence. For example, I was troubled by the low certificate given to *Home Alone*. He was editing out any violence which he thought was troubling or disturbing. What was left was very palatable and very stylized with no consequence, and I thought more dangerous for not showing a reality. There was no pain, misery, suffering, psychological destruction or damage allowed to be shown in films at the time but lots of comic book violence. But the BBFC have completely changed their policies of late.

"Violence and the portrayal of violence..." BOY MEETS GIRL was banned on home video in Britain for several years. Now it isn't. Director RAY BRADY tells why.

Boy Meets Girl.

So how was this challenged by Boy Meets Girl?

Boy Meets Girl challenged the censors on nearly every aspect of censorship and we thought while we're at it we might as well talk to them about other things such as bad language and sexuality. I was interested in using the slight S&M images on the poster to get an audience to come in but then, when they were there, to challenge their preconceptions about what they were watching and why.

I read a Sight and Sound review saying that it's hard to see what the film's meant to be — a cautionary tale, an S&M fantasy or a black satire on violence and voyeurism.

The film could be interpreted in many different ways. Half the audience would find the film very amusing and entertaining and the other half would be absolutely, abjectly repelled. People would get up and walk out and the only time I've ever seen that before was when I watched *Man Bites Dog*. I think James Ferman said to me that he didn't understand why anyone would want to make a film that wasn't entertaining, but there is another part of cinema which actually provokes the way people think.

Isn't there a risk of the film just coming across as confusing?

I don't think there's anything wrong with confusion. I think it's good not to be too simplistic, since it is basically a kitchen sink drama. It's mostly two people in a room.

Did you see Funny Games?

It's annoying because that was in the Cannes selection and we had been banned in England a couple of years prior to that for actually coming up with the same sort of arguments and making a film just as challenging.

Impressive as Funny Games *was in some ways, I actually found it deeply conservative.* Boy Meets Girl *invites the audience to half-identify with the torturers whereas in* Funny Games *they're monsters outright.

Well, the point you're making is interesting but we didn't want anyone to identify with our lead either. I didn't want to paint a bad guy/good guy scenario. The more you find out about the main character, Tevin, the more you get to dislike him. At times you begin to like the people that are abusing him. Some of the things they are saying are quite interesting, even though they are completely mad.

There is something rather endearingly bubbly about the first of the two serial killers.

Well she's enjoying what she's doing

Boy

Meets

Girl

and she's got some good arguments, attacking him for being a homophobic racist misogynist, cheating on his wife, sleeping with prostitutes and possibly bringing AIDS home to his wife, but I think Tevin takes so much abuse that after a while you start feeling sorry for him. He is tragic at the end because I think he has learnt that he was wrong and if he had got out of the room, he would have been a much better person and maybe gone away and re-evaluated his life and his relationship. He'd never really taken the time to think about his actions before, but sitting in a chair alone in a darkened room waiting for this terrible person to come in and torture and abuse him some more, he actually had a chance to finally reflect.

Was the subject dictated as much by practicalities as anything else?

Yeah. I'd watched a film from Canada called *H*. It's about heroin basically. Two addicts lock themselves up in a flat and they close all the doors as they're going cold turkey. That was quite an influence in the fact that we kept it all pretty simple because we were working from a budget of about £13,000, and we shot on 16mm. We had to be ingenious in the way we moved the camera and how we revealed different areas in the room. I still think it was quite beautifully shot. We kept on throwing the inter-titles up now and again which were

provocative and sometimes confusing. Sometimes you'd work backwards and figure out what we're talking about. But some of them we just threw in to inspire people to leave wondering, for example, what "Good Americans when they die go to Paris" means.

What was the idea behind the final twist at the end of Boy Meets Girl?

It's just to pull the rug from the audience's feet. Just when they were getting comfortable and cosy we thought "let's present Tevin as just one victim of this serial killer". If there were any strong feminists in the audience who thought that some of her actions were permissible and acceptable, I just wanted to subvert that argument and take it back. I wanted everyone to leave feeling that they were wronged and had been abused in the cinema, basically. James Ferman found that very awkward. He thought that it completely undermined the whole film. He suggested that we go away and shoot an extra scene where the police break in and I thought "Come on James, in reality serial killers practice for many years, even decades". It's a nihilistic film, this.

Why did you choose that title?

It felt like a nice romantic love story, and it was just to subvert it. Leos Carax tried the same thing about ten years

previously. But I think most people would be aware of what they are letting themselves in for.

Where did you get the cast?

We went to colleges and theatre schools and also pub theatres. The music was written by my co-writer Jim Crosbie and Jeff Southall who lives up in Wolverhampton and they wrote a great score, really quite powerful.

There's about ten seconds of a quite pleasant pop song at the start.

Yeah, the theme tune. They wrote that as well. There was another which Pam Hogg wrote and sung, and Des Brady, one of my brothers, sung a song in it as well. They didn't appear in the final edit.

What was the whole history of the film being banned?

Metro Tartan who wanted the UK video rights had an arrangement with the BBFC where they unofficially presented the film to James Ferman to look at. He said this film will never get a video certificate and so the deal fell through. Ironically eight years later when we did receive a certificate, it probably wasn't that topical anymore.

Given your view at the time that you were making a film that was designed to provoke the BBFC, did you

Boy Meets Girl

**Boy
Meets
Girl**

*imagine that you were go-
ing to have difficulties with
them?*

Oh, we knew what we were
running into. *Boy Meets Girl*
wasn't a very expensive movie
and at the time it didn't seem
an awful big risk.

*But you were aware there
was a risk it might be
banned?*

Well, there's not very many
ways of going about challenging a British institution and
Tom Dewe Matthews was
having a go at it in literature
at the time. I thought the best
way to present the argument
was in the medium of film
because that's what they were
censoring. Trying to ban the
film, if anything, helped to put
it around festivals and stuff.
Glenda Jackson wrote a letter to the video censor at the
BBFC asking why the film had
been refused a certificate. It
was only a small part of a large
swirl that eventually brought
about changes at the BBFC
and brought about the demise
of the old school.

*Did you ever consider
restructuring it, say as a
little piece of theatre? You
could probably get away
with some scenes of torture.*

We did think about it, but then
we'd moved on. I had put on a
couple of pieces in the theatre
at that time.

Do you think there is a

place for the BBFC?

I think it's quite redundant
really in the fact that there
are already laws that govern
what is and is not permissible
and I think those laws could
easily regulate filmmakers.
Most filmmakers make films to
make money, so if they limit
the amount a film could make
their investors will never allow
it to be made. The very fact
that the BBFC exists means
that there are people who will
actually go out of their way to
try to become banned. Some
filmmakers do that to draw
attention to themselves.

Like you with **Boy Meets
Girl.**

No, we made the film to challenge the censors. We weren't
being provocative just to make
lots of money. That wasn't our
intent.

*Do you think that things
have improved in terms of
trying to make experimen-
tal or provocative films in
the UK today?*

No. I think it's gone the other
way. Nobody's making experimental or provocative cinema.
Most of the cinema art theatres have gone now or have
been subjected to at least half
mainstream viewing. It's much
harder now to make anything
of interest.

*Your films are made for
Boudicca films. Is that your
own company?*

Yeah, mine and my wife's. We set it up because it's nearly impossible to find distribution. There's only a few Independents left in the UK and they're up against the big global machine.

Where does the name Boudicca come from? I thought initially of Boadicea...

It is. Boadicea was the name the Romans gave her. The idea was that it was a strong, British independent.

Boy Meets Girl *is a very intense film, but from the shooting scenes you get the impression that there was quite a lot of humour whilst making it.*

Um, no. We were very hot. It was the summer and we'd blacked out the whole place and closed it all down. It was quite claustrophobic and the only moment of light relief was when one of the actresses Georgina Whitbourne was screaming her head off and then all these policemen rolled up and ran into the room. Unfortunately, the cameraman had turned the camera off instead of turning the camera round and filming the police running in. We could have shown that to James Ferman and seen if he'd been happy.

Tell me about your other films?

Kiss Kiss Bang Bang is just a kooky little murder mystery with some strange twists and some very weird characters. Then we made a film called *Day of the Sirens* and that's a thriller set in London with Rik Mayall playing a non-comic part and Saeed Jaffrey.

From the trailer I saw, it seems to have some split screen parts.

It has some bits, yeah. One of my favourite films is *Twilight's Last Gleaming* and Robert Aldrich used a great split-screen effect where you actually got to see different events going on at the same time. It's been picked up by Mike Figgis in *Timecode*.

You've done stuff for TV, haven't you?

We did a piece called *Little England* which got quite amazing reviews in all the broadsheets and even the tabloids. It was just a strange little piece about young people talking about what it's like to live in the UK. They talked about major themes like love, hate, death, war, dreams, money and stuff like that. Unfortunately I never managed to persuade Channel Four to commission anything. Maybe they were worried about me being a bit too confrontational. I don't know.

Is the 2002 version of Boy

Meets Girl *in any way different from that of the 1994 version?*

The sound was appalling before. We managed to work with that a little bit. It was to do with remastering for quality more than anything else. We didn't take anything out of the edit as such.

Has it been a big success since coming out on video and DVD?

There's a little cult interest, I suppose. It's probably the most intelligent of my films except possibly *Day of the Sirens*.

Would you make another film in the manner of Boy Meets Girl?

Um, I don't know. You have to wait for something that actually winds you up that much or angers you enough to actually go out there and spend a few years of your life trying to promote and make it. It's hard enough actually trying to market it and if you don't get it out there quick enough and fast enough, then your argument's going to become dated very quickly. Also, most people seem to think that controversy's great but we almost went bankrupt at one time. GF

Boy Meets Girl is available on Imaginary Films [w] www.imaginaryfilms.com

WATCH YOUR WALLETS AND STAY OUT OF THE BATHROOM!

by Jan Bruun

From its debut in June 1980 until Fall 1985, Bill Landis edited the seminal exploitation film zine SLEAZOID EXPRESS, living the life on Times Square. SLEAZOID was resurrected by Landis and his wife MICHELLE CLIFFORD (editor of METASEX) in 1999. The couple spoke recently to CREEPING FLESH.

Bill Landis is a living legend in the world of exploitation movies and obscure seventies porn. Back when New York's Times Square area was the world's leading sleazepit, he worked in the theatres and put out his fortnightly SLEAZOID EXPRESS newsletter. His choice of material and writing style has been a guiding light for every trash film writer since, but no one could outdo his maniacal attention to detail and intense knowledge of the most wretched movies ever made and the people making, distributing, showing and watching them.

When the grindhouses of 42nd Street started to be torn down to make room for what later became Mayor Guiliani's new squeaky clean Disney-fied version of Times Square, Landis stopped making his newsletter. He spent his time writing for other magazines and kicking an IV drug habit. ANGER, his revealing biography on Kenneth Anger, was published by HarperCollins in 1995. In 1999 he brought SLEAZOID EXPRESS back as a seventy page zine, co-edited with his wife Michelle Clifford. Michelle also edits METASEX, which specifically deals with porn movies, many of them made and shown in NYC. A lot of this is very obscure and unknown material that would've slipped into oblivion had this couple not been here to document it.

At the end of 2002, Simon & Schuster published their SLEAZOID EXPRESS book.

Meet Mr and Mrs Sleazoid!

Inside!

TERROR!
VIOLENCE!

GROSS ME OUT!

Bill Landis'
SLEAZOID
EXPRESS

The largest circulation of anything
of its particular type

Vol. 2, No. 5   September 1981

50¢

Send cor\
Subscrip   respondence to: Bill Landis c/o ~~Newsletter~~.\
            tions $8 per year.

CREEPING FLESH *Where were you born? I assume it wasn't in Times Square?*

BILL LANDIS (BL) This takes a bit of time: Nearly forty-four years ago, I was born of American parents in Landes de Busac, France. Hence, the name Landis — Landes is the Euro spelling — like Corleone in the Godfather movies — it's a taken name from where I was born.

I grew up until age five at a full service hotel in Christine Keeler era London. Fun reading about her in the scandal sheets though I didn't comprehend all the "mechanics" then. It was 66 Lancaster Gate, for American military personnel. The location of the hotel changed when I was last in London in 1972.

Interestingly, my cousin Patti Pallidin — of Johnny Thunders notoriety, she sang with him, produced some of his records; she was in the Cale group Snatch with Judy Nylon — is an American expatriate in London.

I first set eyes on the Deuce when returning to NY around 1965. To a little kid it was a neon palace, sexually driven. It was still the era of the "midnight cowboy" so they were around, looking weird and delusional, like something dropped off Hollywood Boulevard.

MICHELLE CLIFFORD (MC) I was born in Boston, Massachusett. Little Ireland. Moved at seven years old to Fort Lauderdale, Florida. Moved then at nineteen in with Bill, on 14th Street, NYC.

Do you have any education pertaining to movies, journalism or anything else, or did you just learn as you went along?

BL I had been writing critiques of movies since age ten or so. With the encouragement of some neighborhood girls. We'd trade tips on movies after seeing them on creature features, late night TV where the censorship was low. Like, "that was Jane Fonda's tit just now in *Circle of Love!*", they'd shout. And that movie was playing theatrically with *Murmur of the Heart.*

Some movies had simultaneous theatrical and edited TV runs, like *Mondo Cane.* By the time I was fourteen, PBS (public broadcasting in the US) ran all the great Euro-movies like *La Dolce Vita*, *L'Aventurra*, all the Bergmans (I liked *Sawdust & Tinsel* best), great Japanese ones like the *Burmese Harp* and *Harakiri*. So I got an early education in art movies by the time I was fourteen, which were stodgy by the time *Sleazoid* came out in 1980.

In high school I was the paper's film critic, as I was in grad school. A self-taught one. In fact, ironically, Michelle found a note from a teacher saying I should expand beyond reviews...

I think I got a B in the required expository writing — the classes were in huge auditoriums and often taught by a grad student who found it an annoyance to their own studies. I got sick of it early. Just read the books, passed the test, then went to 42nd Street all the time to catch new movies since I was sixteen. I was in a perpetual state of competition — how many new flicks could I see a week? Ten, fourteen, more even? John Friday* went on for the ride for some, and got shocked by *Last House on Dead End Street* though we both thought the race hate *Black Gestapo* was hilarious — well paced and delivered roughie elements.

MC It's passion. What I write about is my religion. I try to tell the truth. Truth is my religion.

* Contributor to the early *Sleazoid Express*.

Watch Your Wallets and Stay Out of the Bathroom!

What were the first movies you saw in Times Square, and when? What kind of impact did it have to go there for the first time?

BL Oh, it's been *so* long ago... the streets were lined with neon... the theatre marquees were a virtual umbrella over the Deuce, which was tiny considering it is just one block 42nd between 7th And 8th.... sex stores abounded for every preference, everything like the Serena S&M classic loop *Girls Behind Bars* to bestiality — *Color Climax* coded ones were ubiquitous.

In terms of movies, cannibal vomitorium *Carnivorous (Last Survivor)* — that was a shocker billed with *I Drink Your Blood*... Andy Milligan's *Torture Dungeon* (didn't live up to the title and the Milligan aesthetic is hard to take the first time you accidentally see it), Bob Cresse's *Love Camp 7* (*did* live up to the title), *Slaves in Cages*... My intro to Jess Franco was *Barbed Wire Dolls*, which showed how much further Euro movies went than US ones — not quite hardcore, not quite softcore. Of course, fave women-in-prison movies like *Big Doll House* and *Black Mama White Mama*. Among the hundreds of kung fu I liked *Streetfighter* for the violence, *Hammer of God* for originality and visuals, *Master of the Flying Guillotine* because the guillotines looked like those little fans sold to hot commuters on NY subways. Saw the edited down version (R-rated) of *Ginger* with the heavy giallo *Girl in Room 2A* — that impressed me with its action and relentless sadism. Eventually I *did* catch up to the uncut *Ginger* and it was everything I'd hoped it would be.

The *cut* versions of *Devil in Miss Jones* and *Deep Throat* played at the Mini Cinema for at least a year after *Animal Lover* was busted. Eventually I saw the uncut versions of them. "Porno chic" flicks I liked included *800 Fantasy Lane*, Alex De Renzy's *Femmes De Sade*, *Waterpower* and a weird one called *The Naughty Victorians*.

WC *Mountainside Motel Massacre* and *Girls for Sale* — my first date with Bill; my first day in NYC. I thought it was like a wee tiny street for such a big reputation.

Did you enjoy the slightly dangerous and half-criminal feeling of the old 42ⁿᵈ Street/Times Square days?

BL Loved it, participated in it, was part of my life as a projectionist/theatre manager there.

WC The crime never scared me, it entertained me. I was never harmed there. The old Times Square reminded me of my mother. My childhood. In the old Times Square you could be yourself. For good or ill.

How does the clean-up completed in the last ten–twelve years make you feel?

BL Well, I took my kid to Toys R Us there for a small ferris ship ride… and kept remembering it used to be the Loew's fiveplex… the topography keeps changing all the time… it's not the same… Took her to see *Thomas the Tank Engine* and it made me sad because it used to be the Empire, where I saw *Blind Rage*, *Battle of the Amazons*, many great triple bills, until you go over to 9ᵗʰ Avenue, 10ᵗʰ Avenue, no theatres there but the Hispanic population has stayed there since the 1950s, with some Irish holdouts.

WC The clean up is "progress". Life changes. The world changes. The values of the world change. Change hurts. But, now we bring our daughter to the multiplex and tell her a book was dedicated to her about how it used to be, a long, long time ago. A history book we wrote… when mom and dad met a long time ago.
But let me add, when Times Square closed, it broke our hearts. Bill stopped writing about the films because there were no more playing. Video companies like Something Weird had yet to

acquire their stocks. He was heartbroken it was demolished. I took photos of its death there. Some are in the book. Some we have of Bill standing in front of places being torn down. It just killed him. It hurt him to see other mags ape his style and claim to have been there when they were lame imitators... He stopped writing over it for a couple years, then I got him to go back to record "all that hath occurred", as Crowley, I think, put it.

The last film we saw there was *Falling Down* appropriately enough. The audience was so sad. Everyone knew the end had come. America had changed.

And we and our kind especially were not wanted. Film mags, periodicals, we couldn't write for because the Deuce wasn't "timely" anymore. We were a figment of the past. And one that NYC was glad to get rid of. They let the buildings rot until, like decayed teeth, needed to be extracted. Which was their plan. The owners of the theatres got rich. Millionaires.

Did the cinemas in the Times Square area show a mixture of porn and horror, or was that always in separate theatres?

BL Always separate, with one funny example. On US holidays, the Victory — a porn theatre right off 7th Avenue north near subway — would have a horror triple bill! Things like the *Curse of the Living Flesh*

thing (an old Mario Bava movie, an Anita Ekberg vehicle), *Kingdom of the Spiders*, *Frogs*, real horror oldies that Aquarius Pictures either got a hold of or had prints lying around.

MC Sometimes the theatres changed what they showed like the Roxy went hardcore, changed to exploitation, then back to triple X.

When was the original version of Sleazoid Express published?

BL Summer 1980, on a manual typewriter, 8 x 11.5 inches offset printed.

That was just a couple of sheets in each issue, wasn't it? How often did that come out?

BL It came out every other week, literally telling what was good, bad or indifferent on the Deuce. A one sheet bulletin. It was also distributed at Club 57 where friends of mine like Kenny Scharf, Basquait, Keith Haring, also encouraged my interest in Times Square. We did performance art pieces — like one where I gave Kool Aid to an audience tripping on LSD pretending I was Jim Jones. I also gave out *Sleazoids* at Artforum parties at the Hellfire Club, record and bookstores. We also did a thing called The Times Square Show, where all these artists did their raunchiest projects and I gave out hundreds of *Sleazoids*. Beth and Scott B were involved — I later played a small part in their movie *Vortex*.

Then it grew to 11 x 17 offset, printed with a cover price of fifty cents. That let me examine genres, directors, campaigns, more explicitly.

owned 16mm prints at Club 57. All my faves like *Big Doll House*, *Manson* (I had a Manson impersonator and the *LIE* album play), *Villain* with a drunk Richard Burton as a gay S&M gangster, the sleaze classic *Toys Are Not For Children*,

> "There was the problem of the mad shitters at the Venus... a black guy in thick glasses with a M*A*S*H Army T-shirt — he got nervous and everyone said 'Don't let him in' — it turned out he was defecating in the aisles." —Bill Landis

Why did you decide to restart it as a thicker zine a few years ago?

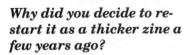 After the success of Michelle's *Metasex*, and seeing how many people copied the *Sleazoid* formula without even venturing to 42nd Street. The latter factor is one factor in my depression — all these imitators — that made me stop putting out the magazine. And Michelle encouraged me to be myself more with the new one — and I had always wanted it magazine length — the love of Eurosleaze films, old chestnuts from the Deuce, obscure films, all together. With the background of the vice there — *Metasex* handles that in-depth.

Did you arrange special screenings of films during the old Sleazoid period?

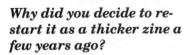 Yeah. A throwback to the smoker era with rented or

Caged Heat, Paul Bartel's best movie *Private Parts*, Warhol's *Flesh*, *Paranoia* with Carroll Baker, Larry Cohen's *God Told Me To* (aka *The Demon*), and, of course, *Mondo Cane*.

You portray the director of Mondo Cane, Gualtiero Jacopetti, as a lying racist paedophile in Sleazoid, but that film remains one of my favourites. I had the local Cinemateque in Oslo dig the film out of their archives to show it for a full house in 2002, with lots of media coverage. It was probably the first time that print had been shown since the sixties... Do you still show movies?

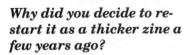 I did it again in 1981. I was the first to revive Herschell Lewis' *Blood Feast* in a decade, since the demise of the Elgin Theater, at the now defunct 8th Street Playhouse, which had a

Previous page
Michelle Clifford and Bill Landis, photobooth pictures. Times Square Playland Arcade, 1986.

Watch Your Wallets and Stay Out of the Bathroom!

midnight movie a night. *Blood Feast* was a midnighter. Then I talked the owner into having a month long sleaze festival — the only constraint that the rental of the movie had to be below $250.

That was March 1983. We had *Pink Flamingos* and *Female Trouble*; a gay triple of *The Back Row* with George Payne and Casey Donovan, *Wanted: Billy the Kid* (freakish straight scene) and *Demi Gods* (an animated short, very rare, with the heads of Sal Mineo, Marlon Brando *et al* in various positions); *The Big Doll House* and *Big Bust Out*; *Night of the Bloody Apes* and *The Last Survivor*; Russ Meyer's *Good Morning and Goodbye* and *Common Law Cabin, Finders Keepers* and *Cherry Harry & Raquel*; *I Spit on Your Grave* (the one Ebert hated) with the extraordinary *Axe*; *Ilsa She Wolf* and *Harem Keeper* (uncut); *The Love Butcher* (great Deuce find) with Cresse's *Love Camp 7*; *The Ghastly Ones* (one of Milligan's best) with *The Headless Eyes* (a fave crazy loner horror, X for violence); *Fight For Your Life* and *Black Shampoo* (race hate mixed with blaxploitation); *The Drive in Massacre* and *I Dismember Mama*; *I Drink Your Blood* and *Don't Look in the Basement*; the tranny documentary *The Queen* (supposedly staged). Years ago, it took legwork to find out who had these films; I got to know a lot of Deuce distributors through this project other than ones I already knew, like Ava Leighton of

Audubon Films.

It was fun arranging this festival from the pay phone at the Bryant Theater, where I was the projectionist.

We started showing movies again in 1999 — did a Sleazoid Festival at Yerba Buena Center for the Arts in San Francisco in 1999 showing *Last House on Dead End Street* (its first theatrical showing in years; people were getting sick!), *Pets*, *The Candy Snatchers*, *Sweet Savior* (Troy Donohue as Charlie Manson) and *Back Row*. We just met with the owner of the Pioneer Theatre/Two Boots on 3rd Street & Avenue A, a nice hipster venue and are planning a Sleazoid/Metasex Festival, similar to that at the 8th Street Playhouse. They have capacity for video projection, which opens up the floodgates for many obscure films (like *Pets*) that are just on tape and the rights are floating in limbo. Also, they are reviving some hardcore movies, so we're looking at *Behind the Green Door* and Bill Lustig's *Violation of Claudia* — we will be doing DVD notes for Lustig's company Blue Underground. So we're back in the swing of doing film festivals; they're far from a thing of the past for us.

Did you make notes continually or do you remember all these details regarding the look and smell of the sleaze theatres, the patrons, the movies, the directors, distributors etc?

BL Both. And the first *Sleazoid*s were so immediate I just went home and typed them down. Whatever was remarkable — the patrons, the film, whether Joe Brenner had slipped a horror title on a stupid Italian crime movie... whether the theatre

twenty-four hours?

BL Some were: The Harem (all porn, "balcony for couples only", people would go in there and change into drag), the Roxy after it became an exploitation grindhouse.
Some of the regular Deuce

"I document this area because of my mother bringing me to The Combat Zone as a child and grindhouses to see films.... She loved film. She was a tough Irish Mick criminal. Reservoir Dogs style crimes. Violent crime and killings."
—Michelle Clifford

---

was packed or empty, freezing or not... Some movies it was worth noting the details, others I couldn't give a damn... like when *Mad Max* first opened it took second place to *Let Me Die A Woman* in the first *Sleazoid* because (1) It wasn't sleazy enough and (2) I didn't like the dumb dubbing or Brian (Queen) May music. Another funny thing — I hated the Romero adaptation of *Creepshow* (I felt he totally sold out by then) and someone got stabbed to death while watching it. So I took note of that — that piece of garbage was the last thing the person saw with his dying eyes.

MC I remember from memory the smell, the look, the floor, toilet, patrons, meeting actors.

Were the theatres open

grindhouses I remember leaving at 3:30am. They were open pretty late.

Did bums "move in" to sleep, or any sex or violence, anything out of the ordinary when you were working as manager or projectionist at the theatres?

BL Oh, you haven't seen (sub-) humanity until you've seen 8th Ave around the time the bars close at 4:30am. There was a curtain behind the Eros theatre that made people adjust their eyes for a minute to get used to the light... and they'd stand and get pickpocketed there. The Eros was open from 10am to 5am.
The Venus had a lot of sleepers, and that's where you had a lot of crazy outbursts. Like in *Metasex* No 1 — real interest-

ing one reeler XXX films. But more of a closety black street clientele than the all-male Eros next door. And the whites that sought them out. Most remarkable scene at the Venus: a dusthead ripped his clothes off, declaring "IT'S ORGY TIME" — the EMS lady who showed up later with an ambulance said "all that trouble for that little thing"... and then the guy would go in again and we'd just hope he wouldn't start it up once more...
There was the problem of the mad shitters at the Venus... a black guy in thick glasses with a M*A*S*H Army T-shirt — he got nervous and everyone said "don't let him in" — it turned out he was defecating in the aisles.
Stabbings — a common summertime thing on 42nd Street... I saw my first stabbing when I was around sixteen, some guy went nuts in front of a massage parlour, then there were cops following bloody footprints to the subway... and we describe this in the book... black robbers often assumed Asian men had hidden sums of gambling money or Indian men were easy marks... they'd take each side of the victim, flash a small sharp pocket knife or object and rob them... the victim would be too terrified to even leave the front of the theatre, fearing the assailants were still out in the throngs of Deuce Street.
One of Chelly Wilson's girlfriends, the obnoxious one named Angela who was paying off some "medical debt"

* Phil Prince had a wife who he worked with in the live sex shows. The police suspected him of killing her to get the life insurance money. Suspect No 2 was Phil's best friend (and possibly homosexual lover) Pat Rodgers, a fellow employee at the Avon Theatre. The whole story is in *Metasex* No 2.

Watch Your Wallets and Stay Out of the Bathroom!

was so nasty to the Venus customers that one night they pistol whipped her. Same thing for Mae. Mae was from Hell's Kitchen, but moved to Brooklyn and continued to take the train at the ungodly hour or 5am. When she'd close the Eros, she'd end up being beaten up or pistol whipped, too. Mae was about eighty, blonde wig, very sweet, why her kids were letting her work there is beyond me... she used to have an apartment on 42nd and 9th, a real old time Hell's Kitchener.

Chelly Wilson's 8th Avenue Theaters had poor security — while the Avon chain had a million people ready to stop a disturbance, from a live show team to a bouncer, so there were no problems like that at the Doll. Only that Phil Prince was a murderer!*

MG Phil Prince was the director of the notorious roughie Avon films like *Kneel Before Me*. All starring George Payne.

BL You could — in a way — conceive of 42nd Street/Times Square as Marco Vassi's ideal of the "metasexual" — except, like many things in human execution, it got way, way distorted from its idealization.

Did you work at making movies as well, writing scripts? You mention some of this in your Andy Milligan article in **Sleazoid's** *spring 1999 issue.*

MG I never worked in film.

BL I did scriptwriting anonymously for certain infamous people under very phoney names... and I was paid but I have no idea what happened to them!

In your Andy Milligan article you mentioned working as "focus finder"?

BL Oh yeah, that's how antiquitated Andy was — a focus finder! they never use 'em on regular flicks any more — and general gofer, I guess, for that production he did *Carnage* — a haunted house thing that went right to video and isn't half bad.

What other magazines have you written for over the years?

MG/BL Many articles for *Film Comment, Carbon 14, Screw, Swank, Hustler, Jersey Voice.*

BL Many for the *Village Voice*. One article I wrote for them got reproduced in two books, an ACLU handbook and a book called *Beyond Crisis* — it was about the needle exchange program by ACT-UP. I wrote for *Soho News* when it was in existence — I had a weekly column on what was playing on the Deuce.

I find it very interesting that you seem to share a lot of your interests re: the sleazy films and the industry. How did you two meet?

BL She wrote me a letter after

Film Comment did a profile of me.

WG I wanted to be a writer. I read Bill's articles and respected his writing. I saw it in a mag in the library in Florida. I was a high school drop out. My mother had been shot in the head by a police officer and I was taking it easy in the library. Reading for my education. Not much to learn in Florida. I would go to the library every day and read a book or two a day. I wrote to him. Moved in with him as a teen. I knew what he wrote was real. He taught me much.

I appreciate your ongoing effort to document these areas of popular culture that most others would scorn or regard with contempt or disinterest. I think it's important to remember and preserve, especially in the light of the clean-up of NYC.

WG Vice is my area. I document this area because of my mother bringing me to The Combat Zone as a child and grindhouses to see films. She took me to see *Taxi Driver* when it came out and *The Godfather*. She loved film. She was a tough Irish Mick criminal. *Reservoir Dogs* style crimes. Violent crime and killings. She was a Madame as well... I didn't grow up with her. I visited. I visited her in jail once. She gave me my first 8mm camera and polaroid. She was a violent criminal. She would tell me the inner workings of the vice

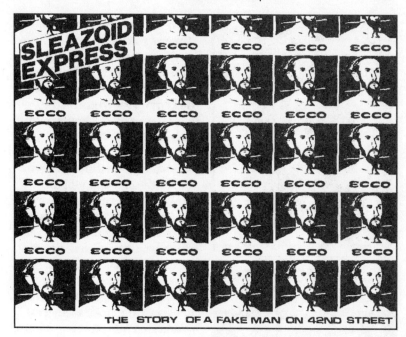

The incredible final edition of *Sleazoid Express* in its original incarnation, Fall 1985.

arena. Her friends, pimps, etc, would treat me like a princess and tell me very personal stories and let me polaroid them as a kid. I document like John Grisham tried to, what I knew to be truth. Inner workings of a secret society. Not a friendly one. One that doesn't like outsiders.

Is it hard to maintain an interest in these movies for such a long time?

BL You know, some of the movies I can live without seeing again, like *Curnvorous*. Or *Farewell, Uncle Tom*, or anything by Jacopetti. Others like *Black Emanuelle* are perennial faves. Or anything with Alice Arno. I think *La Comptesse Perverse* is her

best role — along with the faithful adaptation of *Justine* where she plays the lead. Alice is like the Sleazoid Marilyn Monroe — her image is on the website and there's the snuff scene hyperlink with her in *La Comptesse Perverse* mentioned in issue No 3. There are the old Times Square chestnuts I love, such as *Barbed Wire Dolls*, although I've taken a liking to more Eurosleaze. *La Punition* with Karin Schubert is pretty unforgettable and it would be hard to make a movie like that in the US. Same thing for *Eden & After*.

I just rented the TV-movie Rated X by Charlie Sheen and Emilio Estevez, about the brothers Jim and Artie Mitchell, who made Be-

The new *Sleazoid* zine and Michelle's *Metasex*.

Watch Your Wallets and Stay Out of the Bathroom!

hind **The Green Door** *and started the O'Farrell Theatre in San Francisco. Artie used even more coke than his brother, became violent and threatening, so Jim brought over a shotgun and killed him.*

BL Actually, the Sheen Brothers didn't do a bad job, all things considered. There are two books about the Mitchells — *Bottom Feeders*, which is very, very good, and *X Rated*, which is more about their legal trials. Personally, I have nothing against Jim... when we had the film festival in San Francisco he donated a brand new 35mm of *Green Door* for the screening — people went nuts, loved it. It was all young couples turning up. But I think the tragedy of the Mitchells — apart from the obvious of what happened — is that they turned into peep show pimps instead of developing as filmmakers. *Green Door, Resurrection of Eve, Reckless Claudia* — the early movies — they are very interesting semi-outgrowths of underground movies mixed with the stag mentality. Quite unique and often aesthetically very good. I assume they just made more money running a dirty bookstore and didn't develop as filmmakers. The later big budget ones like *Insatiable* are pretty dull compared to the early seventies' ones.

MG With the survivalist mentality Jim had, the attitude was if you are being physically threatened, you hurt or kill the aggressor. No questions asked. So I understand why Jim would do this if the brother kept acting nuts and threatening his girlfriend.

I was in San Francisco recently and lived around the corner from O'Farrell Street, so I walked by their cinema, still owned by Jim, I suppose. It's a strip club now. I didn't go in, though.

MG When I was in SF for the Sleazoid Film Fest, I went into the Mitchell Theater. It's a very friendly place. We were running *Behind The Green Door* at the museum, Yerba Buena. Although a crazy stripper did start a fight with our driver right outside the theatre while we were inside, saying it was her "handicapped parking zone"...

When you did the **Anger** *book, did you ever talk to Kenneth Anger or get any co-operation at all, maybe early in the process?*

BL I was friendly with him when I got him on the cover of the *Soho News* in 1980. Then by the end of the year I started seeing why people thought he was a jerk and a leech — though he never got to leech off me. This is the difference between art and exploitation — the guy's been on the scam and he's only made two-and-a-half hours worth of film in his life! Exploitation is a one time sale, but the filmmakers are so, so, prolific.

I've heard that Anger is quite difficult to have anything to do with.

BL This is true. Even when you're attempting to help or be friendly with him. So after the last straw — the Danceteria incident — I turned him into a subject for ridicule for a while. He was supposed to read from his then current book *Hollywood Babylon 2* and he was on acid and freaked out and ran down the street like a nut. He refused to go on. The incident is all in the *Anger* book.

MC I was co-author, but didn't take any credit on that book… I was an odd duck. Shy. Anger wrote to me. After appealing to me to stop the book, he cursed me, in a ridiculous scroll letter which Bobby Beausoleil, designed years before.* Kenneth Anger didn't know I was friends with Bobby, so the "curse" was useless to scare me. Big red lettering. Ooga booga… I had a pleasant time working with him and wish him the best.

I just saw a video copy of Paul Morrissey's **Forty Deuce,** *which is about hustlers around Times Square…*

MC That film sucks. It's like a filmed high school play. Terrible, and Kevin Bacon played an excellent hustler in the film *JFK*. So it was the director, not the actors.

Do you have any memories of Hubert's Museum and freak shows on 42nd Street?

BL By the time I was there, Hubert's Museum was a sleazy hustler arcade in the process of turning itself into Peepland, the thing with the giant quarter.

What kind of movie is Russ Meyer's **Steamheat?** *I saw it mentioned in one of your articles.*

BL It's a nudie. And a rare one, because William Mishkin put it out. Supposedly the idiot son who died of brain cancer could have melted that down for the silver content too. It was made before Russ was big, meaning it could have been a one time sale to Mishkin. He made it four years after *The Immoral Mr Teas*.

How did the deal for the **Sleazoid Express** *book come about?*

MC We were approached by an editor at Simon and Schuster, through our wonderful agent, Craig Nelson. The book is all original… all about theatres, films, genres.

BL There's a lot of unpublished stuff, all within a historical/grindhouse/etc context. You can think of the book as both magazines with new material and new outlooks on some of it.

Will the **Sleazoid** *and* **Metasex** *zines continue to come out?*

MC Both mags continue. We'd like to do a documentary and maybe another book. GF

Read review of the *Sleazoid Express* book on p.159

* Michelle interviewed Bobby Beausoleil for the *Anger* book. The letter is some stationary that Bobby Beausoleil designed for Anger.

RAINDANCE FILM
£3 / pb / Raindance Limited, 81 Berwick Street, London W1F 8TW, UK / info@raindance.co.uk

CINEMA SEWER
$4 / pb / 44pp / 2002 / mindseyecomics@telus.net / 320-440 E.5th Ave, Vancouver, Canada BC V5T 1N5 / $2 postage and handling / US Dollars cash or IMO only

AGITATOR
£16.99 / $24.99 / 408pp / ISBN 1903254213 / FAB Press / 2003 / www.fabpress.com

ASIAN CULT CINEMA
£10.99 $14 / pb / 317pp / ISBN 1572972289 / Boulevard 1997 / The Berkley Publishing Group, 200 Madison Avenue, New York 10016 / www.penguinputnam.com

ZINES BOOKS REVIEWS

RAINDANCE FILM
Vol 2 No 2 Summer 2003

This generally impressive magazine accompanies the Raindance Film Festival, the LFF's little sister, and suits it; as opposed to, say, The Exploding Cinema's *Kinokaze* publication, there is a generally glossier, less underground (and less passionate) feel to the thing. You do get some DIY invective from Crass' Penny Rimbaud (who is still worth paying attention to, despite coming over as something of a luddite in his dismissal of almost all modern media) or The Salivation Army (on subverting the documentary form). More interesting is a likeably humble Wayne Kramer (who clearly doesn't feel the need to bang any counter-cultural drum and instead focuses on the difficulties of writing film scores) and Rory O'Donnell and Rachel Castell on funding shorts (a perennial bugger for aspiring film-makers). Most fascinating is an article on Richard Elfman's "missing film" *The Forbidden Zone*, whilst most irksome is an attempt by some tosspot named Steven Grasse to wind up liberals by insulting Michael Moore; Grasse clearly wants to be Jim Goad but lacks his wit, style and intellect. *Raindance Film* is a little too sterile to get really excited about, but is well worth the time of anyone with an interest in films that play festivals then vanish; the production values are also quite impressive. [Anton Black]

CINEMA SEWER 11
Movie Journal of the Odd and Extreme
Robin Bougie

Bursting with enthusiasm and personality, this Canadian zine does exactly what it says on the cover. Using the right mixture of humour and insight, *Cinema Sewer* reminds me of the very best British horror zines of the early nineties. Before they decided glossy production values and snobbish intellectual shoegazing were more important than opinions and fun.

Issue eleven is an all horror issue, something of a departure for *Cinema Sewer*, having given equal coverage in earlier issues to sleaze, porn, Category Three and anime. Often with startling results — one page extolling the virtue of the latest super cute manga would be juxtaposed with a summary of the "10 Most Violent Porn Films of All Time". Boasting a wide variety of contributors and material, all readers with an interest in fright flicks should find something to their liking within the forty-two pages. Which includes lengthy reviews of *Ecco*, *Texas Dildo Massacre* and *Terror on Alcatraz*, a report from the Cinemuerte Film Festival, a contribution to the "do they or don't they" snuff film debate and an overview of that much neglected genre Bigfoot Rape Rampage films (coming to a Blockbuster near you!).

Judging from the hand-lettered pages, DTP has yet to reach Canadian shores but this only adds to *Cinema Sewer*'s charm. It's like receiving a giant piece of airmail from some smut addled, gore-film loving transatlantic pen pal. Layouts and script are crystal clear and Mr *Cinema Sewer*, one Robin Bougie puts his talents as a cartoonist to effective and often hilarious use by recreating scenes and characters from the films discussed. Prime example being "the chainsaw dildo in action". A unique approach and a blessed relief from the same old muddy stills and video covers so beloved of other publications. Harsher critics and jaded cynics would accuse *Cinema Sewer* of covering the same old ground. And they're probably right, but it's executed with such verve and attitude that I don't care. And nor should you. [Justin Bomba]

AGITATOR
The Cinema of Takashi Miike
Tom Mes

"Shoot! Don't fucking talk to me! Shoot!" Takashi Miike has stated in interviews that you can only be described as a director when you're actually making a film. By this definition Miike is one of the only full-time directors around, having made over fifty films since 1991, and with four or five new projects a year shows no signs of slowing down. In a salutary lesson to the likes of Terry Gilliam, who lurches from one fatally grandiose project to the next, Miike accepts almost all of the proposals offered to him, as long as he feels he can do something with the material. He does not stick religiously to scripts, preferring to let his films evolve on set, and makes a virtue of his characteristically low budgets, using audacious claymation sequences ostensibly for scenes too expensive to shoot live, and filming wild on the streets to avoid dealing with Japan's restrictive authorisation processes.

Miike is best known abroad for his more visceral work — *Audition*, described by the director as a film "about cutting off someone's foot", the *Dead or Alive* trilogy and *Ichi the Killer*. But while he has returned again and again to yakuza films, he has also made films (and TV series) in pretty much every other genre going, bar 'pink' films: from pop-group promo (*Andromedia*) to demented musical (*The Happiness of the Katakuris*).

This exhaustively researched book charts Miike's film career from production assistant on a TV crew through to international festival favourite, giving detailed synopses and some analysis of each of his films. While the difficulty of even seeing most of these films makes such an account indispensable in working out the true nature of Miike's achievements, the synopses begin to pall after a while — if you're not intending to track these films down, the entries will often be of severely limited interest — and the analyses are sometimes sketchy and repetitive.

Mes lacks either the fannish enthusiasm of a Steve Pulchalski or the incisive commentary of a Kim Newman or Stephen Thrower, and his prose (which could, incidentally, have done with a better copy-edit) is too dry to go down very easily. *Audition* and *Ichi the Killer*, as two of Miike's more interesting and well-known films, fare better than most of the others in terms of analysis, but Mes' workmanlike style is thrown into stark contrast by the final sections of the book. There Miike's 'making of *Ichi*' diary and an in-depth interview allow the director's ebullient unconventionality to add full-spectrum colour to what is otherwise an often lifeless read; and the director's response to a criticism of misogyny — "Generally if the audience feel that it's like that, then they are right" — makes a refreshing change from Mes' contorted justifications of the violence in *Ichi*.

While Mes draws on previous Japanese critical commentaries of Miike's films as the basis for his own critical analysis, the book could do with more details of the critical reception of his films, especially in Japan. What analysis there is skips over what (with my limited experience of Miike's films) has seemed a key stylistic element: his audacious use of non-narrative imagery. Mes' reductive view of Miike's claymation sequences as being simply ways to cut live-action costs glosses over their high weirdness; and other startling images, such as those at the end of *Dead or Alive: Final*, meet disapproval for not fitting the film's 'tone'. This, it seems to me, is to miss the point: Miike's films are about breaking rules, confounding expectation. As he writes in his *Ichi* diary, "What good is life without adventure? We don't need a manual for making a movie... we make movies but we're not authentic filmmakers. We are artisans and amateurs rather than professionals. We are agitators fiddling around with something that gives us enjoyment."

These caveats aside, if you're interested in Miike, *Agitator* is still an indispensable guide, offering a complete and detailed filmography, hundreds of stills including a colour section, details of the director's films available on DVD and a great cover. But some of the excitement of watching Miike's films seems to have been lost along the way. [James Marriott]

ASIAN CULT CINEMA
Thomas Weisser

This is your essential guide to a movie culture virtually ignored in the West unless you're lucky enough to live near a cinema that screens real full-on Asian movies. You should have this book if you are either already into Hong Kong action movies or you need ideas for your own scripts since the reviews here condense hundreds of movies down to their essential plot points and best scenes. Thomas

THE COMPLETE FILMS OF ALFRED HITCHCOCK
£16.99 $21.95 / pb / 256pp / ISBN 0806524278 / Citadel Press 2003 / www.citadelpress.com

THE EXORCIST: OUT OF THE SHADOWS
£9.99 / pb / 190pp / ISBN 0711975094 / Omnibus Press 1999 / www.omnibuspress.com

FEAR WITHOUT FRONTIERS
£19.99 $29.99 / pb / 320 pp / ISBN 1903245159 / FAB Press 2003 / www.fabpress.com

Weisser is a true fan who's seen just about every movie produced in the Far East since the 1980s. Even the worst of them he describes with wit and real enthusiasm, and he doesn't care about telling you the ending of the pictures since what happens isn't really as important as how it happens in these stories of ghosts and gangsters. Far more so than in Westernised cinema, the creativity of these films stems from their physical execution, their fights, stunts, and spectacle, so plot twists take second place to the choreographic twists taken by the hero or heroine in fighting off the marauding zombie gangster witches or whatever the enemy happens to be. Weisser never misses a trick at this and is happy to tell you which bits of the story can be fast-forwarded to get to a really good chase or fight scene.

Also included are director filmographies, filmographies for the major actors, a mini-guide to martial arts movies and the many heirs to the throne of the late great Bruce Lee (because you wouldn't want to get caught buying a Bruce Le film when the one you want stars Bruce Li instead, would you?). There's also details of where to obtain the movies. Weisser even takes trouble to explain how Chinese names work, which is useful to understand if you're into tracking the careers of your favourite stars (see the perils of Bruce, above.) Even without seeing the movies, *Asian Cult Cinema* is good read. [Jerry Glover]

THE COMPLETE FILMS OF ALFRED HITCHCOCK
Robert A Harris &
Michael S Lasky
Bergmanesque. Godardian. Felliniesque. And Hitchcockian. Not many film directors get their names turned into adjectives, but then not many are as great as Alfred Hitchcock. Indeed, he was such a prolific director*, and he became so closely associated with a particular kind of taut suspense thriller, that his work practically constitutes a one-man genre. My local arthouse video rental shop has a separate Hitchcock section. My video collection contains an entire shelf of his films (it also contains an entire shelf of Russ Meyer films, but that's a different review!). Is there anyone who is remotely interested in the history of cinema who doesn't hold his work in high regard? Is there anyone who doesn't have a favourite Hitchcock film (for the record, make mine *Vertigo*)? Just look at the run of films he made between 1958 and 1964: *Vertigo* (1958), *North By Northwest* (1959), *Psycho* (1960), *The Birds* (1963), *Marnie* (1964). Every one's a winner, baby, that's the truth. Only with *Torn Curtain* in 1966 did Hitchcock falter. *Frenzy* (1972) was his last truly great film. But that magic run from 1958 to 1964 is what most people remember him for these days. If he'd never made any films other than those five, he would still be accounted a major *auteur*. But of course, he made literally *dozens* of other films, some of them every bit as good as the Famous Five — off the top of my head I remember *Rear Window*, of course, *The 39 Steps*, *Spellbound*, *Notorious*, *Strangers on a Train*, *Rebecca*, *Rope*, *The Lady Vanishes*, *Foreign Correspondent*, *Dial M For Murder*, *Suspicion*… you get the picture. It's the achievements of people like Alfred Hitchcock that make me want to give up on creative endeavours entirely. And to think he never won an Oscar…

Small wonder, then, that there are reference books available covering Hitchcock's long and prolific career. *The Complete Films of Alfred Hitchcock* (hereafter referred to as *CFAH*) is a large and handsome volume with a separate chapter for every film after 1934 (the silents are bundled together), taking you all the way from *The Man Who Knew Too Much* (the first version) to *Family Plot*. It also, valuably, has a section on his *Alfred Hitchcock Presents* TV series, which ran from 1955 to 1962.

My major criticism of the book is that it was originally published in 1976, whilst Hitchcock was still alive (he died in 1980), and it hasn't been sufficiently revised to take into account the developments in appreciation, restoration, print availability etc, which have occurred in the intervening twenty-seven years. For instance, there's no mention of video, let alone DVD, availability — and in fact the press release specifically promises "an up-to-date listing of all Hitchcock's movies available on VHS and DVD", but I can't find it at all, which is not good. And when you read, for instance, in the chapter on *The 39 Steps*, "Hitchcock rates [this] as one of his favorite films. He feels that its tempo is perfect," that present tense is pretty jarring. Couldn't the publishers have done something about this? It seems very careless simply to reprint a book from 1976 without revising the text at all — although curiously on page eighteen we read, "Sir Alfred Hitchcock died April 28, 1980", so *some* revision has gone on, just not enough of it.

The individual film chapters contain some interesting trivia and production stills, however, and in fact *CFAH*'s major asset is its many pictures (which are all black and white, sadly). See Cary Grant running from that crop-dusting plane, Anthony Perkins' silhouette at the top of the Bates Motel steps, Kim Novak's flawless profile, the staff of Manderley assembled to greet Joan Fontaine, Rodert Donat and Madeleine Carroll on the Scottish moors (in Lime Grove Studios!), Leslie Banks pointing a flintlock pistol at Maureen O'Hara, and Cary Grant (again!) coming up the stairs with that suspiciously luminous glass of milk. So the book is a visual treat.

For serious reference purposes though, I would recommend instead *The Complete Hitchcock* by Paul Condon and Jimmy Sangster (Virgin Books, 1999), which is considerably more up-to-date and organised into neat little thematic sections for each film, starting with production details and a detailed synopsis. *CFAH*'s film chapters tend to be more discursive (though shorter than those of *The Complete Hitchcock*), and the writing is workmanlike at best, and plodding and clumsy at worst: "*Vertigo* is a sensation of dizziness or a confused, disoriented state of mind. It is also the name of one of Alfred Hitchcock's finest films." Yawn. Serious Hitchcock afficionados might find this book a worthwhile acquisition, but if you're only going to buy one book on Hitchcock, this isn't the best choice available.

Did he direct fifty-three, fifty-four, fifty-seven, or fifty-nine films? My various reference books disagree, mainly because there are a number of marginal cases. Harris and Lasky count fifty-three, but they ignore the French-language shorts he made during for the British Government during the Second World War, as well as (I think) a couple of early silent co-productions. Whatever — he directed a bloody lot of films anyway! [Simon Collins]

THE EXORCIST: OUT OF THE SHADOWS
The Full Story of the Film
Bob McCabe

I find it hard to believe that anybody needs yet another "full story" of the making of *The Exorcist*. There have been so many "definitive versions", especially since the release of the restored print, that we seem to have reached saturation point some time ago. McCabe's book tends mainly to re-hash material already discussed in greater depth by Mark Kermode, in his BFI guide to the film, and presented in *Fear of God*, the BBC documentary on the making of the movie. *The Exorcist: Out of the Shadows* is clearly written, but rather basic and simple, with occasional annoying errors in grammar and factual detail, and without sources for any of the quotations or references. If you're an *Exorcist* completist, I'd avoid this book and try to track down a copy of Peter Travers and Stephanie Rieff's *The Story Behind the Exorcist*, which locates and reprints all the original reviews from film critics in America and elsewhere. McCabe's book adds very little to what has now become an often-told tale. [Mikita Brottman]

FEAR WITHOUT FRONTIERS
Horror Cinema Across the Globe
Ed. Steven Jay Schneider

Which would you rather watch: *Jeepers Creepers*, *Wrong Turn* and *Ghost Ship*, or *Ichi the Killer*, *The Devil's Backbone* and *Dark Water*? Horror fans have long since turned

FILTHY
£10.99 $15.99 / pb / 220pp / ISBN 1555836259 /
Alyson Books 2002 / www.alyson.com

HAMMER FILMS
£19.95 / pb / 368pp / ISBN 1903111447 / Reynolds
and Hearn 2002 / www.rhbooks.com

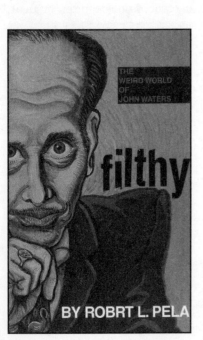

to foreign markets (particularly Italy) in search of fear kicks, and as Hollywood churns out increasingly vacuous and derivative genre fare — and not even much of that — mainstream film audiences are following in their footsteps. The massive success of *Ring* is only part of the story: *The Devil's Backbone* (Spain), *Brotherhood of the Wolf* (France) and *The Eye* (Singapore) all played in subtitled form in local British cinemas to some success, and copies of films such as *Uzumaki* and *Evil Dead Trap* are now readily available on DVD in your local HMV, or any one of a number of websites: this is the acceptable face of globalisation.

American film studios seem to recognise that there's something going on, as evidenced by remakes of *Ring*, *Abre Los Ojos/ Close Your Eyes* (remade as *Vanilla Sky*) and *The Vanishing*, notoriously saddled with a risible happy ending in the remake. Stories are bought, ideas rehashed and foreign directors brought into the Hollywood fold, only to lose their dark creative spark in the California sunshine. The occasional bright new American idea — *The Blair Witch Project*, for instance — is soon swamped in a glut of substandard sequels and remakes all jumping on the ghost train. The one notably atmospheric American haunting that follows — *The Others* — turns out to be set in Jersey and directed by a Spaniard.

An excellent introduction by Kim Newman sets the scene for this timely book, pointing out that the shock of novelty when faced with a foreign country's genre product soon wears off when the viewer becomes familiar with that country's generic clichés; and that the trash aesthetic often associated with these films

comes largely from US involvement, in dubbing or re-cutting, rather than the films themselves. That said, some of the material covered here — particularly the Indian, Filipino and Turkish horror films — looks like it's no stranger to trash. Nothing wrong with that — the Filipino horror films I've seen have had a gleeful delirium rarely found elsewhere — but fans of more serious films will be glad to see that these are balanced out by pieces on more serious fare, from austere Austrian Michael Haneke (*Funny Games*) to Polish genre directors such as Wojciech Has (*The Saragossa Manuscript*) and Roman Polanski.

As a general overview of European and world horror, *Fear Without Frontiers* is not as thorough as the two indispensable Pete Tombs volumes, *Immoral Tales* and *Mondo Macabro*, but then nor does it claim to be. It's more of a grab bag of essays, ranging from close looks at key individual films to overviews of countries' genre industries. The book is divided into four sections: "Artists, Actors, Auteurs" features essays on Jodorowsky, Naschy and Anthony Wong, among others; "Films, Series, Cycles" covers obscurities such as the 'exotic Pontianaks' and more well-trodden territory in pieces on Italian *giallo* and zombie films; "Genre Histories and Studies" features general overviews of genre material from countries ranging from France to South Korea; and the final section is a case study on Japanese horror cinema, comprising a feature on and interview with Takashi Miike and features on the *Ring* cycle and *Suicide Club*.

The book's catholic range is reflected in the selection of authors, who range from the (relatively) well known — Pete Tombs, Travis Crawford — to a host of writers I've never come across before. This makes for a refreshing mix of styles, and while some pieces are slightly dry, others get the space between slavering fandom and highbrow criticism just right. The best pieces closely relate the genre material covered to the countries that spawned them, making them interesting reading even if you don't intend to explore the areas in question. But you'll probably want to.

One of my only criticisms (and it's more of a request, really) is that I want more. Pieces on directors Jerzy Skolimowski and Joraj Herz (Czech Republic) and Sogo Ishii (Japan) would have been welcome: they're all of interest to genre fans, but I've seen very little written about them, and a book like this is the right place for it. Sequels, please!

Some of the pieces that *are* here could do with being expanded: Jodorowsky, for instance, deserves a book of his own, and my favourite of these essays, David Galat's "Secret History of Gallic Horror Movies", could go on to cover directors such as Gaspar Noe and Philippe Grandrieux, who effectively bridge the horror/art-house gap Galat mentions. I would also like to have seen more new material at the expense of areas that have already been covered — such as replacing Italian zombie films with a piece on, say, German horror — but the balance between varying levels of obscurity (none of this stuff is "mainstream") is a difficult one to maintain, and this collection gets it pretty much right.

All in all, then, characteristically great stuff from FAB Press, chock-full with rare stills, ad mats and a blood-soaked colour section, and the attention to detail we've come

to expect from these publishers. One final caveat, though: the cover, which looks a bit — er — trashy. [James Marriott]

FILTHY
The Phenomenon of John Waters
Robert L Pela

This is a fun, lively guide to the white-trash world of John Waters, director of tacky underground masterpieces like *Pink Flamingos*, as well as more mainstream fare such as *Serial Mom* and *Pecker*. Pela is a true Waters addict, and his guide takes us on a wild trip from East Baltimore — Waters' home turf and the setting for all his films — to the wacked-out New York movie world, with plenty of peculiar stops along the way. These include a visit to Suki, a Baltimore woman who has a shrine to the director in her bathroom, and a session with spiritual medium Calvin Sharpee, who specialises in contacting dead celebrities and claims to be in touch with the spirit of Divine, the twenty-five-stone drag queen who became Waters' best-known star. Pela spends a little less time on Water's later, more mainstream work — films like *Pecker* and *Cecil B Demented* — that, at least to many of his fans, constitute a wholescale Hollywood sell-out. If this is also Pela's view, he wisely keeps mum. The book is rounded off by a detailed and annotated filmography, including notes on recurrent or especially peculiar themes, styles, casting coups and lines of dialogue. This is neither a biography nor a serious study, but a fun romp through the world of a bizarre man — just the way John Waters would have wanted it. [Mikita Brottman]

HAMMER FILMS
The Bray Studio Years
Wayne Kinsey

Sometimes I have to pinch myself. Sometimes I wonder if I've dreamed that a book like Wayne Kinsey's monumental opus on Hammer's Golden Years is a hallucination, having been brought up in the relatively impoverished era of the seventies, when the going seemed good if you managed to find anything better on Hammer than the three-minute reading experience which was *Monster Mag*, or the affectionately remembered, but equally tawdry, Lorrimer books (which took, perhaps, a whole twenty-five minutes longer to digest!) Yes, genre publications have certainly come on with exponential leaps and bounds since those hallowed days of yore, and books which were merely once an ephemeral jog to the memory in the seventies have become in the late nineties/early 2000s tomes to equal the best scholarly research in any given field in terms of diligent research and pains taken attention to detail.

Anyone who thought there was little left to mine out of Hammer will, therefore, be pleasantly surprised by Wayne Kinsey's exemplary study, which will without doubt be the benchmark for some time to come. Recent years have seen a plethora of Hammer material, some of it good, little really awful if truth be told. Probably the most impressive on first sight is Marcus Hearns and Alan Barnes' *The Hammer Story*, but previous to Kinsey's present effort the most detailed has got to have been Dennis Meikle's 1996 book from Scarecrow Press, *A History of Horrors*. Though a fine work of detailed analysis in every sense, Meik-

HOLLYWOOD COMEDIANS
£13.99 / pb / 224pp / ISBN 0415235529 / Routledge
2002 / www.routledge.co.uk

LARS VON TRIER
£13.99 / pb / 216pp / ISBN 0851709036 / BFI
Publishing 2002 / www.bfi.org.uk

**THE REMARKABLE
MICHAEL REEVES**
£16.99 / pb / 360pp / ISBN 0951179314 / Cinematics
Publishing 2002 / Lee Road, London, NW7 1LJ, UK

le's study has a major flaw which Kinsey's lacks. Somewhere along the line Meikle seems to have realised that *he doesn't actually really like Hammer films*! Much of the book is taken up by the author's weary and disparaging assessment of nearly all Hammer's major product after *Brides of Dracula* (1960), which despite this, is still viewed as the film in which "the rot began to set in" — a phrase Meikle seems to use with regularity, unless my memory of the whole frustrating experience of reading his book is exaggerating things. Be that as it may, when an author chooses to write a detailed, minimally paid, 'labour of love'-style study of a company like Hammer, only to dwell dolefully on the "unabashed contempt for its audience" (Meikle, p.243) it's safe to say his energy might have been better served in choosing a subject he actually liked. There is no such problem in Kinsey's book which maintains throughout an engaging, scholarly tone which also manages to communicate his enthusiasm for his subject, creating a perfect balance. There is a wealth of minutiae even the most die-hard Hammer enthusiasts will find new, and this too is put across with skill — even when some of the material may come into the category of trivia. But surely that is the sign of a good author who is engrossed by his material to the extent that even the most piddling of facts and figures are made to make sense as part of the over all scheme of things....

I cannot recommend Wayne Kinsey's book highly enough. In fact the only complaint I have is that such a perceptive and enthusiastic champion of Hammer (the architect behind the equally interesting fanzine/part-work *The House That Hammer Built*) should have limited his study to the Bray Studio years. Perhaps this was decided to ensure that his book stood out from previous studies. If that was the case it wasn't necessary. Let's hope Kinsey turns his attention to Hammer's latter years in an equally detailed follow up volume sometime soon. The House of Hammer has at last found its perfect chronicler. Wayne Kinsey's book makes previous offerings look like the bare skeletal frames of unfinished houses in contrast to his magnificently constructed edifice. [Stephen Sennitt]

HOLLYWOOD COMEDIANS
The Film Reader
Ed. Frank Krutnik

Routledge's In Focus imprint consists of a series of film readers that cover much of the academic research that's been done in the analysis of various film genres, from horror and musicals, to experimental cinema. Debates on the subjects are situated in their appropriate academic context, and the central issues identified and explored. The intended audience for the series is students — both undergrad and graduate — in film and cinema studies courses. *Hollywood Comedians*, therefore, is not for the casual movie buff or film fan. It's a collection of densely-written theoretical essays on classical film comedy situated in an academic context, which means there's a lot about Keaton, Chaplin and Jerry Lewis, and not much on contemporary comedians. All the essays have been previously published in academic film journals, there are no pictures, and you may need a magnifying glass or monocle to read the print. That said, Frank Krutnik is a good writer and a thoughtful critic, and for those with a scholarly interest in the subject, *Hollywood Comedians* brings together all the fundamental research in one nice, tightly-produced package. [Mikita Brottman]

LARS VON TRIER
Jack Stevenson

It's maybe a little odd that as of writing this the first book devoted to art-house sensation Von Trier. Having infuriated, exhilarated and wound up discerning film-goers for many years now, his film studio Zentropa is now the largest such organisation in Europe (we'll ignore the recent audit that put them $7 million in the red); as well as a filmmaker of major importance, he is a player in the film world. Yet much information regarding Von Trier exists in the form of rumour, slander, gossip and innuendo: we know that he never flies, that he strips off himself to film nude scenes, that he pushed Björk to the brink of insanity in filming *Dancer in the Dark* (and it shows onscreen), but such myths are all we really have to go on. Now expat Yank Stevenson has written a book on the insane genius, one that comes not a moment too soon.

Stevenson is renowned for his detective work on the forgotten corners of exploitation and "invisible" cinema, and there is no doubt that he is an excellent scribe on such subjects. However, he acquits himself just as well here, dealing with an altogether loftier subject, yet one just as fascinating as John Waters or WWII propaganda movies. In temperament, Von Trier most closely resembles Alexandro Jodorowsky; as a showman, he has the wisdom to always play everything deadly seriously and never to let you know if you're

being put on or not. Like Chris Morris, he has the media savvy never to explain what his "work" "means". Stevenson, to his credit, takes a neutral line on his subject, neither damning him as a charlatan nor praising him as a visionary. This leaves him more room for the diligent research and measured analysis of which he is quite capable, and this book is a definite eye-opener — everything you wanted to know about Von Trier but had no idea whom to ask.

A detailed examination of the myriad contradictions inherent in the subject's life allows us a context in which to understand his films. We learn that Von Trier had libertarian parents that sent him to an ultra-strict school, the discombobulating nature of which led to his being barred from compulsory military service due to psychological issues; on her death bed, his mother told him that the man he thought to be his father wasn't; he called Roman Polanski "a midget" and claimed it would be better if Imgmar Bergman were dead... Von Trier remains fundamentally impenetrable, but this book goes some way to reconciling the paradoxes within him; also, Stevenson's knowledge of Danish idiosyncrasies — such as the emphasis on "the group", i.e the vast mass of Danes — is of invaluable worth to non-Danish readers trying to understand one of the country's favourite/least-favourite sons.

Stevenson treats us to a wealth of information about Von Trier's early, difficult-to-see movies such as *The Element of Crime* and *Epidemic*, before moving on to the shattering classic that made his international name, *Breaking the Waves* (a film which, amazingly, started life as a straight adaptation of De Sade's

Justine!). From there we see how his celebrity led him down even more mischievous avenues — bizarre art installations, twenty-four-hour-long chat shows, no-shows at almost every film festival to which he was invited, and the wonderful concept of Dogma '95 which led to remarkable films such as *The Idiots* and *Festen*. Von Trier often suffers incomprehension from bewildered foreign movie-goers, but I suspect he's not especially bothered; referring to the haphazard running of *Zentropa*, Stevenson says: "This wasn't America, as (producer Aalbaek Jensen) no doubt would have happily enlightened the ignorant, if anyone could be that stupid".

Self-hatred on the American-born but Danish-living author's part? Dunno, but the sentiment wins my vote. Another winning tome from Stevenson, about a director whose films you *need* to see, this book adds much clarity to Von Trier's character, outlook and body of work. Recommended. [Anton Black]

THE REMARKABLE MICHAEL REEVES
His Short and Tragic Life
John B Murray

You wait ages for one biography of Michael Reeves and then two come along at once. As I write this, Benjamin Halligan's book on horror cinema's young genius is but a few months away. Finally, this enigmatic figure is now getting the full treatment for the first time since his untimely death in 1969. After David Pirie wrote about Michael Reeves in his seminal 1973 book, *A Heritage of Horror*, the director of *Matthew Hopkins: Witchfinder General* became the Holy Ghost of British horror: his films have been lauded, analysed,

SLEAZOID EXPRESS
£11.99 $16 / pb / 315pp / ISBN 0743215834 / Simon
and Schuster 2002 / www.simonsays.com

torn apart and put back together again by writers and critics (myself included) seemingly frustrated by the few solid facts available. John B Murray's *The Remarkable Michael Reeves* will bring an end to such theorising, though. Amazingly, I first read about this project in a 1987 issue of *Shock Xpress*, and the fact that it's taken fifteen-odd years for the resulting book to emerge is understandable when you discover how *many* people Murray has interviewed and corresponded with. He even lists those he couldn't contact! Add to this access to Reeves' personal cuttings scrapbook, diary and letters, and every question you ever wanted to ask is pretty much answered…

Michael Leith Reeves was born in Surrey on October 17, 1943. He was cinema-mad from an early age, and whilst at Radley College kept up a correspondence with the American director Don Siegel. At the age of sixteen he inherited a vast amount of money that made him virtually a millionaire, but, despite enjoying a comfortable life (his second passion was for fast cars), he was determined not to let the cash buy him into the film industry. Thanks to the multiple opinions of those interviewed (the most eager ones being actors Ian Ogilvy and Nicky Henson, co-writer Tom Baker, composer Paul Ferris, producer Tony Tenser and members of the Reeves family), the well-documented early days — visiting Siegel, involvement in the Italian horror industry — are fleshed out even more, and a few unconfirmed facts — such as Reeves working in the TV and advertising industry — are dismissed. In fact, a number of myths are roundly shattered here, with Murray going over every event in Reeves' life in minute detail, and then getting

someone else to comment on it: for every 'concrete' opinion there is an opposing one. This sometimes adds to the confusion of what actually happened, but with so much information available, it's hard to be too concerned.

Reeves was *obsessed* with cinema — particularly American cinema — to the point that he rarely spoke about anything else. His favourite directors were Siegel and Roger Corman; his favourite film was Siegel's *The Killers* (he once found Lee Marvin drunk in a nightclub and took him home to meet his friends), one of many he'd show on his 16mm home projector. He was determined to make good movies on low budgets. His first shoot, the Italian abomination *The Revenge of the Blood Beast* was a fair start, but it was with *The Sorcerers* that he really came into his own as an independent director. This had all the exploitation elements intact: an aging star (Boris Karloff), a gesture or two towards the youth market, a good story, a bit of sex and a few exciting moments achieved by guerrilla film making: the massive car explosion at the end of *The Sorcerers* was highly illegal and cast and crew had to scarper before the cops arrived! Susan George — in her first screen role — hated the film, apparently.

But it's for 1968's *Witchfinder General* that Murray saves his highest praise. Two long chapters deal with the making of the film and its subsequent censorship, and this is the real meat for the reader: Reeves and Tom Baker scouted for locations before even starting the screenplay; all the interiors were filmed in a disused — and extremely cheap — aircraft hanger; the incredibly downbeat ending was brought about by time and budget constrictions more than anything else; Robert Russell, who played Hopkins' assistant, had to have his voice completely redubbed because it was considered too high; and Vincent Price and Reeves did *not* get on (how about this for a rumour: Price's animosity towards Reeves was because he was in fact bisexual and fancied the pants off the handsome young director?). It was only after the film was released that Price realised his error, but the success of *Witchfinder General* was the beginning of the end for Reeves. Always teetering on the edge of manic depression (a condition perhaps inherited from his father, who committed suicide), he finally succumbed to the illness due to numerous factors: the sudden praise and attention, the unexpected censoring of his film and the final walkout by his girlfriend Annabelle (screenwriter Charles Griffith said she "had the best body I have ever seen in this life"!!). Also, how to follow-up his biggest success was a constant nightmare. Murray lists a number of projects: some personal, some that were made anyway, some offered by producers that never came to anything. *Witchfinder General*'s backers, AIP, wanted Reeves to helm exploitation flicks such as *Bloody Mama* and *De Sade*. Reeves, fearful of being pigeonholed, had no enthusiasm for them; he wanted a change of direction. Due to his fragile state he walked off the production of *The Oblong Box*, and it looked likely that his next film would have been *O'Hooligan's Mob*, an IRA thriller for Tony Tenser. Other projects — some refreshingly non-horror — are speculated upon by interviewees, and flights of fancy such as Reeves being lined up to direct *Easy Rider* are dismissed entirely.

Reeves' last months were a hideous montage of private hospitals, money-grabbing doctors, large amounts of pills and EST; and, just when it looked like he would pull through, he was found dead of an overdose. Like every other incident in the book, it's commented on from multiple angles; but, from where I'm reading, it appeared to be a simple mistake made in a drunken moment.

If *The Remarkable Michael Reeves* has faults, it's that it is too sprawling and contradictory. Some decent editing would have been welcome, cutting down repetitive and sometimes downright unnecessary comments. As it is, Murray has let these interviews take up the bulk of the book, and, if his own style is occasionally grating ("Mike got cold feet just days before the wedding and called it off, which is of course a terrible thing to do to a girl") then the sheer *amount* of Reeves information more than makes up for it. Rumour, secret and unknown fact, it's all here. Such an overload invariably adds more fuel to the myth, but Murray's years of dedication — plus thirty-two pages of excellent photos — make *The Remarkable Michael Reeves* a welcome and vital addition to any British horror bookshelf. [Martin Jones]

SLEAZOID EXPRESS
A Mind-twisting Tour through the Grindhouse Cinema of Times Square!
by Bill Landis & Michelle Clifford

The press release for this book says: "In *Sleazoid Express*, Landis and Clifford reproduce what no home video can — the experience of watching an exploitation film in its original fight-for-your-life Deuce setting."

That's a pretty fair description.

The original "grindhouses" in New York's notorious 42nd Street/7th & 8th Avenue district were mostly torn down by the mid eighties, but Bill Landis draws upon his decades of experience working and spending his time in and around the sleaze industry. He worked as manager and projectionist at several theatres, also hiring couples for live sex shows and taking care of the box office from time to time. Landis brings the whole spectacle right back to life, skilfully assisted by his wife and co-editor Michelle Clifford.

The chapters in the book are themed by specific film genres and linked to the old, flea-ridden, crusty grindhouses that were showing them back in the good old days, when Times Square was crammed with porn shops, titty bars, gun stores and drug pushers. Chapters have titles like "The Liberty and the Cinerama: Showcases for Eurosleaze", "Taking Their Show on the Road: Times Square Mondo Movies" and "Blood Horror: Chopping 'Em Up at the Rialto". The book is illustrated with many rare ads and a few of the couple's own photos of the area, including some sad snapshots from the decline, when all these venues of grimy fuck flicks and grainy cannibal epics started to close and were torn down.

Some of the movies discussed are familiar to any exploitation fan, like the *Ilsa* movies and *Mondo Cane*, but Landis and Clifford always deliver more behind-the-scenes info than any other writers. Their real strength though, is when they dig up movies that even most of today's sleaze fans wouldn't know about, and wouldn't want to touch with a ten foot pole anyway. Like *Olga's House of Shame*, *The Rape Killer*, and *Nigger Lover*.

SPIKE LEE
£3.99 / pb / 96pp / ISBN 1904048072 / Pocket Essentials 2003 / www.pocketessentials.com

Just like the old NYC theatres, they mix American exploitation with imported Eurosleaze and provocative art movies. Any movie with sex, sex-changes, violence, kung-fu, drugs, torture, rape or S/M is fair game.

Generally the style of writing is very straightforward, but with spots of dry wit and a little tinge of *schadenfreude* when they touch upon the personal destiny of some of the movie makers, actors and theatre owners. The parts dealing with the rise and fall of the movers and shakers in the biz reads like an East Coast sleaze version of *Hollywood Babylon*. And I mean that in a good way. They also provide loving, detailed descriptions of all the hustling, drug use and robberies taking place in the theatres and their often overflowing, stinking toilet stalls.

Even if you have shelves full of books on exploitation movies, you have nothing like this. Just get hold of it. [Jan Bruun]
Bill Landis & Michelle Clifford are interviewed on p.138

SPIKE LEE
Pocket Essentials
Darren Arnold

The wit and wisdom of Spike "only whites can be evil" Lee's oeuvre, comprising of short reviews and brief essays. Lee is an infuriatingly uneven filmmaker, capable both of remarkable work such as *Do The Right Thing* or *Clockers* yet also of eyewank like *Malcolm X* or *Crooklyn*. Plus, he gets away with the sort of racism that would lead to him being run out of town were he a honky. Like the other books in the Pocket Essentials series, this gives you a brief overview of the man's work, and if that's what you want then this is your book. Anyone seeking more in-depth analysis is advised to look elsewhere. It's not bad at all, though contains one major blooper: Arnold identifies "tension" as being one of Lee's major themes, when "tension" is very bleeding obviously one of the cornerstones of any narrative fiction! Duh… [Anton Black]